T
=

A CULTURAL HISTORY OF THEATRE

VOLUME 4

VOLUME 4

A Cultural History of Theatre

General Editors: Christopher B. Balme and Tracy C. Davis

Volume 1
A Cultural History of Theatre in Antiquity
Edited by Martin Revermann

Volume 2
A Cultural History of Theatre in the Middle Ages
Edited by Jody Enders

Volume 3
A Cultural History of Theatre in the Early Modern Age
Edited by Robert Henke

Volume 4
A Cultural History of Theatre in the Age of Enlightenment
Edited by Mechele Leon

Volume 5
A Cultural History of Theatre in the Age of Empire
Edited by Peter W. Marx

Volume 6
A Cultural History of Theatre in the Modern Age
Edited by Kim Solga

A CULTURAL HISTORY OF THEATRE

IN THE AGE OF ENLIGHTENMENT

VOLUME 4

Edited by Mechele Leon

Bloomsbury Academic
An imprint of Bloomsbury Publishing Plc

B L O O M S B U R Y
LONDON · OXFORD · NEW YORK · NEW DELHI · SYDNEY

Bloomsbury Academic

An imprint of Bloomsbury Publishing Plc

50 Bedford Square	1385 Broadway
London	New York
WC1B 3DP	NY 10018
UK	USA

www.bloomsbury.com

BLOOMSBURY and the Diana logo are trademarks of Bloomsbury Publishing Plc

First published 2017

British Library Cataloguing-in-Publication Data
A catalogue record for this book is available from the British Library.

ISBN:	HB:	978-1-4725-8575-2
	HB Set:	978-1-4725-8584-4

Library of Congress Cataloging-in-Publication Data
A catalog record for this book is available from the Library of Congress.

Series: Cultural Histories

Cover image: William Hogarth, *The Children's Theater in the House of John Conduit*, 1732. Public domain

Typeset by RefineCatch Limited, Bungay, Suffolk
Printed and bound in Great Britain

To find out more about our authors and books visit www.bloomsbury.com. Here you will find extracts, author interviews, details of forthcoming events and the option to sign up for our newsletters.

CONTENTS

LIST OF ILLUSTRATIONS

CHAPTER TEN

NOTES ON CONTRIBUTORS

Helen E.M. Brooks is Senior Lecturer in Drama and Deputy Director of Research in the School of Arts at the University of Kent. Her research is on theatre and performance during the long eighteenth-century. She has published on the topics of women's involvement in theatre during the eighteenth century, cross-dressing, acting theory, histories of gender and sex, the economics of the stage, amateur and private theatricals, and the theatre as a site of social engagement. She is author of *Actresses, Gender, and the Eighteenth-Century Stage* and winner of the Southeastern American Association of Eighteenth Century Studies, Annibel Jenkins prize for the essay '"One Entire Nation of Actors and Actresses": Reconsidering the Relationship of Public and Private Theatricals'.

Pannill Camp is Associate Professor of Drama and Director of Graduate Studies in the Department of Performing Arts at Washington University in St. Louis. He studies performance theory, theatre architecture and the history of modern Western theatre, in particular exchanges between theatre and philosophy in seventeenth- and eighteenth-century France. He is the author of *The First Frame: Theatre Space in Enlightenment France*, which received an honourable mention for the Association for Theatre in Higher Education (ATHE) Outstanding Book Award for 2015, and was shortlisted for the 2015 Kenshur Prize, awarded by the Indiana University Center for Eighteenth-Century Studies.

Mita Choudhury teaches in the Department of English at Purdue Northwest and serves as director of the Liberal Arts Study Abroad Program in the UK. Before assuming her current post, she taught at New York University and at the Georgia Institute of Technology. An expert in eighteenth-century British literature and culture, Professor Choudhury has published extensively in the field. In the summer of 2016, she served as Senior Faculty Fellow at the School of Humanities and Social Sciences of the Technische Universität Dresden (TUD), Germany. Professor Choudhury has been invited in recent years to give lectures and talks at the Newberry Library, the University of Minnesota and the University of Athens, Greece. Author of *Interculturalism and Resistance in the London Theater, 1600–1800* (2000) and co-editor of *Monstrous Dreams of Reason* (2002), her current research is on eighteenth-century British conceptualizations of imperial space.

Logan J. Connors is Associate Professor of French at the University of Miami (FL), where he teaches graduate and undergraduate seminars on French theatre, early modern French literature and the history of emotions. He is the author of *Dramatic Battles in Eighteenth-Century France:* Philosophes, *Anti-philosophes and Polemical Theatre* (2012) and of a critical edition of Pierre-Laurent de Belloy's *Le Siège de Calais* (2014). In 2015, he was the guest editor of a double-issue of *Restoration and Eighteenth-Century Theatre* dedicated to anti-theatrical discourses in early modern Europe. His most recent articles have appeared in the *Revue de l'histoire du théâtre, Eighteenth-Century Fiction*, the *French Review* and *PMLA*. His current book project traces the connections between dramatic theories and theories of the emotions in seventeenth- and eighteenth-century France.

Lisa A. Freeman is Professor of English at the University of Illinois at Chicago. She is the author of *Character's Theater: Genre and Identity on the Eighteenth-Century English Stage* as well as the editor of the Sarah Siddons volume of the Lives of Shakespearean Actors Series. Her new book, *Antitheatricality and the Body Public* (2017), explores the politics of anti-theatrical incidents from the seventeenth to the twentieth centuries.

Mechele Leon is Associate Professor and Chair of the Department of Theatre at the University of Kansas. She is author of *Molière, the French Revolution, and the Theatrical Afterlife*, winner of the Barnard Hewitt Award for Outstanding Research in Theatre History, as well as articles and chapters on French theatre and theatre historiography. She is currently working on a history of French theatre and cultural diplomacy in the United States. In addition to her publishing activities, she is a theatre director experienced in a variety of genres and has translated and adapted Molière's plays for the stage.

John O'Brien is the NEH/Daniels Family Distinguished Teaching Professor at the University of Virginia, where he teaches in the Department of English. He is the author of *Literature Incorporated: The Cultural Unconscious of the Business Corporation, 1650–1850* (2016) and *Harlequin Britain: Pantomime and Entertainment, 1690–1760* (2004).

Daniel O'Quinn is a Professor in the School of English and Theatre Studies at the University of Guelph. He is the author of *Entertaining Crisis in the Atlantic*

Imperium, 1770–1790 (2011) and *Staging Governance: Theatrical Imperialism in London, 1770–1800* (2005). He is also co-editor with Jane Moody of the *Cambridge Companion to British Theatre, 1730–1830* (2007).

Deborah C. Payne has published extensively on seventeenth- and eighteenth-century theatre and drama, having written on topics ranging from the Restoration actress to Samuel Pepys and spectatorship. The editor of *The Cambridge Companion to English Restoration Theatre* and *Four Restoration Libertine Plays*, she has just completed a new history of the seventeenth-century theatre. Her next major project entails re-examining current assumptions about seventeenth- and eighteenth-century acting styles. Professor Payne is currently an Associate Professor at American University in Washington, DC. In addition to her scholarly activities, she frequently provides dramaturgical support for resident theatre companies, having served as the Humanities Project Consultant at the Shakespeare Theatre Company from 2000 to 2007.

David Worrall is Emeritus Professor of English at Nottingham Trent University and Senior Visiting Research Fellow, University of Roehampton. He has received fellowships and awards from AHRC, British Academy, Leverhulme Trust, Panacea Society, Folger Shakespeare Library, Lewis Walpole Library and Australian National University. He is the author of *Theatric Revolution: Drama, Censorship and Romantic Period Subcultures, 1773–1832* (2006), *Harlequin Empire: Race, Ethnicity and the Drama of the Popular Enlightenment* (2007), *The Politics of Romantic Theatricality, 1787–1832: The Road to the Stage* (2007) and *Celebrity, Performance, Reception: British Georgian Theatre as Social Assemblage* (2013).

SERIES PREFACE

A *Cultural History of Theatre* is a six-volume series examining a cultural practice that emerged in antiquity and today encompasses practically the whole globe. Theatre is generally acknowledged to be the most social of artistic practices, requiring collectives to both produce and consume it. Theatrical performance's ability to organize and cohere markers of cultural belonging, difference and dissonance are the hallmarks of social life. Its production and reception have, however, altered significantly over the past two and half thousand years. Despite these changes the same chapter headings structure all six volumes: institutional frameworks, social functions, sexuality and gender, environment, circulation, interpretations, communities of production, repertoire and genres, technologies of performance, and knowledge transmission. These headings represent significant cultural approaches as opposed to purely regional, national, aesthetic or generic categories. This allows for comparative readings of key *cultural* questions affecting theatre both diachronically and synchronically. The six volumes divide the history of theatre as follows:

Volume 1: A Cultural History of Theatre in Antiquity (500 BC–1000 AD)
Volume 2: A Cultural History of Theatre in the Middle Ages (1000–1400)
Volume 3: A Cultural History of Theatre in the Early Modern Age
   (1400–1650)
Volume 4: A Cultural History of Theatre in the Age of Enlightenment
   (1650–1800)
Volume 5: A Cultural History of Theatre in the Age of Empire (1800–1920)
Volume 6: A Cultural History of Theatre in the Modern Age (1920–2000+)

Christopher B. Balme and Tracy C. Davis, General Editors

EDITOR'S ACKNOWLEDGEMENTS

I wish to thank series editors Tracy Davis and Christopher Balme for inviting me to participate in *A Cultural History of Theatre*. They brought vision, leadership, expertise and solid judgement to every stage of the project. I am particularly grateful for their guidance on my introduction to the volume and contributed chapter. I am honoured to have worked with the nine contributors to this volume. They each brought a wealth of knowledge and maintained patience and good cheer throughout the months of discussion and revision. It has been a pleasure to work with Bloomsbury. Their commitment to quality publishing in theatre studies is a gift to the field.

This volume forms part of my ongoing research into eighteenth-century theatre history and its resonance in contemporary theatre. I am happy to acknowledge the University of Kansas for providing an exemplary level of research support. I wish to thank, in particular, College of Liberal Arts and Sciences Deans Danny Anderson and Carl Lejuez, and Associate Deans Liz Kowalchuk and Henry Bial. My graduate assistant, Kathryn Nygren, performed yeoman's service in the organization of illustrations for this volume as well as numerous other important tasks. Finally, I would like to thank my colleagues in the Department of Theatre, where I serve as Chairperson, for their advice and support.

Introduction

Theatre and the Enlightenment Matrix

MECHELE LEON

In the time between Marvin Carlson's *The Theatre of the French Revolution* (1966) and Mark Darlow's *Staging the French Revolution: Cultural Politics and the Paris Opéra* (2012), something happened more than simply the passing of forty-six years. This corner of eighteenth-century theatre history – namely, the intersection of theatre and revolution – has changed significantly over half a century. How and why it changed is helpful for revealing some of the ways eighteenth-century theatre historiography more broadly has shifted from traditional critical frameworks prevalent to theatre scholarship until the 1970s and 1980s, to those recognizable today as cultural history. These shifts encapsulate changes in prevailing scholarly theories and practices, providing a privileged view of the developments around, and influences of, cultural history, and especially the impact it has had on the way we approach eighteenth-century theatre, history and culture.

Carlson's comprehensive historical study, still widely referenced for its wealth of information as well as its clarity and succinctness, is the model of a long-standing disciplinary approach that situated theatre in relation to a 'background' of contemporaneous political, societal and intellectual events and ideas. For example, the prologue to *The Theatre of the French Revolution* recounts the political events around the time of Beaumarchais's *Le Mariage de Figaro* and describes how the play, which 'fairly bristled with references to inflammatory contemporary issues', gained fame and incited passions among audiences in the explosive political and social environment of 1783 and 1784.[1]

In contrast, Darlow's recent study of opera performance in Revolutionary Paris, as well as the many books that have preceded it over the past several decades, demonstrates a change in thinking about theatre and performance that shifts it from an accessorized or secondary place in relation to the 'background' of politics, culture, ideas and events (what we generally regard as the 'real stuff' of history) to an active and central player that is *constitutive* of history. Darlow offers a meticulous history of the Paris Opéra from 1789 to 1794 by examining such traditional archives as box office records, management practices, newspaper articles, pamphlets and governmental records. But his history is on how the Opéra, not merely (another metaphor) a 'reflection' of its times, is generative of it. Darlow shows that during the Revolution 'culture is conceptualized by a wide range of agents: creators, performers and critics, but also municipal bureaucrats, crown officials, and deputies in the newly created National Assembly'.[2]

In *Politics, Culture, and Class in the French Revolution*, a seminal study published in 1984, the historian Lynn Hunt summarized a (then) new approach to Revolutionary history that was cultural in focus and which regarded politics not simply as the direct expression of such phenomena as 'economic and social interests'. Instead, politics is generated, expressed and sustained through 'symbolic practices, such as language, imagery, and gestures'[3] – in other (my) words, politics shares with theatre a basis in symbolic practice. 'Historians can no longer assume that politics exists in a clearly separate realm from culture', writes Hunt.[4] In making this claim, she drew on a number of groundbreaking works that were redefining the historiography of the French Revolution since the 1970s, including (and specifically relevant to this introduction) Mona Ozouf's *The Festivals of the French Revolution* (in French 1976; first English edition 1988). Ozouf's study disrupts the received model of performance as background to historical events and instead reads the great public open-air festivals of the 1790s as events that performed fundamental social and political functions for the Revolution – functions such as reformulating the shared meaning of time and space, reinterpreting France's past, recasting former social hierarchies into neutral communities of consensus, and voiding the religious sacrality that had undergirded the Old Regime and reassigning it to the new deity of republican politics. Similarly, in another work that is smaller in scope but still significant, Marie-Hélène Huet in *Rehearsing the Revolution: The Staging of Marat's Death, 1793–1797* (1982), does more than situate the half-dozen plays recounting the trial and murder of Jean-Paul Marat in relation to the trial and 1793 execution of Louis XVI; she situates both theatre *and* the historical events within a regime of interrelated Revolutionary representational practices and symbolic interventions. The influence of Huet's work can be seen in Paul Friedland's *Political Actors: Representative Bodies and Theatricality in the Age of the French Revolution* (2002) which links theatre and the Revolution interdependently as 'conceptual siblings' to suggest that the French Revolution is 'fundamentally related to a revolution in the theory and practice of theater'.[5] Other prominent studies around Revolutionary historiography that reinforce theatre and performance as history-making, not merely historical, include Jeffrey Ravel's *The Contested Parterre: Public Theatre and French Political Culture, 1680–1791* (1999) and Susan Maslan's *Revolutionary Acts: Theatre, Democracy, and the French Revolution* (2005).

Of course, the cultural history of theatre in the Enlightenment does not begin or end with French Revolution studies, however much the Revolution continues to exert a teleological influence on studies of the eighteenth century. However, the studies of theatre and the French Revolution discussed above serve the purpose of providing good illustrations of the growth of the cultural history of theatre. They show us theatre in the centre of the historical landscape and not limited to aesthetic isolation or simply characteristic of the 'thoughts and feelings of an age', as Peter Burke defines the basis of cultural activity in older traditions of cultural history.[6] These studies demonstrate theatre's generative and reciprocal roles in political practices, physical environments, material and economic life, and social interactions, as well as its presence in far-flung geographical sites of cultural intervention, political control and social anxiety. As series editors Tracy C. Davis and Christopher B. Balme describe theatre in the context of the development of cultural history: 'theatre history has largely reorientated towards understanding performance as a social entity: normatively constitutive of sociability, productive of the public sphere, received by socially constituted units and subunits, and reflective of wider social conditions in both its ostensible content and the reactions it engenders'.[7]

THE ENLIGHTENMENT AS MATRIX

The assigned period under the microscope in this volume is the 'Age of Enlightenment'. One of the first questions I faced as editor in curating the volume was to determine if the best approach to Enlightenment meant (a) the periodization marker for the eighteenth century, or (b) theatre within the context of a determined set of text and ideas indicative of Enlightenment thought. The answer is obvious: it is both. Theatre is not restricted to a collection of texts; it is a cultural institution of artistic, material and social practices. As such, it cannot but be integral to the Enlightenment when the Enlightenment is conceived – as it is in contemporary scholarship – as a set of practices and not a canon of texts and ideas. In *The Cultural Origins of the French Revolution*, Roger Chartier writes:

The term [Enlightenment] seems easy to define as long as it is held to be a corpus of doctrines formulated by the Philosophes, diffused through all classes of the population, and articulated around several fundamental principles such as criticism of religious fanaticism, the exaltation of tolerance, confidence in observation and experimentation, critical examination of all institutions and customs, the definition of a natural morality, and a reformulation of political and social ties on the basis of the idea of liberty. Still, faced with this classical picture, doubt arises. Is it certain that the Enlightenment must be characterized exclusively or principally as a corpus of self-contained, transparent ideas or as a set of clear and distinct propositions? Should not the century's novelty be read elsewhere – in the multiple practices guided by an interest in utility and service that aimed at the management of spaces and populations and whose mechanisms (intellectual or institutional) imposed a profound reorganization of the systems of perception and of the order of the social world.[8]

Thomas Munck writes that the Enlightenment in contemporary scholarship is now viewed less as a 'specific reform movement' and more as a 'process rooted in particular local and cultural circumstances'.[9] Foucault warns of collapsing distinctions that dehistoricize the Enlightenment while at the same time he emphasizes its active basis:

We must never forget that the Enlightenment is an event, or a set of events and complex historical processes, that is located at a certain point in the development of European societies. As such, it includes elements of social transformation, types of political institution, forms of knowledge, projects of rationalization of knowledge and practices, technological mutations that are very difficult to sum up in a word, even if many of these phenomena remain important today.[10]

Intrinsic to these elements, Foucault suggests, is a special kind of 'reflective relation to the present' involving a particular 'type of philosophical interrogation – one that simultaneously problematizes man's relation to the present, man's historical mode of being, and the constitution of the self as an autonomous subject'.[11] Dan Edelstein, expanding on Foucault's point that Enlightenment involved both practices and a state of mind, writes that it was 'never just the sum of its parts'. 'Instead of an aggregate of ideas, actions, and events', he writes, the Enlightenment 'provided a matrix in which ideas, actions, and events acquired new meaning. To partake in the Enlightenment, it was not enough simply to pen a materialist treatise or frequent a salon: it took the awareness, by oneself or others, that a particular action belongs to a set of practices considered "enlightened"'.[12]

Matrix, process, practices, systems of perception, reflection and awareness: all these suggest that we can regard the Enlightenment as a *context*. It may be regarded as both a physical and abstract space in which ideas are manifested and expressed through practices and action – in other words, a kind of theatrical stage. In developing the volume, therefore, I avoided tasking my contributors with addressing 'The Enlightenment' as if it were a contained or fixed set of ideas that can be 'applied' to theatre. I aimed to avoid the false binary of asserting the volume's periodization in purely temporal or conceptual modes. That is not to say that throughout the volume the authors do not examine theatre according to intellectual trends of the eighteenth century, or that they do not cast their investigations in Enlightenment terms, but I welcomed the ambiguity that prevails when historians move fluidly through historical spaces that are conceived in ways that allow for the contrasts and contradictions emerging from competing structures of periodization.

Similarly, I welcomed the diversity of approaches that contributors brought to the problem of geographical perspective. Clearly, no one viewpoint – continental, transatlantic, global or country-specific – can be applied equally to every chapter without impinging on the success of the research they contain and expertise of the contributor. British theatre looms largest in the volume. This is in part a welcome counterbalance to the dominating French context that for a long time defined 'Enlightenment'. (As Edelstein points out: 'Forty years ago, it was deemed redundant to bother qualifying the Enlightenment as French'.[13]) But it is also worthy to note that it is through the perspective of British theatre, with its strong influence on the development of commercial theatre, theatrical labour and grand touring networks, as well as wide colonial reach and cross-channel relationships, that we can see major trends that obtained for theatre in the period more globally. However, as one can expect when dealing with a period as complex as the eighteenth century, the chapters reflect the importance of interpreting the cultural history of theatre precisely and embracing specific determining factors such as national, economic, material and cultural practices. In the simultaneous diversity of their material and in the different ways they telescope from the discrete to the continuous, the chapters herein are a reflection of the explosive scattering of the eighteenth century, of its multiple centres of power and philosophy, multivalent social influences, of the secularizing power of its market, and the disruptive energy of its colliding and competing ideas.

The metaphor of the Enlightenment as a matrix of ideas, actions and events (matrix defined as an environment or material in which something develops) offers rich possibilities for understanding the special synergy founded on practice between the Enlightenment and its theatre. This synergy appears throughout this volume in discussions of such topics as stage patronage and censorship, audience behaviour, actresses and theatrical labour, private theatres, touring spectacles, pictorial staging, actor sociability, affect and audience, stage lighting and celebrity. While no one framework can contain these topics and more as they are interwoven in the ten chapters of this volume, I will shed some further light by casting them in the context of theatre and society, subjectivity and material existence, and focusing on three key thinkers and texts of the period – Rousseau, Diderot and Voltaire – that serve to illustrate them.

ROUSSEAU AND THE SOCIAL BASIS OF THEATRE

'The starring role played by society in the enlightened narrative', writes Dan Edelstein, 'comes as little surprise: historians in recent years have drawn attention to how society during the Enlightenment became "the ontological frame of our human existence", or, in César Dumarsais's oft-cited word, "a divinity . . . on earth"'. [14] Proceeding from Edelstein's observation that the very basis of the Enlightenment experience was the obsession with society, or the 'world of all human interaction',[15] a fitting place to highlight the eighteenth-century theatre as a social institution is a seminal text of the period, Jean-Jacques Rousseau's *Lettre à d'Alembert sur le théâtre*, in which he questions the function and role of theatre in a civil society and brings to the fore the integration between society, culture and nation. Rousseau's 1758 *Lettre* is a signature item in the Enlightenment canon of criticism and philosophy about the theatre, even while it challenged ideas presented in another key publication of the Enlightenment: Diderot's *Encyclopédie*. In 1757, the encyclopaedia article 'Geneva', which was authored by Jean le Rond d'Alembert, contained several passages influenced by Voltaire that criticized the Republic of Geneva's current ban on theatre. Rousseau's response to the encyclopaedia article and its criticisms the following year contains a fascinating thesis on the uses and function of theatre within a social context that, in its widest sense, is broader than the issues of Geneva alone.

The first facet of Rousseau's *Lettre* that resonates strongly with the concerns of the period and yet is quite novel to it is the notion that forms of theatre and drama are specific to the unique features of the nation it entertains – nation here referring to the 'prodigious diversity of morals [manners], temperaments, and characters' founded in differences in 'religions, governments, laws, customs, prejudices, and climates'.[16] For Rousseau, the 'diversity of entertainments' in the world is the result of the 'diverse tastes of nations'.[17] Thus, to ask 'if the theatre is good or bad in itself is to pose too vague a question; it is to examine a relation before having defined the terms. The theatre is made for the people, and it is only by its effects on the people that one can determine its absolute qualities'.[18] Rousseau's idea of nation here is not yet fully the sharply bordered sociopolitical one that would define nineteenth-century conceptions of nation and nationalism; it is rather in line with the notion of a 'spirit of the people' as subject to the influence of environmental factors like topography and climate. But what might be called Rousseau's thesis of 'national theatrical relativism', as well as his overall framing of theatre as a national product, is a red thread that runs throughout the period. Theatrical art in the context of national interests informs the use of theatre as cultural intervention in foreign affairs, from entertaining visiting diplomats in British theatre to the imperial/colonizing efforts to bestow theatre upon foreign shores, from Jamaica to Calcutta. These aspects are discussed in this volume in chapters by David Worrall and Mita Choudhury. The British actor David Garrick's circulating tours throughout Europe reflect cultural exchange, but they are also reflective of a new commercial value found in the exportation of nationally inflected differences in theatre performance. That Shakespeare emerges for Garrick as a privileged object of export is significant. The construction of Shakespeare as a national poet and the use of his plays as part of an effort in British global expansion is an important eighteenth-century phenomenon, as Choudhury shows. Daniel O'Quinn points most particularly to the use of Shakespeare in the development of national identity. The eighteenth century also saw several instances in the growing movement of national theatres, most particularly German theatre. Gotthold Ephraim Lessing's efforts for the newly founded Hamburg National Theatre articulated a vision of German theatre that was particular to its people and that could, as Deborah Payne discusses, transform the people and advance a German drama that was not indebted to the dominating influence of French neoclassicism. Theatre as a national product is evident in views held by Carlo Goldoni, who argued for the traditions of *commedia dell'arte* in the Italian context, and Luigi Riccoboni, who sought with his direction of the Comédie-Italienne in Paris to elevate the reputation of Italian drama and performance on foreign soil. Throughout the chapters in this volume are examples of theatre emerging in a new context, differentiated traits of social identity and the concomitant development of national promotion. We see this in the invention of pride in a nation's theatrical product, the recognition of differences in performance, and circulation of theatre and the colonizing project of bestowing theatrical product upon foreign shores.

Rousseau's *Lettre* also disputed the notion of theatrical representation as a means of correcting the ignorance, immorality and vices of a people. He challenged the model of theatre as means of catharsis or cleansing that since the time of Aristotle had provided defenders of theatre with justification for the civic value of theatrical arts. Rousseau rejects the ancient and subsequent theories of theatre as having any salutary or corrective influence on social behaviour by inciting fear (in tragedy) or laughter (in comedy) of misdeeds, vices and faults of human character. Rousseau takes a position on this that is both pragmatic and philosophical. Theatres are in the business of pleasing audiences. To survive, dramatists must write plays that please audiences and theatres must entertain them. By definition, therefore, theatre cannot be truly challenging to the manners and beliefs of the people they serve. 'It follows from these first observations that the general effect of the theatre is to strengthen the national character', he writes,

> to augment the national inclinations, and to give a new energy to all the passions. In this sense it would seem that, its effect being limited to intensifying and changing the established morals [manners], the drama would be good for the good and bad for the vicious . . . I know that the poetic theatre claims to do exactly the opposite and to purge the passions in exciting them. But I have difficulty understanding this rule.

Forced by the basis of its very existence to appeal to the tastes of its public, theatre must appeal to the dominant interest. 'If an author shocks these maxims, he will write a very fine play to which no one will go'.[19]

In challenging these notions of the salutary function of theatre and asserting its power as an agent of societal practices within the context of comparative national differentiation and distinction, Rousseau's *Lettre* reflects important themes in eighteenth-century theatre that are familiar yet new. In this, Rousseau is not alone. In 1698, for example, Jeremy Collier condemned the 'profanity' of the English stage. In doing so, his arguments were not simply those of an ages-old, theological anti-theatricalism. John O'Brien points out how Collier's position cast the question of the morality of theatre in a national context. Throughout this volume, we can read in its histories this important facet of the cultural history of theatre in the Enlightenment: theatre as a social practice and implicated in the development of nation-specific strategies of identity and propaganda, as well as the role of dramatic literature in confirming societal mores, social structures, civic behaviours and state politics.

DIDEROT AND ENLIGHTENMENT SUBJECTHOOD

The eighteenth-century specialist Daniel Brewer describes how scholars of the period have shifted away from 'intellectual history towards a more social, cultural, and indeed material history', and he links this shift to a new way of viewing history that is spatially informed and predicated on visuality, or the 'investigative gaze'. As a critical framework, space has become the 'master metaphor of late twentieth-century epistemology' in a variety of fields, he writes; for the study of the eighteenth century it is particularly productive. The eighteenth century is a world of new and developing spaces both physical and abstract – academies, salons, libraries, the republic of letters – through which new subjectivities are revealed. 'Real physical places in the eighteenth century undergo change and transformation, and in the process they are invested with meaning and value, thanks to particular representational practices'. As Daniel Brewer proposes, eighteenth-century social identity comes into being in relation to one's position vis-à-vis a multitude of new spaces, bringing eighteenth-century subjecthood into being.[20]

The theatre as an Enlightenment space that brings into being new subjectivities and where the gaze is investigative and epistemological is revealed most clearly in two writings by the dramatist and *philosophe* Denis Diderot. The first set of writings is actually a collection of two plays and accompanying materials in the form of framing dialogues that together theorize and demonstrate the performance and reception of middle-class serious drama: the *drame bourgeois*. Diderot's theory of the *drame* shaped new values of performance and spectatorship in the theatre founded on emotional sensitivity and nuance, that are visually (not textually) oriented, and that speak to the spectator's experience of contemplation and feeling in the theatre. The second text similarly deals with audience experience and feeling, but in regards to the craft of acting. As matters for the cultural history of theatre, these texts reveal eighteenth-century perspectives on the relationship between feeling and the stage, visual aspects of performance and audience experience. They are explored in several chapters in this volume in relation to topics such as dramatic genre, performance and the construction of the spectator in the realm of the gaze.

With the *drame bourgeois*, Diderot advocates the use of a new genre: a middle ground of serious plays that are neither in the vein of classical tragedy (with its characters of high birth and tragic endings) nor comedy (with risible characters of low birth in happy endings). He also advocates staging practices that place actors in lifelike positions on the stage, scene designs appropriate and specific to the play, plots that avoid improbable coincidences and unlikely reversals, and dialogue that reflects everyday patterns of speech by allowing, for example, silence on stage when that would more accurately reflect the moment as it might happen in life. Diderot's attempt to create this stage world that is more representative of reality as lived seriously and privately through moral characters was put into action in two dramas, *Le Fils naturel* (*The Natural Son*, 1757) and *Le Père de famille* (*Father of the Family*, 1758). As Diderot sees it, the theatre of his time is overwhelmed by exaggeration and falseness. His *Entretiens sur Le Fils naturel*, the fictional dialogues between the leading character 'Dorval' and 'Moi' (Diderot) which frame the play of the same name, contain a harsh critique of the contemporary French stage. The instructional goal of drama to 'inspire men to the love of virtue, and horror for vice', depended on the power of performance to truthfully imitate life, which the French stage sorely lacks.[21] It is in support of greater stage truth that Diderot calls for removing audience members from the stage (a current practice at the time), asserts that actors should be allowed to face one another (and if necessary, turn their backs on the audience), and decries the practice of actors stepping out of their roles to address spectators directly. The audience should be ignored, he says. It is within this context of creating a convincing truth that Diderot advocates what he calls the *tableau*, or the silent depiction of 'characters on the stage, so natural and true that they would make a pleasing canvas if rendered in a painting'.[22] *Le Fils naturel* is woven throughout with detailed stage directions suggesting what he means by such *tableaux*. For example: 'Rosalie is sadly bent over her sewing work. Justine is seated to her side with hers. They work. Rosalie stops her sewing only to wipe some tears falling from her eye before taking it up again. The silence lasts a bit, during which Justine looks up from her work to look at her mistress'.[23] Diderot abhors the contrived arrangement of actors in contemporary staging practices which place them in unnatural positions across the front of the stage. He advocates the illusion of privacy between actor and audience that in acting technique we have come to call the 'fourth wall' or 'public solitude': 'Whether you compose or act, think no more of the beholder than if he did not exist. Imagine, at the edge of the stage, a high wall that separates you from the orchestra. Act as if the curtain never rose'.[24]

In an influential study of the period, *Absorption and Theatricality: Painting and Beholder in the Age of Diderot*, Michael Fried posits that such depiction of figures absorbed in private action was a driving aesthetic in mid- and late eighteenth-century French art. Based on his analysis of paintings from the era, Fried defines absorption as 'the state or condition of rapt attention, of being completely occupied or engrossed'.[25] Diderot's practices of the *mise en scène* for the *drame* – his emphasis on silent simple gesture, on *tableaux*, fourth wall and natural arrangement of actors on the stage as well as his disdain for artifice in language and self-conscious actorly display for an audience – are all constituting practices for the depiction of absorption in the theatre. To effectively engage absorption, art must maintain what Fried calls the 'supreme fiction', or pretence of the absence of a beholder. Paradoxically, it is through this kind of rejection of the beholder that the eighteenth-century artist aimed to have the maximum effect on viewers. In Fried's thesis, the visual ethos of absorption involved a changing sense of subjecthood that was particular to the period. The creation of 'a new sort of [art] object' in the eighteenth century called for the constitution of a 'new sort of beholder', one whose 'innermost nature would consist precisely in the conviction of his absence from the scene of representation'.[26] The *mise en scène* of the *drame bourgeois*, with its acting as if 'the curtain never rose' fostered new subject identities in beholding audiences of attentive and feeling spectators. Deborah Payne's discussion of the 'contagion' of emotions in theatre, as well as David Worrall's points about the theatre space in terms of new audience social behaviours reflect the influence of this idea of a mutually constitutive relationship between audience and the Enlightenment stage.

Diderot's notion of inciting the emotions of audiences through purely truthful stage depiction seems to have altered in his later years, when he devoted time to writing about acting. His ideas were shaped in part as a result of his contact with the actor David Garrick, 'whose virtuosic demonstrations greatly influenced his speculations into the inner nature of acting',[27] and whose impact throughout the continent is very fruitfully explored in this volume by Mita Choudhury. *Le Paradoxe sur le comédien* (*The Paradox of Acting*), written around 1773 but first published in 1830, offers a complex theory about the nature of acting, 'approaching it as a craft rather than as a diabolic or sacred mystery'.[28] His central argument is counter-intuitive: namely, that audiences feel most when the actor feels less. Diderot is not presenting a thesis against truth and feeling on stage; rather, he is supporting the idea that the experience of truth and a sincerity of feeling is a deeply social endeavour, invented by an audience bound together in illusion. In *Listening in Paris*, James Johnson writes of the collective power (and importance) of feeling as a social practice: 'These were the years of sensibility in France, when to feel at all was to feel passionately, and to show it in public *de rigueur*'.[29] In his chapter, Logon Connors remarks the new 'codes of sensibility' that are embedded in the development of audience experience for Diderot's *drame*. Lisa Freeman explores a range of sentiment as conceived on the eighteenth-century British stage through an in-depth discussion of the play *Isabella; Or, The Fatal Marriage*. The importance of Enlightenment spaces, particularly theatre, in the development of subject identities can also be read in places beyond plays and genres. The social practice of perceiving truth and sincerity, and its stakes, can be seen in the history of actresses and motherhood which, as Helen Brooks points out, are revealed in the eighteenth century in the space between the depiction of motherly goodness in women's roles and the reality of the professional lives of actresses.

THEATRE IN THE MATERIAL WORLD: VOLTAIRE

As Pannill Camp argues in his book, *The First Frame*, the spectator of the Enlightenment was seen a 'sense function' and spectatorship was recognized by theatre architects 'to be foremost a sensory activity, and sensation a function of material interactions between bodily organs and the physical world'.[30] Many in the period wrote about theatre architecture – well documented in studies by Daniel Rabreau and Michèle Sajous D'Oria, among others. Within the huge volume of writing by Voltaire, his thoughts on theatre architecture, stages and audience occupy just a small fraction; as a major figure in the French Enlightenment, however, his thoughts about these subjects are worth exploring. Voltaire wrote about the importance of playhouses in the urban landscape, about the stage and how the audience views it, and about the audience space. It is a helpful entry point to a theme that appears throughout this volume: theatre in the physical world as an Enlightenment practice, and about the physical world as form and expression of societal relationships.

Voltaire's essay *Discours sur la tragédie ancienne et moderne* was published in 1749 as a preface to his play *Sémiramis*, which had premiered at the Comédie-

Française the year before. The essay compares ancient Greek theatre to opera, and French tragedy to Greek tragedy. Voltaire also takes the opportunity to enter into a discussion regarding theatres, stages, audience behaviour and spectatorship. He writes of emulating ancient models in writing *Sémiramis*, but acknowledges its failure to achieve the same 'dignity as in their representations', or productions, of Greek theatre. He blames this on the French habit of seating audiences on the stage: 'One of the main obstacles that prevents our stages from having strong and moving scenes, is the crowd of spectators, mixed up on the stage with the actors. This indecency was most sharply felt at the premiere of *Sémiramis*'.[31] This distraction not only affects the performance of plays, he writes, it also has a chilling effect on the development of other masterworks that surely would be performed if France could build respectful theatres 'such as exists in other nations of Europe'.[32]

The presence of spectators on the stage that Voltaire so despised was an artefact of medieval performance that had thrived in French theatres throughout the seventeenth century and well into the eighteenth. Indeed, by the 1730s, the Comédie-Française had *increased* the number of spectators on stage:

Two rows of tiered seats initially installed on each side of the stage were replaced by five rows of benches, of which four were free-standing and one backed against the stage boxes. At the cost of a somewhat radical shrinkage of the space available to actors – the stage opening was 'reduced to 15 feet in front, and to 11 at the opposite end' this change created enough permanent seating for 140 spectators.[33]

In part because of Voltaire's campaign against the practice, seating on stage at the Comédie-Française ended ten years later and France would eventually achieve the prestige of the grand theatres Voltaire desires, as described in my chapter here on the environments of theatre.

In addition to audiences impeding the stage space, the other 'grand fault' of French playhouses, according to Voltaire, was the presence of the audience 'standing in what is called the Parterre, where they are constrained and pressed indecently, and where they launch at times into a mêlée, one against the other, in the image of a popular riot'.[34] It would take much longer before this unruly standing pit, with its street-riot behaviour, would be disciplined in more orderly fashion with the installation of benches in the 1770s. Charles de Wailly, architect of the new playhouse for the Comédie-Française that would be completed in 1782, pictured in his illustrations of the interior a ground space filled with well-behaved gentlemen seated politely on banks of benches while the rabble inhabit the uppermost balconies: 'The architect offered his patrons and the salon public a sanitized image of the social world of the theatre, one where the tumult of the standing parterre would be hidden from sight in the third balcony and *paradis*'.[35]

Voltaire's critique of the stage and audience practices of his time, with the disruptive presence of self-displaying spectators seated on the stage ruining the dignity of the great literature being performed and unruly audiences in the *parterre*, is meaningful beyond the particulars of Voltaire's complaint. It is indicative of an era gaining a new awareness of the interaction between spectatorship and the material practices of theatre space. Two chapters of this volume speak most directly to this, Pannill Camp's discussion of architecture, scenery and lighting in 'Technologies of Performance' as well as my chapter on 'The Environment of Theatre'. Throughout the volume's chapters, however, are discussions that highlight the value of Voltaire's 'brick-and-mortar' focus on theatre.

The brief look at historiographical developments in the study of theatre and the French Revolution I presented at the beginning of this introduction contains a cautionary tale and a bit of irony. There is a progressivist narrative implied in my tracking the movement from a simple or 'traditional' view of theatrical cultural history to its new, sophisticated, more complex form. I am also guilty of the common tendency to make hierarchical valuations about prior scholarly investigations and methods. Both points demonstrate how easy it is to fall into patterns of constructing historical knowledge in ways that, despite exaggerated reports of its death, are still dominated by the Enlightenment hope that progress, growth and greater truth has led us out of the darkness. To echo Daniel O'Quinn in his chapter on 'Knowledge Transmission', writing about the status of knowledge in a volume on the Enlightenment is 'doubly vexed'. With that awareness in mind, perhaps a useful way to regard this volume's contribution is to acknowledge that, despite the apparent definitiveness and publishing prestige of a six-volume set of books, the cultural history of the theatre is never finished nor fixed.

CHAPTER ONE

Institutional Frameworks

The State, the Market and the People in the Age of Enlightenment

JOHN O'BRIEN

In a 1771 letter, David Garrick, in every imaginable way the central theatrical figure of the Enlightenment-era theatre in Britain, urged his correspondent, a young writer who wanted his feedback on the draft of a play, that 'If Your inclination leads You to the Stage, the Study of the frame-work will be absolutely necessary for without that Mechanical part all ye Wit, humour &c Character, Which we know You are possess'd of, will be thrown away'.[1] 'Frame-work' here constitutes a play on words; Garrick is critical of the play's plotting and character relationships, what we might think of as its framework in a conceptual sense. But he also puns on the literal sense of framework as a 'Mechanical part', associating plotting with the other material aspects of the stage that his correspondent has to learn as well: scene construction, costuming, lighting – all of the elements of a production that, as Garrick testifies here, are essential to the success of a play. Garrick's pun is testimony to the way that theatrical performance at once takes place in the physical world and seems to transcend it, to reach for abstraction. Given the broad scope of the topic, and the fact that the mechanical structures of the eighteenth-century stage have for the most part disappeared, this chapter on the institutional frameworks of the Enlightenment theatre will of necessity have to be fairly abstract, but I invoke Garrick here to underscore how one of the unique things about theatre is how its abstractions are in the service of live, embodied performance. Following Garrick's lead in proposing a trio of ideas that the material and the conceptual framework of the stage supports ('wit, humour and character'), this chapter will plot out the frameworks of the theatre of his age by attending to a triumvirate of concepts: the state, the market and the people.

In most European countries, the state gradually took over the role of patron from the monarchs and wealthy noblemen who had sponsored, protected and subsidized theatrical companies in the major cities. Well into the eighteenth century, the princes and monarchs of nation states licensed theatres. Most theatres in Europe, even when they called themselves 'Theatres Royal', were not, however, owned by the prince or the state; they were typically private institutions, owned by individual entrepreneurs, partnerships or joint-stock companies. Theatres created and then served a market for performance, one that was fully a part of the emerging capitalist economy. What is more, both the state and the market addressed themselves to new conceptualizations of the people, who were at this point both the population to be managed and an audience whose desire for entertainment called out to be served. Attending to the topics of state, market and people will enable us to compare the various ways in which these elements were combined in different national traditions over the period. It will also help us see how this is when theatre began to take its modern form throughout Europe, where it became on the one hand a symbol of each nation's distinctive culture and on the other hand a part of the entertainment industry. Theatre companies spread widely throughout Europe and its colonies, with hundreds of theatres opening in provincial cities. By 1789, there may have been as many as 120 provincial theatres in the British Isles and seventy-two in France.[2] Colonial cities like Philadelphia, Baltimore, Williamsburg, Kingston, Port-au-Prince and Calcutta (among many others) all boasted purpose-built playhouses. Theatre was for many Europeans the central institution of their culture, linking them to the classical past while also creating a way for them to imagine distinctiveness of their own nations.

In this chapter, I will attend primarily to the English-language theatre from the 1660s to the 1790s. This was a theatre that had its base in London but that would in these decades radiate out to provincial cities and towns in the British Isles and then to the larger cities in the colonies of the Americas and then India. Britain is useful as a place from which to survey the Enlightenment theatre, in part because it is a well-documented example, in part because the tensions between the state and the marketplace were felt and often articulated in particularly acute ways, and also because English performance traditions were widely known and recognized on the Continent from the Renaissance onward. Travelling groups of 'English comedians', small companies of actors, dancers and acrobats from England toured Germany and Scandinavia beginning in the late sixteenth century; the name was then used for many decades to describe indigenous companies even when there were no longer any English-born performers among them. I will also pay some attention to the French theatre, both in its own right as an interesting and contrasting case study, but also for the way that it informed the English-language theatre as a prominent counter example. As a more autocratic realm, in France, particularly early in the period, the institutionalized theatre was particularly strongly associated with the monarch and the court. English playwrights mined French (and also Spanish) plays for raw material, plots and characters that became the basis for many popular works. English critics also drew extensively upon French literary theory. The trajectory of the theatre in Germany and Scandinavia offers useful points of contiguity and divergence. Theatre in Scandinavia in the late seventeenth and early eighteenth centuries, for example, was strongly modelled on the theatre of the French court. As in France, many performances were staged at the behest of the kings and other aristocrats, and the repertoire in the early decades of the eighteenth century consisted largely of works by French playwrights like Corneille, Racine and Molière. Starting in the 1720s, when Ludvig Holberg wrote an extraordinary series of comedies for the royal theatre in Copenhagen, Danish theatre developed its own trajectory as an institution that attempted to represent the fundamental characteristics of the nation and its people to itself. In Germany, theatre similarly became one of the institutions through which writers would advance and help create the conditions for a national literature and culture. Because Germany, divided into multiple principalities, did not have a central city on a par with Paris or London (or for that matter Copenhagen or Stockholm), it developed several regional theatrical centres: Hamburg, Weimar, Mannheim, Berlin. None of these cities was large enough to sustain multiple companies at the same time, or, for that matter, to train many professional performers, and early in the century, many performances were undertaken by amateurs.[3] This meant, however, that extraordinary figures like Gotthold Lessing, Friedrich Schiller and Johann Wolfgang von Goethe were able to manage theatres in those places, and the comparatively small size of the enterprises with which they were associated may have meant that they were freer than their peers in London or Paris to introduce innovations in performance practices and critical theory. Lessing, for example, in effect invented the role of the dramaturg, the critic who works *within* the theatre, shaping a theatre's repertory according to the best principles of the art, when he worked for the Hamburg National Theatre in the late 1760s. His *Hamburgische Dramaturgie*, probably the most influential treatise on the drama written in German in the eighteenth century, derived directly from that experience and, in creating the discipline of dramaturgy, gave a name to the practice of studying play texts with a new kind of professionalism. Goethe directed the Weimar Court Theatre from 1791 to 1817, raising it from an amateur troupe in a small town to become one of the most important centres of theatre in Europe. In each of these places, the theatre had a different trajectory and developed different performance traditions. There is much common experience as well in this period, however, and the British stage is a useful case study, offering lessons that can be extended to understanding the institutional structure of other national theatres. Throughout the period of the Enlightenment, the theatre as an institution was thus never just one thing, but the name we assign to a dynamic cultural process, an interaction between the state, the market and the people.

THE STATE AS LICENSOR

Throughout the eighteenth century there were many performances in Europe offered by itinerant companies who set up for a few days at a time in a market town, or a place such as Smithfield in London, that held annual fairs at harvest time in which performers, sometimes from a professional theatre, staged performances on temporary platforms erected for the duration of the fair. The vast majority of such performances have left no trace in our records because they flew, in effect, under the radar of any official authority. But a permanent acting troupe performing in a purpose-built playhouse was something else entirely. For a group of investors and performers to establish such a thing was understood to be a right derived from a sovereign, much like the right to form other companies that operated mines, lent money or traded in defined regions of the globe, like the Royal African Company or the East India Company. Because they had been authorized by a monarch, many theatrical companies in this period in Europe denominated themselves a 'theatre royal', and often performed in a building that carried that name as well.

The affiliation with the monarchy usually meant less in practical terms than the name might seem to imply, however. Monarchs officially authorized theatre companies and some of them patronized theatres fairly frequently. Probably the monarch with the greatest enthusiasm for the stage was Gustav III of Sweden, who reigned from 1771 until his assassination – fittingly enough, while attending a masquerade ball in the foyer of an opera house – in 1792. Gustav wrote and even performed in his own plays, commissioned operas and is credited with founding the Swedish Royal Theatre, the Royal Swedish Opera and the Royal Swedish Ballet. Other monarchs also believed that supporting the theatre was an important part of their job as supervisor of their nation's culture. Charles II, for example, saw that publicly supporting the theatre was a way of turning the clock back to the period before the unpleasantness of the English Civil War, reminding his subjects of the proud tradition of drama and entertainment that had characterized the reigns of his father Charles I and grandfather James I earlier in the seventeenth century. Yet although theatre companies needed the monarch's support for the right to perform, this did not come with a reciprocal obligation on the monarch's part to subsidize the theatres financially. Charles II doled out gifts to performers and playwrights here and there when they particularly pleased him, but it was impossible for those who were running the theatres to count on the court as a source of income. This was even truer in the eighteenth century. Neither Queen Anne (who reigned from 1702 until 1714), nor the three successive Georges who served as monarch from 1714 to the end of the century, cared much for the theatre. George I, for example, did not speak particularly good English, so he took little pleasure in plays. But opera boomed during his reign in part owing to the remarkable fact that George Frideric Handel had been George's kapellmeister – director of music for the court – when George was the Elector of Hanover. Handel made London one of the great centres of opera in Europe.

In the early years of his reign, Louis XIV of France he took a great interest in the theatre. Louis founded the Comédie-Française in 1680, merging two established companies, and he provided an annual subsidy of 12,000 *livres*. British writers sometimes pointed jealously to France as a place where theatre received the support that it deserved.

Louis's support waned, however, when he became influenced by religious reformers who increasingly found the theatre to be morally objectionable. He attended the theatre only rarely after the mid-1680s, although he occasionally hosted performers at court.[4] Theatres were closed in Copenhagen entirely during the reign of Christian VI (1738 to 1746), who banned theatrical performance because he believed it to be impious. (His successor Frederick V reversed course and issued a patent for a new theatre; the Royal Danish Theatre,

FIGURE 1.1: *The Comédie-Française*, Antoine Meunier, late eighteenth century. By permission of the Bibliothèque nationale de France.

now one of the central cultural institutions in Denmark, has operated continuously on the same site in Copenhagen since 1748.)[5] The title of 'Theatre Royal', then, conferred what were considered to be essential rights to build playhouses, hire and train actors and stage public performances. It also gave the businessmen who owned and ran the playhouses some protection from potential competitors. Monarchs did not, however, own the theatres in their capital cities, nor did they tend to subsidize them in any systematic or sustainable way. Outside capital cities, even those institutions that called themselves Theatres Royal were pretty much on their own.[6] The benign neglect of sovereigns belied the impression they tried to convey of being active supervisors of their peoples' entertainment.

Even though personal supervision on the part of monarchs was uneven and infrequent, it was widely understood that the state had a role in overseeing the smooth operation of theatres and the policing of their repertoires to prevent moral contagion and political unrest. Actors appealed to government ministers when they believed that theatre managers were treating them unfairly or reneging on terms to which they had previously agreed. This happened with some frequency, as the Lord Chamberlain's office was called upon to adjudicate even fairly minor disputes. It did so in 1720, for example, when the then-Lord Chamberlain, the Duke of Newcastle, ordered the Drury Lane Company not to allow any performer to have their benefit performance night – a special performance during which the gate receipts, minus expenses, would go to an actor or actress – before those of the established stars Anne Oldfield and Mary Porter.[7] More consequentially, the state monitored theatres for transgressions of morality, sexual suggestiveness or religious impiety. Monarchs were not only in theory responsible for their people's entertainment, but for their morality as well; the British monarch was officially the head of the national Church. It is no surprise, then, to note that the most famous anti-theatrical treatise of the period, Jeremy Collier's *A Short View of the Immorality, and Profaneness, of the English-Stage* (1698), was written by a man who had been trained to be a minister in the Church of England. At the time he published his treatise, Collier was at odds with the official Church (he disagreed with its hierarchy for endorsing William and Mary's legitimacy), but his chief complaint in *A Short View* was that the Church had squandered its moral authority and was not exercising its supervision of the stage aggressively enough. The result, Collier argued, was that playwrights had run amok, filling their plays with sexual innuendo, double entendre and anticlerical satire that the state had an obligation to take action against.

In arguing that the English state, just now settled into the post-Glorious Revolution era and beginning to embrace norms of modern finance and cosmopolitan urbanity, was neglecting its responsibility to supervise the stage, Collier was urging that it return to the example set by the ancient states of

Greece and Rome. 'Notwithstanding the Latitudes of Paganism', Collier claimed, 'the Roman and Greek *Theatres* were much more inoffensive than ours'.[8] Collier's prose is clumsy but effective, and reminds us of the degree to which Europeans of this period looked to the classical past for models as they navigated the new hazards of modernity. Especially in the early part of the eighteenth century, playwriting throughout Europe was heavily influenced by ideas that have been called 'neoclassical' for the way that they looked back to the norms of the ancient Greek and Roman theatre. Playwrights crafted many plays about heroic figures from the ancient world. Joseph Addison's 1712 tragedy *Cato*, for example, which staged the last hours in the life of Cato of Utica, the last holdout of the Roman republic before Rome turned to empire and tyranny, was performed again and again throughout the English-speaking world. George Washington ordered the play to be staged at Valley Forge in the brutal winter of 1777 to encourage his troops to accept their hardships with the same Stoic resignation as that portrayed by the play's titular hero as he faces his own death; their reaction is unrecorded. Johann Christoph Gottsched adapted Addison's play for the German-language theatre as *The Dying Cato* in 1732, and Gottsched's version remained part of the repertory in that tradition for decades as well.

The most obvious way in which playwrights were urged to model their works on the classics was the way in which they were for decades pressured by critics to follow the doctrines of the 'unities' of place, time and action, which decreed that plays should take place in a single location (place), in the course of a single day (time) and should follow a single line of plot (action). The unities had been introduced by French playwright-critics like François Hédelin, abbé d'Aubignac, whose *Pratique du théâtre* (1657, translated into English in 1684 as *The Whole Art of the Stage*) was widely influential, and French playwrights in particular were disposed to follow them, which was particularly important since in many places like Germany and Scandinavia, French was spoken in the courts in which performances often took place in the early part of the century.[9] The unities were based on what we would now think of as a misreading of Aristotle's treatise from the fourth century BCE, the *Poetics*. While Aristotle was trying to describe the Greek stage and the qualities that the most successful plays of that repertoire had in common, the French playwrights, theorists and their followers throughout Europe took his findings as setting out hard-and-fast rules for playwrights to follow. Collier, for example, supported the unities, and mocked John Vanbrugh's still-popular comedy *The Relapse* (1697) for deviating wildly from them. It was not until the 1760s or so, when writers like Voltaire, Samuel Johnson and Gotthold Lessing all independently argued against the unities, that their hold was finally broken.[10]

Collier's work makes it clear that aesthetic principles do not take shape in a vacuum, and that these rules were just the means to an end. Only by following this set of precepts from the ancients would playwrights be contributing to an 'English stage' that encouraged the people of the modern English state to emulate the virtues of the ancient nations. Theoretical claims like Collier's worked hand in hand with the interest of all the monarchs and states of this period in making sure that the theatres which they licensed did not do anything to threaten their authority. Governments could close the theatres entirely, as had happened in England in the 1640s and 1650s, and as happened, as we have already seen, in Denmark in the 1730s. In most places, at most times, things rarely went that far, because the men running the theatres and the playwrights working in them internalized norms that supported the structures of power from which they derived their authority. They knew the boundaries of what would be acceptable to their royal and aristocratic patrons and the government, and did not often push against them. In seventeenth-century Britain and France, theatres were nominally under the supervision of court officials like the Master of the Revels or the *procureur du roi*, but it was very rare that such men had to intervene to censor the repertoire.

The willingness of government officials to intervene in the day-to-day operations of the playhouses changed in eighteenth-century Britain, with decisive effects. The Stage Licensing Act, enacted in 1737, is the most famous and influential example of government intervention in the licensed playhouses, the two theatres in London that were officially authorized by the government.[11] The story has often been told that Robert Walpole, the de facto prime minister of Britain, put the Act forward because he was annoyed at being ridiculed by Henry Fielding's political satires. That is at least partly true. Fielding wrote a series of ingenious satirical short plays in the 1730s that mocked both the managers of the playhouses and the management of the nation, which he saw as analogous to each other, *statecraft* being by these lights just another form of *stagecraft*. Fielding's satires feel very modern at times in the way that they imagine the government as putting on a show designed to obscure its incompetence and corruption from a credulous public. Walpole's move against Fielding's mockery is only part of a much larger story, however. The middle-class tradesmen of London, worried about the effect of all forms of entertainment on their apprentices and other young people, had already been agitating for a crackdown on the stage and Fielding's barbs provided a convenient excuse. Moreover, the kind of arguments that Collier raised against double entendre and other kinds of bawdy language still had purchase among many observers, who had long argued that the state should intervene in order to restore the British theatre to its lost glory.[12]

Whatever the constellation of forces that led to the passage of the Licensing Act at this moment, its impact was substantial. The Act had the effect of closing down a number of unlicensed playhouses that had sprouted up in London, ending the boom in theatrical performance that had taken place in the 1730s.

Eventually, such performance venues would return. Most importantly, the Act had a long-standing effect on dramatic literature in English. From this point on, well into the nineteenth century, theatres had to submit plays to the Lord Chamberlain's office in advance of production for approval, and the impact of such censorship – either imposed by the licensor or pre-emptively undertaken by playwrights who had internalized the censor's norms – was enormous. (Remarkably, the Stage Licensing Act was not fully repealed until 1968.) The number of new plays produced for the English-speaking stage dropped as the theatres turned to revivals and spectacles, relying on the skill and celebrity of performers to draw audiences to familiar works. Even though provincial theatres were largely ignored by the Lord Chamberlain's office, they drew their repertoire from the London playhouses, so the scope of their performances was limited by decisions he made.

The relative decline in the production of new dramatic works in English in this period had some interesting and unplanned side effects. First, it is probably no coincidence that the rise of William Shakespeare as 'The Bard', the quintessence of all that is great about English literature, dates to the 1730s and 1740s.[13] Shakespeare's plays had been in the repertoire in the London theatre since the restoration of the monarchy in 1660, though often in heavily adapted versions, such as the one of *The Tempest* written by John Dryden and William D'Avenant, or in the extensive revision of *King Lear* undertaken by Nahum Tate in 1680 that (among many things) changed the ending of the play so that Lear survived and Cordelia married Edgar. Shakespeare's works continued to be reprinted, and in fact the eighteenth century was when critics like Samuel Johnson and Edmund Malone developed the standards of scholarly editing that inform our understanding of Shakespeare's texts to this day. The works of other English Renaissance playwrights such as Ben Jonson, Francis Beaumont and John Fletcher had been kept alive as well – at least until the 1730s. These authors were often put on a par with (or even ahead of) Shakespeare and considered equally interesting and significant contributors to the nation's cultural heritage. By comparison with Jonson, in particular, Shakespeare failed the new test posed by the neoclassical critics. Thomas Rymer, for example, had mocked the plot of *Othello*, which turns on the discovery of a handkerchief, as absurdly improbable; he criticized the language of Shakespeare's tragedies as falling frequently into '*bombast Circumstance*, where the Words and Action are seldom akin, generally are inconsistent, at cross purposes, embarras or destroy each other'.[14] It is hard to imagine a critic writing anything in this vein about Shakespeare now. In the 1730s and 1740s, Shakespeare filled a felt need for a theatrical figure who was untainted by the controversies of the moment. Faced with state-enforced limitations on the scope of new plays in the present, the English-language theatre turned back to the past, and advanced Shakespeare to the position of cultural authority that he has occupied in European culture ever since.

So, too, does the so-called 'rise of the novel' in England at mid-century owe more than a little to the limitations imposed on the drama in the late 1730s. Samuel Richardson, a wealthy London printer who was one of those most concerned with the impact of popular entertainment on his own apprentices and other young people, had campaigned against the playhouses in several tracts that he published during the 1730s. In 1740, he published his novel *Pamela; Or, Virtue Rewarded*, in which a young woman born in respectable rural poverty rises to the gentry by following examples of good behaviour learned, not by attending uplifting theatrical performances that would demonstrate exemplary virtue, but by reading the Bible and moral tales. Henry Fielding, his successful theatrical career cut short by the Walpole government's intervention, started his career as a writer of fiction first by writing parodies of *Pamela* (*Shamela*, published in 1741, and *Joseph Andrews*, published in 1743), and then branched out with a novelistic masterpiece of his own, *Tom Jones* (1749). Other writers had the trajectories of their career redirected by the fact that the new regime of prior censorship made it so much more difficult for new plays to be staged and new playwrights to enter what up to that point had been a plausible profession. Samuel Johnson, having failed as a provincial schoolmaster, came to London in 1738 with the draft of a verse tragedy called *Irene* that he hoped would make his fame and fortune. Frustrated by the high hurdles to new plays imposed by the Licensing Act the year before, Johnson turned to journalism, making a career as a writer for the *Gentleman's Magazine* for more than a decade before finally achieving fame as the author of his *Dictionary of the English Language* in 1755. (*Irene* was eventually produced, in 1749, to middling commercial and critical success; Johnsonians have worked hard to forget about it.) Tobias Smollett arrived in London in 1739 from his native Scotland with the hopes of making his career as a playwright: he too discovered that this was now all but impossible. He spent close to a decade as a surgeon in the Royal Navy before returning to London and finding literary fame at last as a novelist with the publication of *Roderick Random* in 1748. To be sure, there were some new plays produced in London every season and the theatres prospered with a menu of well-staged revivals, farces, dances, music and spectacle. For several decades, however, many ambitious writers directed their energies elsewhere. One way or another, the relationship between the state and the theatre shaped the entire course of literary culture in the eighteenth century.

THE MARKET AND THE ART OF MANAGEMENT

Because no monarch or government provided sustained financial support even to the playhouses that carried royal titles in their names, the theatre had to be a commercial institution, supporting itself through box-office receipts. Playhouses in the major European cities were run as for-profit businesses, their managers determined to extract their own incomes from the nightly performances. The managers were in many cases actors themselves, but sometimes they were businessmen or even speculators who came from outside the world of the theatre; Thomas Harris had been a successful manufacturer of soap and John Rutherford an importer of wine when they invested £60,000 (something like £9,000,000 in current value) to purchase the patent for the Covent Garden company in the late 1760s and joined George Colman, a playwright, and William Powell, an actor, as co-managers.[15] Run poorly, theatre then and now is a very good way to lose a lot of money very quickly, and the history of theatre in the eighteenth century is riddled with bankruptcies, closures and other financial crises brought about by mismanagement, overreaching or simple bad luck. Theatres could also be highly profitable, and there never seems to have been a shortage of people eager to get into the business. Theatrical patents and licences were valuable pieces of property in their own right, in some ways more enduring and valuable than any physical component of the playhouses such as sets, costumes or the buildings themselves, which were prone to wear, decay and disaster in ways that the rights conferred by the patents were not.

How did theatres make their money? What was, to use a modern term, their business model? We do not know everything, but enough documentary evidence has survived to give us some idea. There were (most of the time) generally two licensed playhouses in London, their rights derived ultimately from the two patents issued by Charles II at the Restoration in 1660.

One theatre was on Drury Lane, on the site of the building that currently bears the name Theatre Royal; it was built in 1812 to replace an earlier theatre built in 1794 but destroyed by fire. That theatre had replaced an earlier Theatre Royal, built in 1674 and designed by Christopher Wren, which itself replaced yet another theatre, built in 1663, that was also the victim of fire. The other theatre company performed in a series of theatre buildings that were located on the edge of Lincoln's Inn Fields from 1661 until 1728, when the company moved to a new, larger theatre just off Covent Garden. The Royal Opera House now stands on that site. Like the vast majority of theatres built in Europe in this period, all of these playhouses had proscenium arch stages and movable scenery. These were fairly intimate spaces, particularly as compared with an open-air Renaissance theatre such as Shakespeare's Globe, which by this point had long fallen into ruin. Where the Globe might have fit 3,000 (tightly packed) spectators, neither of the patent houses fit more than 700 or so spectators, particularly in the early part of the century. (Successive renovations generally found ways to add seats, and the 1794 and 1812 Drury Lane playhouses were designed to accommodate the larger audiences now possible with a much larger urban population.) The spectators were put in tiers, an arrangement that often demarcated social standing. The side boxes were generally occupied by the wealthy and until the 1760s in London, the very rich were often able to become part of the performance by buying seats on the stage itself. Seats in the lower circles were generally occupied by members of what we might now call the middle class: merchants, bureaucrats, tradespeople. The upper gallery was often occupied by the footmen who had come early to secure seats for their employers, and other servants, apprentices and members of what we might now call the working class. The benches in the pit area were generally occupied by young men, either attending the theatre alone or in groups. Ticket prices varied and we do not know all of the details, but we do know that at the end of the century, seats in the pit went for three shillings and box seats generally sold for six.

From these receipts, the managers of the theatres had to pay all of the considerable expenses associated with doing live performance several nights a week: salaries for performers and staff, sets, costumes, building maintenance. Precise figures are hard to come by, but in London, the cost to run a playhouse ranged from about £32 per day in the early part of the century to about £83 by the 1780s.[16] Candles and oil to light the stage and the auditorium were a large and ongoing expense (and an ongoing hazard, as the number of playhouses that succumbed to fire makes clear). Probably the largest outlays, though, went to actors, singers and other performers. Unless they also had a stake in management, actors were generally on salary; a star could earn several hundred pounds a year; a featured player might get a base salary of a fraction of that, plus a bonus for every night they acted. This was not enough for anything more than a fairly modest middle-class lifestyle, and many performers relied on their annual benefit performance, through which they would receive one night's gate receipts minus house expenses, as a necessary supplement. For their part, playwrights were entitled to the receipts from every third night's performance of a new play minus the house expenses; if a play ran for nine or twelve nights (a good run at the time), this could translate into a substantial sum. Playwrights also retained the publication rights to their works, which was helpful, although windfalls such as the substantial profits that Addison made off the multiple editions of *Cato* were pretty rare.

After expenses were accounted for, managers were generally able to reserve substantial incomes for themselves, and in some cases became quite wealthy. Perhaps the most spectacular example was David Garrick. A former student in Samuel Johnson's failed boys' school, Garrick walked with Johnson to London in 1738, but his success came much sooner than that of his former teacher. Garrick became famous in the role of Richard III in 1742 and was the leading star on the London stage for the next three decades. He became the manager of the Drury Lane Company in 1747, at the age of thirty. By the 1750s, he was able to purchase a large country estate, achieving the dream of many upwardly mobile Englishmen. Garrick was particularly talented and canny, but in general the fact that patent holders held on to their rights for a long time makes it clear that these were valuable pieces of property; managed competently, the theatre could be a profitable business.

The men who exercised the rights conferred by the theatre patents and licences were not supposed to not say this very loudly, however. All theatre companies had to claim to be operating in the interest of the monarch and the country that he or she led, providing entertainment and moral uplift for the sake of the public and the nation. It seems entirely possible, of course, that many managers believed this themselves, and saw the profit motive as incidental or a necessary evil. Richard Steele, who became the patentee of the Drury Lane Company in London in the late 1710s, did so in part on the basis of his professed desire to reform the British theatre, to become its 'Censor' on the ancient Roman model of the official responsible for public manners. Although Steele was often criticized as an opportunist and profit-seeker, it seems likely that he was at least partly sincere about his intentions to use his position to advance the public good; for Steele, as for many people, motives of self and of public interest were often in a state of uneasy detente. Yet it seems fair to say that most of the men – and they were all men – who actively ran playhouses had cash flow near the top of their minds a good deal of the time. They had little choice; theatre has always been a capital-intensive business, requiring considerable resources of material and personnel.

Theatre is almost always risky as well, since it can be very challenging to predict what will succeed and what will fail. Theatre managers sought to contain that risk whenever they could. They tended to program familiar, tested plays, and to introduce new plays that followed familiar conventions. They developed star systems where predictably audience-pleasing performers became typecast in familiar kinds of parts, and in many cases performed the same set of roles for decades. The London theatre companies rarely poached performers from each other; in this way, they kept salaries, one of the biggest ongoing expenses, in check. Rather than operating on the model of a truly free market, the professional theatres in major cities tended to become cartels, tacitly following norms that preserved their collective prerogatives and kept out upstart rivals. The managers of the patent houses in London were therefore not as unhappy with the passage of the Stage Licensing Act in 1737 as one might expect, since it had the substantial benefit from their point of view of cracking down on the unlicensed playhouses that were outside of the cartel system and therefore represented a threat.

That the theatre managers professed to be pursuing moral uplift while chasing box-office success was an open secret that periodically fuelled conflict. Collier, for example, at the outset of his *Short View*, addresses the conflict between profit and moral purpose directly: 'The business of *Plays* is to recommend Virtue, and discountenance Vice ... Our *Poets* write with a different View, and are gone into an other Interest'.[17] To be sure, Collier's immediate complaint is with playwrights ('Poets') rather than with management. But his invocation of 'business' makes clear that he understands well the commercial context within which such works were being produced, and that he wanted to push back against the tendency for theatre to pander to its audience's interest in titillation and scandal. Similarly, the satirical print *A Just View of the British Stage* (1723), which alludes to the title of Collier's treatise, draws its energy from its claim to be drawing the curtain back on the inner workings of the commercial theatre.

Here the managers of the Drury Lane Company (Colley Cibber, Barton Booth and Robert Wilks) are exposed as they rehearse their newest entertainment, an amalgam of *Harlequin Doctor Faustus* (a hit of the 1723–4 season), *Harlequin Sheppard* (which had opened on 28 November 1724) and *Scaramouche Jack Hall*, a pantomime that existed only in the artist's imagination. Like many

FIGURE 1.2: *A Just View of the British Stage*, 1724. This image has often been attributed to William Hogarth, but there is no firm evidence to support that.

satirical images of the period, *A Just View of the British Stage* is filled to the brim with significant visual detail and allusions that well exceed the space of this essay to explicate in full: a statue of the hero of *Cato*; dragons that refer to the climax of *The Necromancer*, a hit pantomime for the rival Lincoln's Inn Fields company; the ghost of Ben Jonson rising to condemn his successors, and so on. The point is clear: the managers have corrupted an institution that should be advancing the national culture, putting their financial interests first as they pursue profits to the exclusion of all else.

By displaying the crassness of the Drury Lane managers, the artist of *A Just View* is also showing how the commercial playhouses ran afoul of what I will call, following the great historian E.P. Thompson, the theatre's moral economy.[18] This economy had to do with money, of course. More importantly, however, the moral economy also had to do with status, with tradition, with many things that could not readily be quantified and that people in the theatre often comprehended under the umbrella of 'custom'. Actors, for example, invoked customary rights to wages, parts and perquisites; this was what Mary Porter and Anne Oldfield were doing when they appealed to the Lord Chancellor to have their rights to the season's earliest benefit performance restored. In the same spirit, spectators protested when performances transgressed customary norms, as for example when a new and inexperienced performer took over a new part, or when the managers dared to raise prices. Audiences rioted periodically when they believed that the moral economy of customary rights had been violated. A famous example was the series of events in 1809 that became known as the Old Price Riots. When the Covent Garden theatre reopened in September 1809 after a fire, the manager John Kemble jacked up the ticket prices to make up for the costs involved in rebuilding and refurbishing the theatre. On opening night, audiences rioted, calling for the restoration of the customary price, and they continued to demonstrate for two months until Kemble finally gave in.[19]

The importance of the moral economy to the theatre demonstrates that neither the state nor the market fully account for all of the forces that shaped it as an institution. The final element of our constellation, the people, is perhaps the most important of all, and writers of the period recognized this. It is no coincidence that the name of the most famous and influential periodical of the age was called *The Spectator* (1711–12) in reference to playgoers, and that its editors, Joseph Addison and Richard Steele were both (among other things) men of the theatre. Modern scholars have argued that it was in the pages of just this kind of journal that Enlightenment writers across Europe created what has come to be known as the 'public sphere', an imaginary place for reasoned debate, removed from the pressures of both the court and the marketplace.[20] The nebulousness of that concept indicates some of the difficulties involved in describing 'the public' with any degree of confidence. Who are 'the people',

FIGURE 1.3: *King John's First Appearance at the New Theatre Covent Garden*, Isaac Cruikshank, November 1809. © Victoria and Albert Museum, London.

exactly? What did those who were involved in the theatre in this period mean when they spoke of 'the audience', 'the public' and 'the people'? I will sketch out some ways of approaching this question in the next section.

PEOPLE, POLICE, NATION

To monarchs and the states that they headed, 'the people' were subjects to be ruled and guided. The state undertook its supervision of the theatre in the first place because of the monarch's role as supervisor and regulator of his subjects, providing officially sanctioned entertainment for their pleasure and edification. But of course subjects are also potentially a source of unrest, and every government worries about how best to manage the people of the nation it rules so as to optimize their potential while keeping dissent within safe bounds. The eighteenth century had a name for this. Taking the word from French, Europeans in many states called it the art of 'police'. European writers in this period used this term a good deal more broadly than we do today. Eighteenth-century theorists on the art of government invoked the concept of 'police' when they argued that the state should promote policies that sought to understand and then improve the lives of the people within national boundaries. So, for example, Sir John Fielding observed in 1758 that 'The Riches and Strength of a Nation are the Number of its Inhabitants; the Happiness of that Nation, their being usefully and constantly employed'.[21] What is particularly interesting for our purposes here is that John Fielding goes on to describe the efforts of his late half-brother Henry (who had died in 1754) and himself to implement strategies of 'police' in London that would enhance the state by improving the lives of its people. These efforts had included the Fielding brothers' creation of the first official 'police' force in London, the Bow Street Runners. Like a modern police force, this was a group specially charged with arresting crooks and investigating crimes, but the Fielding brothers' agenda went much further than that. They had also, for example, opened a 'Universal Register Office', a central office where workers and employers, renters and landlords, sellers and buyers could, upon paying a subscription fee, post their information in the hopes of being matched up.[22] The Universal Register Office does not seem to have been financially sustainable, but the Fieldings' impulse to rationalize broad swathes of the casual economies of employment and housing fit well within the goal that theorists of police articulated of making the most of a state's human resources.

Theatre could be seen as part of this effort, too. As a playwright, Fielding is remembered as a scathing satirist of the government and the established playhouses, but it is not hard to imagine that his scorn is largely directed at the way that both were failing in their duty to promote the public interest. For many writers, the theatre was an institution that needed to be harnessed in the service of managing the urban population. The state's periodic legislative interventions into the theatre were often then motivated by concern about the effect of the theatre on audience members, particularly on younger, unsophisticated viewers who were believed to be in danger of taking the wrong messages from performances and following the bad examples of some of the rogues, rakes and whores who featured in the more scandalous works in the repertoire.

To the managers, playwrights and performers, 'the people' were the paying customers whose ticket purchases sustained the enterprise. This audience was only a subset of the entire population. The economic system of Europe and its colonies was still overwhelmingly based on agriculture, which meant that these were still largely rural societies, with large peasantries. Because playhouses were all in cities, there was a huge proportion of the population that would rarely if ever be in a position to attend the theatre. Even in the cities, the proportion of the population who attended the theatre regularly was not all that large, particularly at the outset of our period. The late seventeenth-century audiences in London, for example, were proportionately more aristocratic than the theatres of Shakespeare's period had been. As the eighteenth century went on, the theatre became a more democratic place, but it never developed a large working-class clientele. 'The people' as relates to the theatre were largely a bourgeois phenomenon in the original sense: city dwellers who owned property.

This group had particular interests that shaped the kinds of plays that the theatres offered. Most comedies in the repertoire from this period are set in cities and feature people much like those who were in attendance: members of the middle classes and up, who were interested in seeing aspects of their own lives staged before them. Such plays always end in marriage. That is pretty much the definition of comedy, but almost invariably the plots of such plays in this period involve the couple scheming, either together or independently, to gain, not just each other, but property. Enlightenment comedies often are really about the way that marriage functions as the means by which property gets passed down from one generation to another. This was true across Europe, as witnessed by the heavy cross-pollination of comic plots and heavy reliance on translations and adaptations of works from one nation to another. Comedies like these entertained their bourgeois audiences by flattering them that the complications of romance and property were always resolvable, sometimes in the span of three hours or so.

Theatre managers faced the constant problem of adapting to an ever-changing public taste. It was the public who were the ultimate arbiters of which new plays succeeded to become parts of the repertoire and which ones would be forgotten immediately. They were perhaps the most important force for changing the dramatic repertoire over the course of the period. To be sure, it is not as though playwrights were passive; they innovated and advanced the art as well. In places like Germany and Scandinavia, the managers of the theatre had tremendous importance in, for example, transforming the repertoire from one dominated by French plays to one dominated by works written in the vernacular. Given the theatre's heavy reliance on box-office receipts, however, it stands to reason that a portion of the shifts in drama over the period had much to do with changing audience desires, which were impossible to predict, much less to direct. Managers, with large investments to protect – not only the patents, but also the buildings, scenery, costumes and personnel that had to be paid no matter how successful the current offerings at a playhouse – saw the theatre-going public as essentially an enormous agent of risk, and they sought ways to minimize that risk by building a repertory that generally evolved incrementally.

The fickleness of audience taste could be very frustrating. Late in his career, Holberg began to resent the way that audiences in Copenhagen seemed indifferent to the quality of a play, not caring whether it 'was well or poorly written but only whether it ends with a song and a dance'.[23] Other writers attempted to elevate the public taste by making rhetorical appeals that seem designed to urge theatregoers to aspire to demand more of themselves. When

Goethe asserted, then, that 'One can show the audience no greater respect than by not treating them as a rabble', it is hard not to hear in this statement something like its opposite, that he was occasionally tempted to pander to the lowest common denominator of his audience's wishes and was hoping that he could persuade them to prove him wrong.[24]

Perhaps most important of all, as the eighteenth century went on, the theatre came to be seen as essential to the way in which the people might be imagined as a nation. The great German dramaturgs frequently saw their efforts as helping to create a vernacular German culture that would create the conditions for a unified German state. As Friedrich Schiller put it in 1784, 'If we had a national theatre, we would become a nation'.[25] At the time of the French Revolution, the Comédie-Française retitled itself the Théâtre de la Nation.[26] And when Cruikshank followed the Old Price Rioters in mocking John Kemble as 'King John', he was alluding to the King John who had signed the Magna Carta, the document from which the rights of British subjects were believed to derive. The theatre became one of the leading ways to develop a distinctive national culture. These efforts were not only responding to the existence of the people and trying to harness their energies but in effect constituting the theatre-going public as the basis of a modern nation.

By the nineteenth century, it would be possible for European states to think plausibly about creating national theatres in the modern sense, theatres that were imagined to embody the national character by performing what were now understood to be a repertoire of national classics. This was part of a larger effort to build distinctive national literary traditions, an effort that was pursued widely in Europe as critics defined canons of great works and significant authors. But the liveness of the theatrical event, the immediacy of the relationship between performers and spectators, gave the theatre a particular pride of place as a new kind of institution in its own right, one where the relationship between the people and their nation could be renewed, brought into being afresh every night.

CHAPTER TWO

Social Functions

Audiences and Authority

DAVID WORRALL

The social function of theatre is invariably linked to its audiences. These are the people who go to see performances and perpetuate theatre's existence either by returning to see more or, in some cases, reacting with a resolve to try to have it closed down. Playhouses are specifically, architecturally, designed to facilitate audience viewing. They are not easily adaptable for any other use. The increase in the number of theatres in the eighteenth century, both in urban centres as well as in provinces, regions and colonies, brought together socially mixed audiences whose assumed susceptibility to moral or political influence challenged government attitudes towards the freedom of expression. Britain's 1737 Theatre Licensing Act instituted the legislative basis for the increasingly comprehensive censorship of the texts of stage plays but even this pales into insignificance with the effective imposition of a period of theatrical prohibition by the new American republic after 1782. For this straightforward reason, this chapter will first of all explain the theatrical infrastructure which enabled theatre's social existence before going on to discuss the political controls that developed to cope with theatre audiences. Finally, it will look at different types of audience experience including individual responses to theatre and its take-up by amateur performers.

Audiences interact in many ways with theatrical performances but, primarily, they interact with each other. The audience's personal relationships extend beyond the walls of the theatre where performances may remain objects of discussion across several types of social network by conversation, letter writing or printed commentary. Our knowledge of theatre's social function flows from these interactions. Sometimes it is possible to analyse the behaviour of entire social groups, at other times one can concentrate on individual responses. At its most basic, theatre reflects and expresses society's shifting identity as it develops across time. This has the consequence that theatre has often provoked political and legal controls as vested interests felt challenged. The presence of socially diverse audiences assembled in theatres, almost invariably located at the centre of urban areas, meant that their propensity to create disturbances or to threaten government or religious order could not be ignored by the authorities. However, whatever its perceived social role, theatres only existed because they were able to access the audience's surplus income. It should be no surprise that economics often defines the boundaries of theatre's social function. Such economic determinants are nowhere more manifest than the way in which theatre shadowed the expanding military and trading empires of the eighteenth century. Amongst these, it is the anglophone Atlantic which provides the most developed example for how theatre functioned socially, with a repertoire travelling along its oceanic trading routes.

Theatre was a powerful cultural driver because it moved along the maritime routes and networks of empires old and new, travelling from London to the new cities of colonial and new republic America. For Britain, theatre's social role was particularly ideologically formative. In Kathleen Wilson's formulation, 'the English stage [w]as the leading site for the enactment of superior national virtue and character', where 'theater was able to transform historical idealizations into historical "realities" that helped structure and confirm English beliefs about their own distinctiveness and destiny'.[1] As Daniel O'Quinn has persuasively argued, theatre also acted as a point of reception for British encounters with the Islamic Mediterranean, Asia and the Pacific, including their exploration, colonization and settlement.[2] In colonial America, as Jason Shaffer has shown, through a combination of theatre and elocutionary training, Joseph Addison's tragedy, *Cato* (1712), fulfilled a similar role, one quite exceptional in its reliance on a single play.[3] In other words, with the new republic of America emerging from its colonial past, and Britain encountering new territories to the south and east, theatre stood at both the beginning and the ends of empire.

THEATRICAL INFRASTRUCTURE

In order to have any measurable political and cultural impact on the sort of transoceanic scale suggested here, theatre needed a built infrastructure, a massive network of venues where performances could take place. For Britain, the best contemporary guide to the national network is James Winston's *Theatric Tourist* (1805). Originally planned as a part-work of etchings illustrating theatre buildings, it also gave enough information for amateurs to look for work as professional actors.[4] Winston commissioned a remarkable set of drawings showing an amazing range of venues from converted barns to new playhouses built, or at least decorated, in the classical style.[5] Winston's *Theatric Tourist* was a direct response to a forgotten spate of theatre building starting after the 1788 Theatrical Representations Act, a piece of legislation conclusively defining that local magistrates could license playhouses. By 1805, most provincial cities, and many small towns and villages, on mainland Britain had access to live theatre for at least one month of the year. These productions were provided by touring companies on established circuits, many described in Winston's book. In America, there were fewer playhouses but, as well as the principal cities of Boston, Philadelphia and New York, there were also theatres at Providence, Annapolis, Charleston, Baltimore and many other places, all of these being traced in Odai Johnson and W.J. Burling's calendar of performances up 1774.[6] Not least, Johnson also discovered touring companies visiting the British-held Leeward Islands in the West Indies from the late 1760s, demonstrating, as at other American venues, that actors were economic beneficiaries of slaving.[7]

The scale of the built infrastructure enabled extensive social responses to theatre. To have social impact, theatre needs to have a material presence and to be attached to networks of theatregoers able to discuss performance meaning as well as, not least, ensure its financial viability. In eighteenth-century London, theatre-going reached a massive scale and became culturally central to the expanding metropolis. Covent Garden and Drury Lane theatres each held about 3,000 persons. By 1813, it was estimated that the capital's total theatre seating capacity, including venues such as King's Theatre and the Little Theatre in the Haymarket, as well as Sadler's Wells and several other playhouses, was around 29,500 seats (although not all of these playhouses were open at the same time).[8] Theatre audiences were extraordinarily socially diverse, a situation which ensured the theatres survived but which was also a by-product of deliberate pricing policies. For Drury Lane in the 1790s, admission prices ranged from six shillings in the boxes to one shilling in the upper gallery with intermediate pricing for the pit and first gallery. However, at half time, when the 'mainpiece' (often a serious comedy of manners or a tragedy) had finished, admission prices were halved for the 'afterpiece' (often a farce or pantomime) making it possible to get in for as little as sixpence.[9] In today's marketing terms, this would be described as broadening the access arrangements. A significant feature of these pricing policies is the noticeably steep differential between the highest possible price for admission (six shillings) and the lowest possible price (sixpence for 'half-price' in the cheapest seats, which were in the upper gallery). Given these policies, theatre attendance in London was enormous. In the season 1813–14, Drury Lane's accountant calculated that the total number of seats sold in that theatre that year came to 484,691.[10] If taken in conjunction with Covent Garden (which had the same seating capacity), and the capacity of the other London theatres, this means that annual seat sales in the capital probably approximated inner London's total population of 879,491 recorded at the 1801 census.[11] It is to these, admittedly rather dry, statistics that any estimate of eighteenth-century theatre's social function and impact needs to be related.

LEGISLATIVE AND LEGAL CONTROLS ON THEATRES

Given this configuration of capacity and distribution, theatres were not places the governing authorities could choose to ignore, even in the smallest urban centres. Like churches, they are architecturally unusual spaces in that gathered assemblies of people are visible to one other, across the building. Since price, and therefore, social differentials of class and rank, was more or less built into the theatres, the potential for disruptive behaviour by audiences was considerable. A frequent response of government was to institute controls over play-acting. People gathering together after working hours, unsupervised, were considered inherently dangerous. Government's instruments of limitation included restrictions on what could be said on stage, either by suppressing theatres outright or, more subtly, to simply devolve control down to provincial authorities to administer repression in a local manner. Indeed, many of the features of repressive state government were continuations of lessons learned about controlling theatres. The potential for plays to be understood by audiences as political allegories was considered alarming. Dramas such as Thomas Otway's repertoire staple, *Venice Preserv'd* (1682), which was perceived as endorsing republican government, were treated with general suspicion but permitted to be played principally because no legislation had been in force when they were first performed. But as urban centres became larger and more socially diverse, restrictions on theatres became more commonplace. New satires on contemporary society provoked clampdowns. It was plays such as John Gay's *Beggar's Opera* (1728), a drama which appeared to invert normal social relationships by apparently glorifying criminality, which helped prompt Britain's 1737 Theatre Licensing Act.

This piece of legislation instituted the censorship of the texts of all new plays in London and other British mainland royal theatres. Censorship was under the control of the Lord Chamberlain (who then appointed an Examiner of Plays to actually read the plays). The censor's scrutiny of new drama increased markedly after 1778 with the appointment of John Larpent as Examiner. Censorship accelerated further in 1824 when George Colman the Younger, a successful playwright, was appointed as Larpent's successor. Such controls over theatre were not confined to Britain. In colonial and new republic America, similar impulses arose but from different perspectives. Theatre was perceived as a colonial imposition on the natural Puritanism of the republic's founders. As state congresses acquired more powers, the social ills of theatre became ever more clearly defined in state legislation. A typical example of legislation was the 1750 Massachusetts 'Act for Preventing Stage-Plays & Other Theatrical Entertainments'. This was aimed at 'avoiding the many and great mischiefs which arise from publick stage-plays, interludes and other theatrical entertainments, which not only occasion great and unnecessary expences, and discourage industry and frugality, but likewise tend generally to increase immorality, impiety and a contempt for religion'. In the colonial era it was renewed in 1750, 1760, 1770 (twice), 1776 and 1779.[12]

However, if these were the legislative changes, it is the transmission into provincial England of such centralized concepts of authoritarianism which tells us much about the perception of theatre as a medium threatening society. One particular incident illustrates how even the temporary presence of players in remoter communities created hostile reactions. Before the 1788 Theatrical Representations Act, local magistrates in the provinces were willing to use their powers of arrest to stop theatre. In 1766 an itinerant theatrical troupe travelling through the small village of Newport, Shropshire, were gaoled by a local magistrate, Richard Hill, on the grounds of their vagrancy. Hill wrote a pamphlet explaining his actions. His testimony is valuable because he describes the pressures exerted on him by local townspeople to stop the players performing:

> some of the sensible and thinking part of the town begun to be apprehensive of the ill consequences which must ensue if they were permitted to continue: Hereupon I had two applications by letter, signifying, that is was the earnest desire of several reputable persons belonging to *Newport*, that I should use my authority to make the players leave the town; and one tradesman in particular told me, that his just debts remained unpaid by such as nevertheless could find money enough to squander at the play. But the persons who thus applied to me, desired I would keep their names secret (which I promised to do) lest it might injure their business among such as were encouragers of the players, and lest the rabble, and *certain lewd fellows of the baser sort*, which were all of the strollers' side, should break their windows or do them some injury.[13]

The social tensions the players had provoked amongst this rural population tell us much more about everyday attitudes than legislative instruments such as the 1737 Licensing Act. Not only were the sources of the allegations kept secret but one glimpses here a contradictory moral economy. One set of townspeople are concerned with the morality of squandering money but another set fear physical retribution from '*certain lewd fellows*' who are quite clearly the fellow citizens of the secretive 'reputable' complainants. What the incident demonstrates is that everyday attitudes to theatre were extremely sensitive precisely because people feared its disruptive power.

THEATRE AS AN EXTENSION OF DIPLOMACY

Given the above, where both government and provincial authorities exerted such interventionist controls, it is only slightly counter-intuitive to learn that theatre also became an extension of political diplomacy. Since theatre's political messages were government censored yet, by their very nature, playhouses provided opportunities for informal entertainment, a night at the playhouse for visiting diplomats was a regular occurrence. Britain's vigorous maritime military and commercial empire brought many overseas dignitaries. Pantomime, together with the taste for adding music to drama, made theatre accessible even to those with limited proficiency in English. In 1756, the Drury Lane prompter noted that at a performance of Shakespeare's *Henry VIII*, 'for ye Morocco Embassador, who, tho' unlearn'd in our Language, behav'd as if he understood nature'.[14] Nor was this purely a London phenomenon. In 1750, *Henry IV Pt I* and Henry Fielding's *Tom Thumb* (1731) were performed at the High Street Theatre, Portsmouth, 'for the entertainment of His Excellency Hadge Mahamed Hajee, the Algerine Ambassador'.[15] It was quite clear that many of these visits were extensions of political diplomacy as Britain engaged with the non-Atlantic world. As early as 1721, for example, 'the King of Delago in Africa' and his 'Two Princess Bro[rs]'. made several visits to Drury Lane. This was the year the Dutch East India Company had founded a factory in Delagoa (present-day Maputo, Mozambique). Its destruction by English pirates a year later gives some idea of the volatility of the diplomatic relations needing to be assuaged by the king and his brothers' trips to see benefit performances of Congreve's *Love for Love* (1695), Dryden's *The Spanish Fryar* (1681) and *The Merry Wives of Windsor*.[16] In 1794–5, the Turkish ambassador, Yusuf Agah Effendi, made a whole series of theatre visits, including some to see afterpieces such as *The Soldier's Festival; or, The Night Before the Battle*, one of a number of contemporary spectacles reflecting the war with France and Britain. The ambassador was a key diplomat in Britain's attempt to realign its links with the Ottoman empire in order to obstruct French ambitions in the eastern Mediterranean.[17] These foreign visitors were visible to, and recognized, by audiences. John Kendall (fl. 1757–95) of Maidstone, Kent, realized how foreign ambassadors were socially valuable to theatre managers when he saw David Garrick performing in Benjamin Hoadly's *Suspicious Husband* (1747) in 1768. Kendall observed that 'he exerted himself Greatly as he performed out of compliment to the foreigners, the French Ambassador, Prince of Monaco etc who appeared highly pleased, they were all to sup with him afterwards'.[18]

FIGURE 2.1: *English Curiosity or the Foreigner Stared out of Countenance*, Thomas Rowlandson, etching, 1794. British trade and a century of war brought many overseas visitors to see theatre in London and elsewhere. Rowlandson's etching captures both their presence and their visibility. Courtesy of the Lewis Walpole Library.

AUDIENCES: SOCIAL CONTROLS
AND AUDIENCE RESPONSES

The unnamed Newport troupe, referred to above, never got to perform but their experience demonstrates how local legal authorities had deeply embedded anxieties about theatre. The magistrate, Richard Hill, had a surprisingly extensive knowledge of the contemporary theatrical repertoire, but one extremely sensitive to what he feared was its ability to trigger moral disorder. He commented on:

> the pernicious consequences which too often result from permitting such gentry among them [the villagers], how many diseases left uncured, how many pockets emptied, how many minds corrupted how many apprentices

and servant-maids commence *Othellos, Desdemonas, Altamonts, Calistas,* Lady *Wrongheads,* Lady *Betty Modeishes,* Mr. *Fribbles, Roman Emperors, Tragedy Queens* and what not, to their high improvement in the arts of debauchery, intrigue, dissimulation and romantic love, the great loss of their time and neglect of their masters' business[19]

The repertoire to which Hill refers, with *Othello* as the most recognizable play, includes Colley Cibber's *The Careless Husband* (1705) and *The Provok'd Husband* (1728), Nicholas Rowe, *The Fair Penitent* (1703) and David Garrick, *Miss in Her Teens* (1747). Hill's comments remind us not only of how unfamiliar we are today with the Georgian canon of drama but also how vehemently it was impugned with originating social ills. Strikingly, in a document originally secretly circulated to members of Parliament in 1825, the Lord Chamberlain's Examiner of Plays expressed very similar sentiments, warning, 'Produce, constantly, before Spectators nothing but fascinating Debauchees, and heroick Conspirators, and the weak part of the multitude, (which is the majority,) would, in time, turn Profligates, and Rebels'.[20]

On the other hand, audiences themselves often acted in a disruptive, even authoritarian, manner by taking control of the theatre auditorium. Theatre rioting as part of a repertoire of social contention had a long history.[21] The Covent Garden Old Price Riots of 1809 were ostensibly disturbances caused by audiences protesting at raised prices but they were also expressing middle- or lower-class prurience at new anterooms located behind the theatre's refurbished boxes which (they alleged) concealed upper-class sexual immorality.[22] Quite clearly, moral authoritarianism or a moral economy could be exerted from below as well as from above. Theatres became legitimated arenas for all sorts of audience unrest. The appropriation of theatres by factional interests was a regular occurrence with significant anti-French riots at Drury Lane in 1755 and 'half-price' riots at Covent Garden in 1763 (protests about removing the half-price-at-half-time custom).[23] Like the 1809 riots, these disturbances were broadly about management policies. However, theatre auditoriums were also regularly used as proxies for other sorts of unrest prevalent elsewhere in society. One of the most culturally significant of these resulted from white people 'destroying property at the Theatre of the blacks' in New York in August 1822. This was the African Theatre in Mercer Street (parallel to Broadway) where 'a number of white persons entered into the pit of said Theatre and from where they climbed into the Boxes . . . then broke the benches and every thing they could get hold of'. The net outcome was that the African-American actors, Ira Aldridge, certainly (who was assaulted during the attack), and James Hewlett, possibly, fled to England to pursue their acting profession.[24] Aldridge went on to have a significant acting career in Britain and eastern Europe, beginning at the Royalty Theatre in the Thames dockyard area, a location which reminds us again of how theatre travelled along the Atlantic trading routes.[25]

As theatre riots demonstrate, audiences bring with them attitudes originating outside the theatre but which materially determine what happens inside. This is seen at its most extreme in the Atlantic slaving economies where high artistic culture and inhumanity coincided. After a disastrous fire in 1811 at the theatre in Richmond, Virginia, during a performance of *The Bleeding Nun, or, Agnes and Raymond*, amongst the deceased was 'Pleasant[,] *a mulatto woman belonging to* Mr. Wm. Rose'. Most of the blacks escaped the conflagration because they were segregated into the gallery which had a less congested exit than the one on the ground floor.[26] Further south, a Christmas Eve 1805 performance of *Hamlet* 'By Particular Desire' at Charleston, South Carolina (advertised as 'Shakespeare's Celebrated Tragedy'), saw no irony in performing the Bard's brand of universal humanism while advising that 'People of Colour cannot be admitted to any part of the House'.[27] In 1837, South Carolina's record high price for slaves enabled the rebuilding of the theatre.[28] In these cases, theatre acts as a perfect mirror of dominant conditions outside of the playhouse walls.

THEATRE AS AN AGENT OF SOCIAL CHANGE

Theatre often acts as a vehicle of social change. This is because it is a social activity which is primarily visual, occurs in real time and at a fixed place, and has performances which can be assimilated and debated with friends or along extended social networks. Although there is no discernible pattern as to whether social changes wrought by theatre are progressive or regressive, it seems to be the case that the display or articulation of variant cultural attitudes on stage helps precipitate the emergence of new perspectives on social behaviour, quite often ones more widely adopted by general society somewhat later. This may occur because theatre creates and validates behaviours which others may wish to emulate but, alternatively, it may also alert others to guard against such changes.

At the most basic level of social intervention, eighteenth-century theatre regularly contributed to benevolence activities. The simplicity of cash paid directly at the door, combined with the potential for substantial audiences, led to 'benefit' performances in support of specific charitable causes. Drury Lane and Covent Garden held at least one annual benefit night for a range of hospitals, including the 'Lying In' (maternity) hospitals in Duke Street, Aldersgate Street, the Middlesex Hospital and the Lock Hospital (the latter specializing in venereal diseases). Similarly, the death of the American actor John Hodgkinson, in 1805, provoked benefit night performances in both New York and Charleston, South Carolina, in aid of his daughters.[29] At Stamford, Lincolnshire, within six weeks of the event, there were performances 'For the Benefit of the Sufferers at the Battle of Waterloo'.[30] Although limited in scope, such theatricals customs delivered direct benefits to local communities.

The enormous scale of eighteenth-century theatricality means that one keeps finding, right across the Atlantic seaboards, unexpected examples of social attitudes undergoing processes of change. As far as evolving attitudes to gender construction are concerned, one might try to imagine how at the Moot Hall, Newcastle-Upon-Tyne, in north-east England, already a coal-mining area dominated by a masculine workforce, a touring company in 1754 could produce an entirely cross-dressed version of Gay's *Beggar's Opera*.[31] In north America, what actually proved to be transient attitudes to native Americans were glimpsed at Lailson's Circus, Philadelphia, in their 1797 'serious pantomime' production of François Arnould-Mussot's *The American Heroine* (sometimes billed as *The Fair American*). Originating at the Théâtre de l'Ambigu-Comique, Paris, in 1786, this seems to have been performed by the same French émigré company. It designated Yarico, its native American heroine, as the 'young American' and stressed the bravery of Yarico in confronting Caribbee Indians who have pursued her cowardly English lover, Inkle (who wants to sell her into slavery): 'Yarico is not intimidated by their threats . . . Frightened at the sight, he re-enters into the hollow of the rock'.[32] *The American Heroine*, which remained a repertoire staple, captures an extraordinary moment when the United States was at ease with representing the nobility of its indigenous peoples.

This ability for theatre to offer variant perspectives, particularly on race and gender, features recurrently. In their inexorable search for talent, theatre managers often remained open to what may have seemed quite radical social experiments. In New Orleans by 1780 (then under French rule), the actress sisters known as Minette and Lise ('mulatas en el teatro') had played in Beaumarchais's *Le Marriage de Figaro* but other 'quadroon' performers also arrived in that city from Port-au-Prince (present-day Haiti) after rioting destroyed the theatre there in 1791.[33] In London, Garrick's farce, *May Day, or, The Little Gypsy* (1775), with music by Thomas Arne, specifically aimed to showcase the Jewish singer, Harriet Abrams, its title probably hinting at Abrams's physical appearance. Drury Lane's prompter carefully recorded her reception, 'Miss Abrams (a Jew) about 17 years old She is very Small a Swarthy Complexion, has a very Sweet Voice & a fine Shake, but not quite power enough yet – both the Piece & Young Lady were receiv'd with great Applause'.[34] Of course, these are not necessarily examples of social assimilation but they do point to theatre's role in ruthlessly identifying talent, wherever it lay, as well as indicating the public's apparent openness to social change.

THE AUDIENCE EXPERIENCE

Inevitably, theatre audiences brought with them all the beliefs, prejudices and expectations of the outside world. To understand the physical conditions and experiences of theatre attendance is also to understand the nature of its centrality in contemporary culture.

Journals and diaries are often excellent sources of information. The richness of some of the accounts provides a real sense of the physicality of the theatre-going experience. In October 1775, Samuel Curwen, an American refugee living in London, went to the theatre in a party consisting of a male cousin, a friend and his wife, all with kinship or other links to America:

> afterwards [we] rode to Drury Lane play House in order to see Shakespeares as you like it, the King and Queen present but the pit and Gallery being filled we . . . adjoined to Covent Garden, which we also found filled but being loth to depart we consented to stay in [the] Gallery which was inconvenient enough being too much crowded to admit my standing or sitting, nor had I a sight of more than ½ the Stage being crowded into a corner, the entertainment was the opera of Artaxerxes[35]

An enormous amount can be deduced from evidence like this. First of all, as the centre of a maritime trading empire, London and its theatres were cosmopolitan spaces; second, when royalty were present, theatres filled to capacity (their financial account books confirm this); third, if one playhouse was full, then another was accessible; fourth, Shakespeare's name is beginning to be attached to his play as an author with name recognition; fifth, while the opera's composer is not considered significant, the work can be identified as Thomas Arne's *Artaxerxes, An English Opera* (1761), its subtitle a reminder to the audience that opera, as a continental European art form, was here made accessible in the vernacular language. It is also important to note, incidentally, even though Drury Lane was packed, Covent Garden was also 'too much crowded to admit my standing or sitting', another reminder that, even with these two very large theatres in close proximity to each other, they sometimes filled to overflowing. On this night, for example, Curwen reported that at Covent Garden he could not see 'more than 1/2 the Stage'. The Curwen party may even have later purchased *The Overture, Songs & Duetts in the Opera of Artaxerxes . . . properly dispos'd for the voice and harpsichord* (?1762), a reminder that popular theatre songs and music had a secondary life outside of the playhouses because amateur singing in the home was commonplace, in this case with the music arranged for solo harpsichord, a keyboard instrument for a domestic space. The crowding, the variety of entertainments on offer, the sense of going as a party, the proximity of royalty, all tell us much about the attractiveness of theatre to huge numbers of people.

It is not difficult to see from this account how theatre stood at the centre of eighteenth-century urban culture, embodying, exemplifying and perpetuating a rich anthropology of behaviour. One is continually struck by how often theatres were crowded. Here is an account of a visit made around 1794 to what was probably the Royalty Theatre, near the Tower of London. The diarist is Jacob

Nagle (1761–1841), an American-born sailor then serving in the Royal Navy (but who had visited Sydney, Australia, by 1790). He goes with a group of friends rather than alone or as a couple. Nagle can be taken as an impartial, culturally disinterested witness, someone who had recently survived combat, shipwreck and life as a prisoner of war. Even though his written English betrays functional literacy, he gives an extraordinarily fluid account of the theatre's auditorium and the ebb and flow of the audience's complex behaviour:

> Arriving at the playhouse, the croud was numerous. Mr. Goodall gave us warning to secure our pockets. We entered the stair case, which was very broad, but so throng that it was difficult to squese [sic] along side each other, the pusser[purser] and his wife next to them, the capt. And myself bringing up the rear, keeping close together. There happened to be a great big bussen[36] gutted gentleman got a long side of me, and being so much scrouged, he would come bump up against me . . . We went to the gallery and seated our selves in a row on one bench. When they begin to act, there was a lady with a large bonnet on sitting in front of Mr. Goodall and me that prevented [sic] us from having a vieu when they ware acting. Therefore Mr. Goodall spoke to her very politely if she would be so good as to [take] hur bonnet off, the [that] we might see, but she would not taken any notice in what he desired hur. He having a light kain [cane] in his hand, he touched hur on the shoulder several times, but would not take any notice . . . Mr. Goodall finding she would not take it off, and beside it being against the rules in the playhouse, he took his kain and put the end into the loop of floroshing ribben behind and twisted it round and hove the bonnet clean off hur head. The cap, being pined [sic] to the bonnet, went with it, and hur head was as bare as a plucked fowl. There was such a cruel laugh and uproar in the gallery, made them stare from all quarters of the playhouse.[37]

With its 'bussen gutted gentleman' and wigged woman, this is an extraordinarily rich memoir. The audience is not only physically densely packed ('he would come bump up against me') but also confined (with Nagle and his friends seated on a 'bench', albeit of the backless type normally used in theatres). Revealingly, he says nothing about the show and does not even name the theatre (although internal evidence suggests it was the Royalty, Tower Hamlets, London). Instead, he is entirely engaged with the theatre's impact on his immediate social network and their intersection with other networks across the auditorium. His description is replete with rapidly changing spatial and temporal alignments, blocked conversational gambits and fluid reorientations in the theatre's material space: 'Mr. Goodall spoke to her very politely if she would be so good as to [take] hur bonnet off'. Indeed, Nagle's awareness of his personal space, and that of his friends, and how it might be threatened are all

FIGURE 2.2: *The Boxes*, Thomas Rowlandson, etching, 1809. This shows Covent Garden's interior during the Old Price Riots but it also captures the crowded proximity of London audiences. Note the two people of colour in the lower boxes. Courtesy of the Lewis Walpole Library.

emphatic: 'He having a light kain [cane] in his hand, he touched hur on the shoulder several times, but would not take any notice'. Eventually, in a wonderful example of interactivity, the disturbance 'made them stare from all quarters of the playhouse'. This contestation of the auditorium's public space described here is profoundly revealing of how deference and politeness were not only prerequisites for acting, but Nagle's account also shows that audiences directly engaged with each other in appropriating and counter-appropriating non-artistic theatrical space.

In Curwen and Nagle's accounts, perhaps because they have the perspectives of outsiders, we get a rich sense of the social make-up of the audiences and, not least, how auditorium tension might edge towards conflict. However, while Nagle only records this solitary visit, Curwen went to the theatre about ten times a year between 1775 and 1784. It is difficult to estimate rates of attendance. Some people went very frequently. The literary editor and book collector, Isaac Reed (1742–1807), went forty-eight times in the season 1781–2 alone.[38] What all of these examples should alert us to is that, perhaps disconcertingly frequently, theatre's social function sometimes had little to do with what was performed on stage.

INDIVIDUAL AUDIENCE RESPONSES

The picture drawn so far is of performances taking place on a massive scale, right across the theatrical infrastructure, but what do we know about individual audience responses? The social function of theatre is overwhelmingly connected to our individual responses and how we interact with others in discussing those experiences. Records of such responses, where they can be authenticated, are extremely valuable for understanding historical theatre.

In 1774, the sixteen-year-old Anna Porter (who later married John Larpent, the Examiner of Plays), wrote withering entries in her private 'Methodized Journal' about her theatre-going: 'At the Play. The Beggar's Opera & Harlequin's Invasion. The first was too shocking to please me, such vice laid open!' 'At the Play. The Inconstant, a low, indelicate, immoral thing'.[39] By contrast, in October 1783 the similarly sixteen-year-old future American President, John Quincy Adams (1767–1848), saw Sarah Siddons at Drury Lane playing the title role in David Garrick's (adapted from Southerne), *Isabella; Or, The Fatal Marriage* (1757). Adams noted in his diary, almost dispassionately, 'Mrs Siddons supposed to be the first Tragick performer in Europe play'd the part of Isabella A young lady, in the next Box to where we were, was so much affected by it as to be near fainting and was carried out. I was told that every night Mrs Siddons performs, this happens'.[40] This testimony strongly suggests that audience responses were very different from those we might encounter today, whether in ourselves or in our friends.

What these incidents may bear witness to is that there is a history of affective emotion. That is, responses which were normal in the past may not be considered normal today. Other incidents bear this out. Adams' diary is no less reliable than that of John Marsh, a Sussex composer and shareholder in the Chichester theatre. In March 1785 Marsh attended a private theatrical in Dover belonging to Peter Fector, a banker. The play performed was *The Orphan of China*, Arthur Murphy's 1759 adaptation of a Voltaire play.[41] What Marsh recorded there was an incident very similar to Adams's witnessing of Siddons two years earlier. When Fector,

> as he represented in y[e] last Act a person dying in consequence of having been tortur'd, his Sister was so affected as to go into fits, on w[ch] the Play was suddenly stopt & he arose & leap'd from the Stage into ye Box wherein she was, & was forc'd to continue for sometime assuring her he was very well & that nothing was really the matter with him, before she c[ld] be pacified enough to be had out [of the box].

Admittedly Fector was performing in front of his sister at his 'private Theatre', but Marsh's presence along with, presumably, other guests must have diluted filial intensity between brother and sister yet Marsh simply characterizes it as little more than 'an instance of Mr Fector's good Acting'.[42] If an amateur actor in Dover in 1785 could inspire responses similar to those experienced by sections of Sarah Siddons's audiences at Drury Lane in 1783, the affective gradient between Fector and Siddons as performers cannot have been abnormally large. Although it may be difficult to account for, these diversely located but similarly affective responses imply that professional and amateur performers fulfilled essentially the same social function in their rendering of emotion.

On account of the snapshot they give of interiorized moral wrangling, some of the most intriguing testimonies of responses to acting come in two letters by Abigail Adams (1744–1818), mother of John Quincy Adams (above). Abigail wrote in 1785 to William Stephens Smith about having seen Sarah Siddons playing Desdemona in *Othello* the previous night at Drury Lane. Othello was played by John Philip Kemble, Siddons' brother. This letter, with its deletions shown here, must count as one of the most profoundly revealing records of individual audience reaction of the entire era:

> She appeard in the tradegy [sic] of Othello, and acted the part of Desdemona. Othello was represented blacker than any affrican. Whether it arises from the prejudices of Education or from a real natural antipathy I cannot determine, but my whole soul shuderd when ever I saw the sooty ~~heretik?~~ More [Moor] touch the fair Desdemona. I wonder not that Brabantio thought Othello must have used Spells and magick to have won her affections.

~~The Character of Othello~~ Through the whole play ~~is that of a Noble Generous open Manly~~ the character of Othello is Manly open generous and noble, betrayed by a most artfull villan and a combination of circumstances into an action that his Soul abhored ~~but I So powerfull was prejudice that I could not seperate[sic] the coulour from the Man and by which means~~ That most incomparable Speach of Othellos lost half its force and Beauty, because I could not Seperate the coulor from the Man. Yet it was admirably well spoken.[43]

Kemble was a white European. He was playing Othello (intended by Shakespeare to be a north African Moor), 'blackface' by wearing black facial paint (usually made from burned cork and lard fixed with beer). It would take hundreds of words to unpick the moral and historical layers of Adams' response. Her writing on paper records rather than removes her deletions, only thinly disguising her 'prejudice that I could not seperate the coulour from the Man'. In a second letter, to Elizabeth Smith Shaw, written about six months later, Adams wrote more fluently about the same performance, repeating how she 'could not Seperate the affrican coulour from the man, nor prevent that disgust and horrour which filld my mind every time I saw him touch the Gentle Desdemona'.[44] However, it is her first letter which demonstrates most completely the confusion of her initial response, one made doubly complex by its reference to a fictional person represented by a fake black man. Abigail Adams's response to blackface acting is a powerful comment on theatre's ability to connect with individuals in the audience and to make them re-appraise their previously held social perspectives. If theatre regularly did this to us, we would have few doubts about the significance of its social role.

PRIVATE THEATRICALS

Not everyone remained a spectator. Theatricality was not confined to the playhouses. In the Caribbean, Kathleen Wilson has identified a sustained public or communal theatricality of the streets, a hybrid outcome of indigenous and African genres interacting with European theatrical forms.[45] In Britain, there was a widespread interest in private theatricals held at the big country houses. The fullest historical analysis is Sybil Rosenfeld's 1978 *Temples of Thespis: Some Private Theatres and Theatricals in England and Wales, 1700–1820*. As the case of 'Mr Fector's good Acting' shows, performances were not diminished in emotive power because they were amateur. One of the most fascinating sources for our knowledge about the social function of theatre comes from records of amateur or private performances. These can be traced to Britain's colonies as well as its provincial regions. The best introduction to their contemporary social nuances is the fictional account given in Jane Austen's novel, *Mansfield Park* (1814), where much of the book is taken up with the comically satiric repercussions of an abortive country house production of Elizabeth Inchbald's *Lover's Vows* (1798), a successful Covent Garden adaptation of an August von Kotzebue play. The significance of private theatricals is that they reveal directly how plays were consumed. They were necessarily collective projects which, as in *Mansfield Park*, involved discussions about text selection, appropriate casting, participation in rehearsals, a collaborative final presentation as well as the careful invitation of suitable audiences, all carried out free of commercial determinants. For these reasons, private theatricals are key signifiers for the public use of theatre.

Race and the representation of transgressive gender roles are particularly explosive indicators of the cultural perspectives present at these private theatricals. The governor's gardens in colonial Madras, India, was the setting in 1788 for amateur productions of Isaac Bickerstaff's *The Padlock* (1768) and James Townley's *High Life Below Stairs* (1759), both of them staged by European women and white army officers in aid of a local charity for female orphans.[46] In Madras, the blackface roles of *The Padlock*'s Mungo and *High Life*'s Kingston were played by British army captains but, more remarkably, the latter's female black servant, Cloe, was played, presumably cross-dressed as well as blackfaced, by one Lieutenant Grant. Around 1774, at Cassiobury House, Hertfordshire, the amateur actor Thomas Orde-Powlett made a souvenir print etching (Figure 2.3), probably for fellow players, of the servants' hall scene in *High Life Below Stairs* which had been played at a house party there. Unique impressions of this print show that players endorsed copies with recollections of their roles ('Blackee you go! . . . Cookey you go! . . . Sambo = Answer the Door'). The derogatory term 'Sambo' is not present in Townley's published text, implying a specifically Cassiobury private theatrical interpolation. As the print shows, English gentry revelled in blackface, ridiculing Cassiobury House's (presumably) black servants.[47] Serving military officers sometimes also cross-dressed at these events. In 1787, at a private theatrical at Hinchinbrook House, near Huntingdon, Major William John Arabin performed the role of Mrs Cheshire in John O'Keeffe's Haymarket comic opera, *The Agreeable Surprise* (1784), 'in a style that drew forth the incessant laughter and applause of the house. In a rich crimson silk, a pair of double ruffles, and diamond ear-rings – he presented the most Agreeable Surprise that could be witnessed'.[48] Whether it was in the seclusion of the English country house, or at an Indian colonial garden party, blackfaced white gentry delighted in counterfeiting black people, choosing to act and observe theatrical performances where complicated nuances of rank and authority could mix with transgressive sexualities.

Amateur or semi-professional theatricals in the British colonies, directly staged under military auspices, are also an important subgroup of private performances. Kathleen Wilson has traced the near-global dispersal of Nicholas

FIGURE 2.3: *High Life Below Stairs*, Thomas Orde-Powlett, etching, *c*.1774. The etching is apparently a souvenir (this is one of two known impressions) of a private theatrical performance at Cassiobury House, Hertfordshire, of James Townley's 1759 Drury Lane comedy. Courtesy of the Lewis Walpole Library.

Rowe's *Fair Penitent* (1703), as its text and the techniques of its dramaturgy were transported along maritime routes of exploration and colonization.[49] Military amateur theatricals performed by soldiers and sailors to entertain themselves while stationed far from home are discussed extensively in Gillian Russell's groundbreaking, *The Theatres of War: Performance, Politics, and Society 1793–1815* (1995). Perhaps the most significant of these was General Washington's sponsoring of a performance of Addison's *Cato*, played by officers of the Continental Army, at their Valley Forge encampment in 1778 together with, barely thirty miles away, an entire season of amateur theatricals staged in occupied Philadelphia by British soldiers and sailors, both warring parties stalemated by the harsh north-eastern winter.[50] Whereas Washington used *Cato* to embody the ideology of a sacrificial heroism he sought to promote in his beleaguered soldiers, the British played their endgame in a range of plays drawn from the contemporary London repertoire. With the British eventually forced out of Philadelphia in May 1778, these military theatrical performances truly mark both the ends and the beginnings of global empires.

This chapter has shown how the Atlantic seaboard cities and ports on the trading routes, as well as inland settlements ranging from towns and villages to country houses, all illustrate the centrality of theatre to eighteenth-century Western culture. Its transoceanic distribution meant that patterns of reception and production were enormously conditioned by differences in time and place. Largely on account of its scale, which was accompanied by the gathering of many people together into concentrated physical spaces, complex systems of control, accommodation, personal agency and patterns of behaviour emerged. The theatre-going experience was clearly different from our own and it is quite challenging to make the imaginative leap to understand those distant times. Inevitably, we will be left wondering at the huge volume of theatre produced during that era as well as, very probably, our own extreme unfamiliarity with the repertoire.

CHAPTER THREE

Sexuality and Gender

Changing Identities

HELEN E.M. BROOKS

During the Enlightenment, a radical change took place in English theatre: the introduction and establishment of the professional actress. In France, Italy and Spain, theatre companies had employed women since the latter half of the sixteenth century. In England however, while women had long been a lively presence in non-legitimate contexts – appearing in court masques, parish dramas, festive pageants and fairs – it was only with the re-establishment of theatre in England after the hiatus of the Interregnum that they were permitted to perform in licensed spaces. It is uncertain who exactly the first professional actress was – Anne Marshall and Margaret Hughes both having some claim to the title – however what *is* known is that when *Othello* was performed on 8 December 1660 at Gibbon's Tennis Court Theatre on Vere Street, the part of Desdemona was played by a woman. This actress was not, however, a solitary presence. Despite taking the name the 'King's Men' for his company of players, Thomas Killigrew – who, along with William Davenant, had been given a royal licence to produce theatre in July 1660 – employed a number of women including Katherine Corey, Mrs Eastland and Mrs Weaver. Initially these actresses' performances were something of a novelty; however, it was not long before women became firmly established within the theatre industry: both as actresses, and also as playwrights, dancers, singers and, albeit to a lesser degree, house servants such as dressers and box keepers.

At the same time as this radical change in the gender composition of theatre was taking place, a wider cultural shift in understandings of gender and sexuality was transforming English culture. By the end of the eighteenth century, this shift would result in men's and women's bodies, social roles and behaviours being seen, for the first time, as opposite and naturally determined. It was a remodelling of the very grounds on which men and women related to each other. And while it was not unique to English culture – with the Enlightenment marking the birth of a new sex/gender system across much of western Europe – what was unique to the English context was that the emergence of the modern gender/sex paradigm took place alongside a specific shift in the gender dynamics of theatre. For while in Europe professional actresses had long been a familiar feature, with actresses performing in France throughout the seventeenth century, and in Spain since the late sixteenth century, only in England did the shift to having women play female characters coincide with broader cultural changes to notions of sexuality and gender. As such, the English theatre provides a helpful case study for this chapter, revealing as it does not only how ideas of sexuality and gender were engaged with within dramatic performance, but also how they shaped the working experiences of the new cohort of professional female performers that quickly emerged after 1660.

It is on these two key areas that the present chapter focuses. The first section, 'Roles and representations', explores how dramatic performance functioned as a means of responding to and shaping changing ideas about gender roles and sexual identities. Looking at the highly popular practice of cross-dressing, it considers in particular how the dramatic text and embodied performance might have intersected in different ways to speak to competing gender ideologies. The second and third sections move away from this focus on dramatic performance and consider instead the often-overlooked ways in which gender and sexual discourse impacted on the material experience of working in the theatre. In the second section, 'Motherhood and marriage', the focus is on the ways in which the biological and legal experiences of being women shaped actresses' working lives. The final section, 'Pay and participation', considers the extent to which gender impacted on women's opportunities to participate in different capacities within the theatre industry, as well as how far it determined what they were paid in comparison to their male peers. Examining theatrical performance, economic structures and material experiences of working in the theatre, as a whole, therefore, the chapter reveals, even if it cannot detail in the space available, the extent to which gender and sexuality permeated every aspect of Enlightenment English theatre.

ROLES AND REPRESENTATIONS

The introduction of the actress in 1660 was a seminal moment in English theatre history. As well as providing opportunities for women who wanted to work as legitimate performers, it also prepared the way for female playwrights who, in the wake of the actress's introduction, began to have their works produced publicly on the legitimate stage. Women like Aphra Behn, Mary Pix, Catherine Trotter and Delarivier Manley all found success in writing for the new theatre companies and by the end of the eighteenth century, women would make up approximately 10 per cent of all playwrights writing for the London theatres.[1] Particularly in the Restoration, plays by these female writers frequently mocked male characters, protested against patriarchal oppression, and gave more lines to female characters (and therefore actresses). Yet female playwrights were not alone in focusing their work on issues of gender relations; the works of male playwrights including John Vanbrugh, Thomas Southerne, George Etherege, William Congreve, William Wycherley, Thomas Durfey and George Farquhar all reveal a similar and unprecedented preoccupation with the topics of gender and sexuality and the social institutions (such as marriage) which controlled them. While in part a reaction to the introduction of women to the stage and the new possibilities that this allowed for exploring such topics, the extraordinary proliferation of plays exploring gender and sexuality during the Restoration was also a response to a social and cultural environment in which understandings of and attitudes towards the body, sexuality and sexual behaviour were all beginning to change.

Over the course of the eighteenth century, a revolutionary shift took place (albeit gradually and irregularly) in constructions of sexuality and gender roles. For centuries, male and female bodies had been conceived of as being variants of one body type placed at different points on a vertical continuum. Within this hierarchical or 'one-sex' model, sexual difference had been a matter of degree and sex had been a sociological rather than ontological category. However, over the course of the eighteenth century a new oppositional or 'two-sex' model slowly gained dominance. With this new framework, male and female bodies existed in a horizontal, incommensurable relationship and were understood to be anatomically and qualitatively different. For the first time, the sexed body became the primary site of identity and difference, and was drawn on to determine and constrain men's and women's social roles and behaviours, economic activities, and sexual desires.

At a time of radical upheaval in the ways that bodies and behaviours were understood and socially regulated, theatre served as an important public forum for responding to, testing and shaping ideas about gender roles and sexual identities. In part, playwrights undertook this cultural work as they wrote their plays, and not infrequently rewrote the plays of others. In fashioning new characters and adapting older types across varied genres, playwrights offered multiple and even conflicting versions of masculinity and femininity, which both voiced and challenged contemporary anxieties over changing gender roles. In the rakes, fops and country gentlemen; wits, coquettes, prudes, maids and ladies of eighteenth-century drama, flawed and idealized versions of masculinity and femininity were presented and problematized: the drama in its multiplicity both resisting and promoting changing understandings of sexuality and gender.

Theatre's engagement with the social and cultural changes taking place within English society was not solely restricted to the dramatic text, however; just as significant were the performances of these works by actors and actresses in the live moment. This was an age in which the performer was pre-eminent and was often as much of a draw for spectators as the play itself. In addition to spectatorial knowledge about performers' 'real' lives and awareness of the ways in which these lives enhanced or disrupted the gender ideologies implicit in the plays, the non-naturalistic style of acting and the direct communication that would often take place between performers and spectators also provided the former with an opportunity to incorporate their own commentaries on contemporary gender attitudes into their performances. The dramatic character was just one part of a much wider signifying system. Through the embodied performances of these parts, actors and actresses had licence to both work with and resist the gender commentaries of the plays they represented.

The nuanced ways in which acting and text might have intersected to speak to changing notions of gender and sexual identity is manifested, in particular, through examples of theatrical cross-dressing: a genre which was exceptionally reliant on the performer's embodied representation of the 'other' to make meaning in the theatrical moment. Cross-dressing – a genre which included female breeches and what I describe as male 'petticoat' roles (where a character cross-dresses within the world of the play), as well as travesty performances (in which a performer took on a part written for the opposite sex) – was generally popular with audiences throughout the eighteenth century. The ways in which cross-dressing spoke to changing notions of gender, however, varied greatly and depended not only on the sex of the performer, but also on the role being performed and the particular subgenre of cross-dressing being presented.

Male travesty performance had a long history in English theatre, being the only means prior to 1660 by which female roles could be represented on the legitimate stage. Over the course of the later seventeenth century, however, not only was its form altered, but its range was greatly reduced. This change was instigated both by the interruption of skills transmission to new boy actors during the Interregnum and by the introduction of the actress in 1660. It was then reinforced by the cultural shift away from a world view in which sexual identity was mutable. The result was that over the latter half of the eighteenth century male travesty performance became limited to secondary roles such as the nurses in Henry Nevill Payne's tragedy *The Fatal Jealousy* (1672), and in Otway's adaptation of *Romeo and Juliet*, *Caius Marius* (1680); the landlady in Thomas Scott's *The Mock Marriage* (1695); Mrs Fardingale in Richard Steele's *The Funeral* (1701); and the first trull in Thomas Shadwell's *Humours of the Army* (1713).

This limitation of male travesty to secondary female characters who were invariably older, lecherous, deformed and/or dowdy suggests an increasing resistance to the blurring of homo- and heteroerotic attraction which serious travesty – in which actors had played tragic heroines, witty maids and everything in between – had allowed. In addition, the comic nature of these secondary roles likely facilitated a more parodic and mocking style of performance in which the actor could be distanced from the role he played. Performed in this way, male travesty was therefore ultimately recuperated within a culture in which the boundaries of sex and gender were increasingly being demarcated, and in which male sexual desire was being contained within the binary categories of exclusively heterosexual or homosexual.

The petticoat role and its better known female equivalent, the breeches role, also reflected the emerging sex/gender model. In breeches and petticoat roles, the play's dramatic action and comic effect both demanded and relied on the parodic gap between the actor's (and character's) 'true' sex/gender identity and the 'other' they imitated. The popularity of David Garrick's portrayal of Sir John Brute – a man who disguises himself as his own wife – in *The Provoked Wife* – was grounded therefore not in Garrick's believable transformation into a woman (although, as the *London Chronicle* commented in 1757, 'you would swear he had often attended the Toilet' so accurate was his imitation of women's mannerisms) but rather in his lampooning of femininity.[2] In a parallel example, the comic effect of watching Peg Woffington mock masculine stereotypes as Sylvia in *The Recruiting Officer* (1706) was only achieved if the actress's femininity was foregrounded. As such, breeches and petticoat roles ultimately reinforced the new heteronormative order in which male and female bodies and behaviours were naturally and incommensurably opposite.

Both petticoat and male travesty performances seem to have reinforced the new sex/gender paradigm; however, there was a distinct difference between the meanings on offer through the two types of male cross dressing. For while petticoat roles, like breeches roles, necessitated a gap between the performer/character's imitated and 'real' gender identity, the cross-dressed element in travesty performances, absent as it invariably was from the dramatic text itself, allowed the performer far more latitude to blur or demarcate these boundaries. As such, while the increasing partitioning of male from female and masculine from feminine seems to have reduced the range of male travesty, the playful blurring of sex/gender boundaries offered by earlier travesty did not necessarily disappear. Instead, actors like James Nokes, William Bullock and Henry Norris could each determine the extent to which they would present a serious or parodic version of femininity with each individual role they played. Being fundamentally performative therefore, male travesty cultivated an ambiguous relationship to both residual and emergent gender ideology.

FIGURE 3.1: *Mr. Garrick in the Character of Sr. John Brute*, James Roberts, 1776. Harry R. Beard Collection, given by Isobel Beard © Victoria and Albert Museum, London.

FIGURE 3.2: *Mr. Bullock the Comedian*, Charles Hall after William Hogarth, 1781. Harry R. Beard Collection, given by Isobel Beard © Victoria and Albert Museum, London.

Female travesty was similarly fluid in its response to competing gender ideologies. In such diverse roles as Macheath in *The Beggar's Opera*, Sir Harry Wildair in *The Constant Couple* and Lothario in *The Fair Penitent*, actresses drew on the audience's knowledge of their real selves and their other performances while embodying, according to contemporary accounts and portraits, a passable masculinity. The result was a performance style which to varying degrees, depending on the performer and role, was provocatively androgynous. Like their male peers, female travesty performers therefore had the potential both to blur the lines between feminine and masculine signifiers in a gesture towards the mutability of gender identity *and* to create the parodic distance between self and character which spoke to the emerging two-sex paradigm.

While male and female travesty performances could speak to both residual and emergent gender models, the sociocultural resonances of each form of travesty were markedly different. For while male travesty performers divested themselves of their sociocultural primacy in taking on female roles (a reduction in status which brought with it connotations of effeminacy and sodomy), female travesty performers took on this social superiority. Not only in their embodied performances, but also in the simple fact of their being freed from the restrictions of long skirts and petticoats, actresses gained a new physicality which signalled strength and masculine privilege. For much of the century this theatrical appropriation of masculine prerogative on stage seemed largely unproblematic, even being mirrored in the kinds of real-life cross-dressing practised by women including Hannah Snell and Christian Davies. By the 1780s and 1790s, however, the growing demand for women's bodies to function as direct signifiers of an internalized, natural and inferior feminine identity resulted in a sudden decline in the practice.

MOTHERHOOD AND MARRIAGE

The growing preoccupation with interiority in the last two decades of the eighteenth century placed new importance on the body – and female body in particular – as the projection of a fundamentally gendered and authentic interior self. At the core of this self, for women, were the roles of mother and wife. In an ideological move which served to erode women's public and economic activities, raising children now became a woman's exclusive function in life. This shift placed the actress, as the most public embodiment of the working woman, in a uniquely difficult position: not only because her professional presence on the stage signified her maternal absence from the home, but also because almost every aspect of theatrical work was in conflict with advice on antenatal and maternal conduct.

In the latter decades of the eighteenth century, pregnant women suddenly found themselves subject to new scrutiny, with an explosion of publications

CONSTANT COUPLE.

Dodd del.   Goldar sculp.

M.ᴿˢ BARRY as SIR HARRY WILDAIR.

_Sdeath I'm afraid I've mistaken the House

Publish'd May 17. 1777. by I Lowndes & partners.   Act II. Sc. 2.

FIGURE 3.3: *Mrs. Barry as Sir Harry Wildair*, Daniel Dodd, 1777. Harry R. Beard Collection, given by Isobel Beard © Victoria and Albert Museum, London.

seeking to regulate almost every aspect of their behaviour. The most frequent advice in such volumes was to avoid, among other things: travelling, physical exertion, fatiguing employments, crowded assemblies (especially at night), strong or excessive emotions and an irregular life. For the many actresses who found themselves pregnant in this period of limited and unreliable birth control, this advice was as much a description of working in the theatre as it was of risky behaviours during pregnancy. With a gruelling schedule that involved hours of rehearsals and line-learning before an evening's performance of sometimes more than one play, a regular London season could be arduous. For those performers working on the touring circuit, whether individually or as part of a strolling company, it was even more intense. On top of rehearsing and performing multiple roles, these performers had the additional challenge of travelling for hours by coach between theatres as far afield as Edinburgh, Glasgow, Exeter and Dublin, often with little opportunity to rest between engagements. For pregnant actresses of course, whether working in London or the provinces, such professional exertions would also frequently have been coupled with nausea, vomiting, swelling, exhaustion, frequent urination and the other common side effects of pregnancy.

Actresses could also find themselves behaving counter to popular advice when it came to the period surrounding the birth. When it came to stopping work, most actresses probably planned to work until the standard one-month confinement period, but due dates were notoriously hard to estimate and some women, like Sarah Siddons, who went into labour on stage in 1775, found the gap between final performance and birth shorter than anticipated. Moreover, while audiences seem to have had no issue with heavily pregnant actresses performing a diversity of roles (including virginal heroines), the physical discomfort apparent in such performances could be a matter of concern. As the *Morning Chronicle* wrote of Isabella Mattocks on 30 September 1773:

> We lament that so good an actress should be in so disagreeable a situation as this lady must have been in yesterday evening. Surely the Managers should now let her rest, and allow a substitute to represent her characters till she has got up from lying-in! [. . .] The painful sensations the audience must feel on such an actress's account form an idea of her being uneasy; [. . .this] was frequently the case with us yesterday evening, when we thought we discovered in Mrs Mattocks's countenance at different times strong tokens of pain and illness.

Similar concern was shown over actresses who returned to work after only a short lying-in period. While conventional medical wisdom prescribed four to six weeks of rest and recovery, actresses frequently returned to work much sooner and were the subject of press attention as a result. As *The Times* commented on 21 November 1788, following Dora Jordan's speedy return to the stage after a stillbirth within the previous ten days, 'Mrs Jordan has just stepped out of a sick room – and she plays three successive evenings – surely the manager of Old Drury has never read the fable of the hen and the *Golden Eggs*!'

The common press insinuation that theatre managers forced actresses to work late into their pregnancies or to return to work soon after giving birth probably has some basis in reality, in particular for lower-tier actresses who could easily be replaced and had little bargaining power. Yet, as sporadic anecdotes of actresses having their workloads reduced during pregnancy reveal, managers could also be considerate of the needs of their female performers. Where women returned to work soon after giving birth, therefore, financial necessity, a sense of professional obligation or fear that a rival would supplant them were often as much the cause.

Whatever an actress's reasons however, returning to work before being fully recovered could be risky, as the story of Mary Wells cautioned. Returning to work reportedly in order to 'oblige the manager of Covent Garden' by performing a particular role, Wells suffered, in her estranged husband's words, a 'revolution of her milk which afterwards flew to her head, and occasionally disordered her brain'.[3] Whether there was any link between her return to work, her experience of what we now know as mastitis, and her subsequent mental health is impossible to know; however, by putting her professional work ahead of her maternal duty – and specifically by neglecting her duty to devotedly breastfeed her child – Wells's maternal body was figured in this narrative as revolting against her failure of femininity.

This attack on Wells for being a poor mother was not unique. By the end of the century, actresses were increasingly being judged in relation to an idealized version of femininity in which women devoted themselves to an exclusively domestic life centred on the happiness and education of their children. Yet both in their working practices and decisions around balancing birth with work, as well as in their very presence on stage (and therefore absence from the home), actress-mothers resisted these ideals. As Richard Cumberland pointed out in discussing Andromache in 1792, when the role was overwhelmingly associated with Sarah Siddons, the problem for actresses was that:

The Andromache of the stage may have an infant Hector at home, whom she more tenderly feels for than the Hector of the scene; he may be sick, he may be supperless; there may be none to nurse him, when his mother is out of sight, and the maternal interest in the divided heart of the actress may preponderate over the heroine's.[4]

Actresses were not alone in finding themselves caught between the discursive ideals of domestic maternity and the practical realities of having to provide economic stability for their families. Women across the social spectrum were also having to align these polarities in their daily lives. Yet while a gap between the high ideals of motherhood and lived experience was a reality for many women, it was actresses, the most prominent group of working women, who provided a focal point for the debate around women's social and economic roles.

Motherhood was not only a challenge to be negotiated, however; it was also a uniquely female identity which actresses could draw on to support their professional roles. Indeed, as Sarah Siddons realized in 1782, being a mother could be used both to justify and to negate other, less acceptably feminine aspects of an actress's identity. Leaving the south-west to move to London in the summer of 1782, Siddons was about to make an ambitious second attempt to establish herself at Drury Lane (her first having failed six years earlier). In her farewell speech to the Bath and Bristol audiences, she explained her decision in terms, not of professional ambition, but of maternal love and duty. Heavily pregnant Siddons brought her three young children out on stage and informed her audiences, 'These are the moles that heave me from your side / Where I was rooted – where I could have dy'd', then continuing by commanding:

> Stand forth, ye elves, and plead your mother's cause,
> Ye little magnets – whose strong infl'ence draws
> Me from a point where ev'ry gentle breeze
> Wafted my bark to happiness and ease;
> Sends me advent'rous on a larger main,
> In hopes that you may profit by my gain.[5]

At a time when being professionally or economically ambitious was the antithesis of femininity, Siddons used her identity as a mother not simply to negate but to justify her ambition. And it was no coincidence that she performed this speech as an epilogue after performing Andromache in *The Distrest Mother*, a role which epitomized late-century ideals of maternal devotion and self-sacrifice.

Siddons was probably not the first actress to use a performance as the selfless mother Andromache to counter criticism; in fact it was a strategy that had reportedly been used almost a century earlier by Anne Oldfield. In November 1712, while performing the play's epilogue which, although witty, ends 'Take then, ye Circles of the Brave and Fair, / The Fatherless and Widow to your Care', Oldfield, like Siddons decades later, is reputed to have brought her three- or four year-old son Arthur out to stand alongside her.[6] If true, it would certainly have made for a poignant image: less than two weeks earlier, Arthur's father and Oldfield's partner of almost ten years, the prominent Whig, Arthur Maynwaring, had died, aged just forty-four. While never legally contracted in marriage, Oldfield was in all other respects Maynwaring's widow: a position indicated by her being named his executrix and inheriting a third of his estate.

Fashion'd alike by Nature & by Art,   *Mᵣˢ Oldfield*   In publick Life, by all who saw, Approv'd

To please, inengage Interest ev'ry Heart.   In private Life by all who knew her, Lov'd.

I. Richardson pinx.   Decus et Deliciæ Theatri.   I. Simon fec. & Ex.

FIGURE 3.4: *Mrs. Oldfield*, Jonathan Richardson possibly after John Simon. Harry R. Beard Collection, given by Isobel Beard © Victoria and Albert Museum, London.

It was this position as widowed mother that Oldfield sought to emphasize in bringing Arthur onstage during the epilogue. After playing the widowed Andromache, a tragic heroine who vows to remain faithful to the memory of her dead husband but has to marry again to save her son, Oldfield used the play's epilogue to position herself as a loyal, grieving widow and mother of a fatherless son. She did so specifically to counter the attacks she faced in the wake of Maynwaring's death and his testamentary decisions.

Oldfield's political leanings and private relationship with Maynwaring had long marked her out as an easy target for press attacks. In the period following his death however, the news that Oldfield was the primary beneficiary of his will gave such attacks new momentum. As William Oldys, author of the 1741 *Memoirs of Mrs Anne Oldfield* wrote:

> a most scandalous and false Rumour was spread, chiefly levelled at Mrs Oldfield, that he [Maynwaring] had died of a Venereal Malady. But to obviate so ungenerous a Reflection, his Body, by her Direction, was opened by two Surgeons [. . .] These Gentleman (sic), all, declared, that there was not the least Symptom of anything Venereal; but that he had died of a Consumption.[7]

Being too much 'admired *upon the stage*, to have any Enquiry made in her Conduct *behind the Curtain*', Oldfield's public persona onstage was evidence, as another scurrilous attack implied, of her sexual promiscuity offstage.[8]

The implication of promiscuous sexuality, which was levelled against Oldfield in the attacks following Maynwaring's death, was not unique to this instance. Female performance had long been associated with sexual immodesty. From the first appearances of actresses in 1660, tracts and poems had emphasized the sexual allure of actresses' performances, while in memoirs recounting their admirers and lovers, and in sexually playful prologues and epilogues, the association between actresses and a potent, often threatening female sexuality had been established in the cultural imagination. Some actresses, including the celebrated Restoration performer Betty Boutell, even seem to have deliberately presented themselves in this mould as a means of courting audience favour.[9] More often however, lampoons and satires which highlighted the apparent sexual promiscuity of actresses were a means of countering the perceived threat posed by these women's new economic and social power.

In many cases these sexually focused attacks relied on their subject being unmarried. For actresses like Oldfield who engaged in long-term sexual relationships outside of the bounds of conventional marriage, professional attacks which cast aspersions of sexual immorality were a familiar challenge. There were, however, a number of reasons why actresses in the long eighteenth century might choose not to marry – reasons not only of a personal nature, but also grounded in the legal status of a married woman as feme covert: a status which meant that a woman's legal identity was 'incorporated and consolidated into that of the husband'.[10] Losing the autonomy to sign legal documents, trade independently, negotiate and agree contracts, take legal action to redress any dispute with an employer and even to receive their own earnings, actresses, like other working women, could be severely impacted by marriage's legal constraints.

This is not to say that marriage was entirely inimical to an actress's professional identity. Throughout the long eighteenth century, marriage continued to be, as it had for centuries, a means of creating and affirming networks of kinship. Within the theatre, just as in wider society, these networks of kinship were drawn on by women and men – including Susannah Cibber, Sophia Baddeley, Ann Dancer, William Gardner and John Bannister – to promote and enhance both economic and professional status. If these partnerships failed however, actresses were uniquely at risk, not least because their estranged husbands frequently retained the legal right to claim their earnings. This was certainly the case for both Sophia Baddeley and Susannah Cibber in the 1760s and 1730s respectively. Yet while Baddeley was able to reclaim her earnings through negotiation with both her husband and Drury Lane's treasurer, almost forty years earlier Susannah Cibber had found the reassertion of financial independence far more challenging.

Susannah's marriage to and acrimonious separation from Drury Lane's manager, Theophilus Cibber, exemplifies the potential risks of marrying for an actress. Over the course of six years, Theophilus tried to force Susannah to play roles she was not entitled to, took her salary to pay off his debts, stole her personal belongings, encouraged her to develop a relationship with a wealthy admirer in exchange for financial loans and, subsequently, when the affair developed into a serious relationship, kidnapped the pregnant Susannah and made her the subject of two public trials for criminal conversation. In the end, Susannah only escaped by exiling herself to Ireland until her mother's successful 1742 injunction which, in preventing Theophilus from interfering with Susannah's career, taking her income or working in the same theatre, enabled the actress to return to England effectively as a feme sole.

Susannah's story is all the more poignant for the fact that prior to her marriage, she and her mother, Anne Arne, had gone to great lengths to protect the young actress's property and earnings from the clutches of her notoriously indebted fiancé. Not only establishing a separate estate (a type of property which a husband and his creditors were meant to be unable to touch) for her income but also stipulating that half her annual salary would be invested in government securities, Susannah had made every effort to guard against the economic and professional pitfalls of marrying Theophilus. Unfortunately, as many eighteenth-century women found, the flaws and loopholes of separate estates meant that they often failed to provide the legal protection they promised.

FIGURE 3.5: Susannah Cibber, Thomas Hudson, 1746. Harry R. Beard Collection, © Victoria and Albert Museum, London.

PAY AND PARTICIPATION

It is hardly surprising that actresses like Susannah Cibber sought to protect their professional earnings when they married, or that others might have considered the financial implications of marriage a strong deterrent. Throughout the long eighteenth century, the theatre provided women a rare opportunity to earn significant amounts of money through their own hard work and skill; not only did most actresses earn more than in almost any other female occupation, but those women who made it to the higher echelons of the industry could equal or even surpass the income levels available to many men within wider society.

In the early years of the century, at a time when the average female wage was five shillings a week (£13 p.a.); when a skilled housekeeper might earn up to £15 p.a.; and when only a few specialist female workers achieved the highest rate of ten or twelve shillings a week (£26–£31 p.a.), novice or aspiring actresses like Anne Oldfield and Mary Porter were comparatively highly paid. In her first year at Drury Lane in 1699, Oldfield was earning 15s a week (£22 per season excluding benefit) while in 1703, Porter was paid a comfortable £35–£40, a figure which had risen to £80 by 1709.[11] Some years later, in 1742–3, the lowest-tier performer in John Rich's company received 1s. 8d. per day (a potential £32 for an 180-day season), a sharp contrast to the £20 p.a. paid to an experienced waiting woman in a large aristocratic London household.[12] This gap between the wages of lower-tier actresses and the earning power of women in other occupations widened even further in the latter half of the century. In 1756, Frances Abington made her Drury Lane debut on thirty shillings a week (a potential £45 per season) and in 1771, Ann Cargill was paid £31 10s. in her debut season at Covent Garden.[13] Around the same time, women in domestic service could expect to be paid only £20 for work as a ladies' maid, £12 working as a cook or £7–£9 working as an 'inferior' woman servant.[14]

Throughout the century, even if a new or low-tier actress was paid for only a proportion of the season, her earning potential could easily match and surpass that of women in other lines of employment. In comparison to the earning potential of men in wider society however, actresses did not fare so well, unless that is they could make it to the higher tiers of the profession. Throughout the century, star actresses including Anne Oldfield, Susannah Cibber, Hannah Pritchard, Kitty Clive, Peg Woffington, Frances Abington, Dora Jordan and Sarah Siddons all achieved income levels which far surpassed those attained by most men outside the theatre. In 1706, Oldfield was earning £120 per season at a time when the cost of keeping a family was around £40 and the lower income threshold for a 'middling class' family was around £100; three years later she was earning almost twice as much and at the end of her career in 1728–9, at a time when the upper-class income threshold was around £500, she earned £878 (including £500 from one benefit performance).[15] In the middle decades of the century, when an educated and trained lawyer earning £200 p.a. was in the top-earning 5 per cent of the population and when successful merchants were earning around £600 p.a., contracted salaries and benefits for an actress could together bring anything from £430 (Hannah Pritchard, 1742–3) to £745 (Kitty Clive, 1742–3).[16] In exceptional cases, actresses like Susannah Cibber and Peg Woffington could even top these rates: Cibber, in 1749, negotiating a £700 salary which was paid out even though she only performed thirteen times that season, and Woffington returning to Covent Garden in 1754 on an £800 contract.[17]

Towards the end of the century, leading London actresses were comfortably earning more than the £200–£300 needed to secure a place in the middling classes. Frances Abington received £600 in 1782 at Covent Garden, and both Sarah Siddons and Dora Jordan earned £30 per week at Drury Lane in 1790, a salary which brought Jordan £641 for forty performances including benefits.[18] Earning slightly more for a ten-month season's work than a college fellow or headmaster might earn for a full year's work, actresses also had the potential to more than double their income through summer touring. So great was the profit that could be made from a summer's tour, in fact, that in 1809 Jordan achieved an annual income of between £3,000 and £4,000. This was an income greater than the £2,600 Patrick Colquhoun estimated was earned by leading merchants and bankers at the turn of the century and close to that of the country's twenty-six bishops on c.£4,000 p.a.[19]

Throughout the long eighteenth century, leading actresses could equal and even surpass the income levels of many men within wider society. Yet this could also be the case within the profession. Women, including among others, Christina Horton, Susannah Cibber and Dora Jordan were all, at different points in the century and in different companies, the highest paid performers below the actor-managers. Contracted by Covent Garden in 1734, Horton's £250 salary confidently exceeded that of her male peers, Mr Stephens (£200) and John Hippisley (£180), while Cibber's £315 Drury Lane contract in 1747–8 placed her second only to actor-manager David Garrick.[20] Moreover, it was not only celebrated London actresses who could beat their male peers to win the highest salaries. In the early 1780s, the novice Dora Jordan negotiated the highest salary – £1 11s. 6d. per week – within Tate Wilkinson's Yorkshire company after her success performing in *The Fair Penitent*.[21]

In addition to such examples of individual achievement, there were also sporadic instances of companies paying more for their female performers, as a group, than for the men in their company. Such was the case at the Queen's Theatre in the Haymarket in 1708.[22] In spring 1708, in a company where there were five male and five female singers, the women earned a total of £1,290 while the men earned slightly less at £930: a wage gap in women's favour of 28 per cent (or 17 per cent if the castrato Giuseppe Cassani's additional £137 for travel expenses is included). Equally noteworthy is the women's £200 median wage compared to the men's £100.

This reverse pay gap at the Queen's was certainly unusual; however, it was not the sole example of a theatre company reversing the conventional gendered pay structure. Later in the century, Anthony Pasquin's [John Williams] 'Authentic List of the Principal Performers engaged at the Opera House for the year 1789' also indicates a pay gap in women's favour.[23] For the eight women and ten men (figures which exclude two couples whose salaries were listed jointly, the ballet masters and the managers) the average seasonal wages were £500 and just over £414 respectively: a pay gap of 17 per cent in the women's favour. In addition, not only were two of the three highest paid performers women, but the median male pay was just £250 compared to £350 for the women: a median gap of 29 per cent in the women's favour.

As well as sporadically exceeding the pay of their male peers both individually and en masse, the wages of actresses more frequently equalled those of the actors they worked alongside. Certainly when the 1703 plan for a new united theatre company was developed, no distinction was made between the wages to be offered to the leading women (Elizabeth Barry and Anne Bracegirdle) and the leading men (Thomas Betterton, John Verbruggen, George Powell and Robert Wilks).[24] For men and women who had succeeded in creating a unique theatrical product, a product for which audiences wanted to exchange large amounts of money, it was the value of their offering within a commercial market, rather than their gender, that determined how much they could earn.

This was not, however, necessarily the case for the vast majority of performers, as the 1703 plan also reveals. While the plan proposes ten women being employed as actresses, this is a sharp contrast to the twenty men proposed as actors. In addition, while the mean average salary for those twenty actors was £83, the ten actresses were to receive an average of only £72: a mean gender pay gap of 13 per cent, and a median pay gap of 25 per cent. With the £150 earmarked for each of the six top-tier performers – Elizabeth Barry and Anne Bracegirdle; and John Verbruggen, George Powell, Robert Wilks and Thomas Betterton (who received an additional £50 as manager) – removed, there was an even starker wage differential. The remaining eight women earned a total of just £420, compared to the sixteen men's total of £1,060: a mean gender pay gap of 21 per cent. It was a gap almost exactly reflected in the 20 per cent difference between Anne Oldfield's proposed £80 salary and the £100 being suggested for her peers Thomas Doggett and Benjamin Johnson. As documents like this reveal, customary notions about the value of women's work as well as the fact that there were fewer female roles available both tended to suppress female wages, creating a gap between men's and women's pay rates as well as an imbalance in participation.

The 1703 plan, listing every performer by intended salary rather than the money they actually received, is invaluable for the insight it provides into the gendered pay and participation structures of an early eighteenth-century theatre company. It is not, however, the only example of gender disparity in wages or indeed in participation, as Richard Brinsley Sheridan's employment of a third more actors than actresses in his first season at Drury Lane (forty-eight compared to thirty-six actresses) reveals. Nor were such practices isolated to low-tier performers or even to companies performing dramatic works. When Felice Giardini, the composer and co-manager of the Italian Opera at the King's Theatre, laid out his hypothetical pay scale in 1763–4, he estimated paying the 'First Man' a maximum of £950 while the 'First Woman' would receive a maximum of £760 'if excellent' (a 20 per cent wage gap) and £552 10s. (a 42 per cent wage gap) 'if middling'.[25] Twenty years later, in 1784–5 at the same theatre, the six male and four female singers earned totals of £2,580/£2,550 (one singer has two variables) and £1,400 respectively: a mean wage gap of 18 to 19 per cent.[26]

Even where there was greater equality of participation, as was sometimes the case in opera companies like the Pantheon between 1790 and 1792, female performers continued to be paid less than their male peers. Yet while there was greater equality in participation at the Pantheon during this period, the known wages of twenty-one out of the twenty-four figurantes for 1790–1 (three of the women's wages being incorporated into the salary paid to a male principle such as a husband) indicate the persistence of a pay gap of at least 11 per cent. In addition, while less than one-third of the male figurants (three) were paid below the median wage of £60, almost half of the women (five) were paid below £50: a wage which placed these women in what Patrick Colquhoun described as the 'lower orders'.[27]

The 1791–2 season, where wages for all the figurants are known, presents a slightly different pattern. While again more women than men were employed in the company, although by only one rather than four as in the previous season, these nine women's total wages were slightly higher than the eight men's: £475 compared to £465. While this only translated as a 9 per cent mean wage gap however, the median wage gap was significantly higher, at 17 per cent, and twice as many women (four) as men (two) were paid less than the £50 median wage. In addition, the two lowest paid members of the company, both women, received just £25 and £35 each.

While women on stage at the Pantheon were well represented, if poorly paid in comparison to their male peers, behind the scenes the situation was far more unbalanced. As in most theatres, the female presence behind the scenes was, if not minimal, certainly curbed; musicians, treasurers, prompters, doorkeepers, brokers, tailors and caterers were invariably male, and women were relegated to roles which involved supposedly domestic skills such as sewing, washing and cleaning. Just as in wider society, these roles were poorly remunerated as a consequence of assumptions about women and men's relative physical strength, the supplementary nature of a woman's income to a household, and presumptions about the ways in which a woman's reproductive status would impact on her work. The Pantheon was fairly typical therefore in having only two women in the eleven-strong scene painting team. Being paid 2s. per day to stitch the canvases together, these women were not far from being the lowest paid members of the team – with only two male labourers remunerated at 1s. 6d. per day beating them – and were paid significantly below the 5s. 8d. mean average. Fifty years earlier at Covent Garden however, 2s. per day (a potential £17 4s. /£17 18s. for a season of 172/179 nights) had been the highest salary for any offstage female theatrical employee.[28] In the 1735–6 season approximately a third of Covent Garden's employees had been women, yet only one, a box keeper (and one of only three women out of seventeen working as box office and house staff) had been paid the mean rate of 2s. This was a sharp contrast to the eleven men who received this amount or higher. Other than these three women, and another three women whose roles are unknown, all the remaining women were employed in the female-only occupations of charwomen (of which there were six), dressers (nine), sweeper (one) and washerwoman (one). The wages of these female-only occupations were also notably low, ranging from 1s. 8d. per day for two of the dressers (£14 6s. 8d. for a 172-day season) to 1s. 6d. per day for the other seven dressers and the sweeper (£12 18s. for 172 days and £13 8s. 6d. for 179 days respectively). At the bottom of the hierarchy was 1s. per day for the six charwomen (totalling £8 19s. for 179 days). Only one man was paid this low and his job was unlisted. Overall, out of the twenty women whose salaries are listed in the 1735–6 roster, seventeen were paid 1s. 6d. and under while only two of the nineteen men listed (excluding billsetters) were paid in this lower bracket. Similarly, while only three women earned more than the median pay of 1s. 8d., only two men earned *below* this figure.

The reality for those women who tried to make a living behind the scenes rather than by performing in front of them was that being female fundamentally shaped both how much they could be paid and what kinds of work they could do. While to an extent this was true for the many female performers whose working lives and experiences were impacted by the legal, biological and social ramifications of womanhood, those women at least had the potential to transcend the economic and professional implications of their gender and earn as much as, if not sometimes more than, their male peers, both within and outside the profession. For female performers however, and particularly ones working at the end of the eighteenth century, there were also additional challenges. Cultural conceptions of gender and sexuality had long shaped both *what* as well as *how* actors and actresses could perform on stage, but in the last decades of the century these ideas started to encroach on performers' lives offstage. In an age of widely available print media, female performers in particular found not only their performances, but every aspect of their lives under scrutiny. Held up against new ideals of feminine behaviour, actresses' working and personal lives were now uniquely interwoven in a way which, while challenging to one extent, also opened up new opportunities: opportunities which the new century would see being embraced to the full.

CHAPTER FOUR

The Environment of Theatre

Power, Resistance and Commerce

MECHELE LEON

Histories of theatre typically focus on what goes on inside a playhouse – on performances that take place within theatre buildings – and the buildings themselves. We do not often think about theatre within the larger context of the physical spaces (like cities or fairgrounds) where theatres are located, nor the social meanings these spaces carry. 'Most works of theatre history present theatre spaces as immobile lifeless containers within which unfold the rich and fecund careers of authors and actors'.[1] To think about theatrical spaces and places as alive to the production of meaning in themselves is a rather a recent methodological development and one influenced by the interests of cultural history. New paradigms for social theories of spatial practices, such as the work of Henri Lefebvre, as well as movements in phenomenology and cultural geography, brought matters of space and place under the umbrella of theatre and cultural history and the environments of theatre have become an important epistemological framework through which to understand past performances. Looking at theatre history spatially means exploring the material existence of places of theatrical performance, on the one hand, and attending to the lived sense of space involved in the human embodied experience of theatre-going, on the other. It also means looking at how these material and embodied realities of space combine and intersect in ways that are culturally, socially, economically and politically meaningful.

This chapter will explore these intersections by considering the eighteenth-century theatre according to three coexisting performance environments that defined the era and which can be seen most vividly in French, specifically Parisian, examples. In the first section, I consider the widespread development of monumental theatre construction and the extent to which the advent of such landmarks were symbolic of theatre's importance in the context of urbanization and civic pride. Second, I explore what could be considered the opposite of theatre as civic monument by taking a look at another defining trend of the period: private theatres, or those 'exclusive spaces' of association and sociability. Lastly, I turn to the Parisian fairgrounds, boulevards and the Palais-Royal. These 'spaces of alterity' were hybrid commercial/entertainment districts where marginalized and exclusionary spatial practices eventually coalesced under the power of the marketplace.

CIVIC SPACE: THE MONUMENTAL PUBLIC PLAYHOUSE

'Place exists at different scales', writes cultural geographer Yi-Fu Tuan. 'At one extreme a favorite armchair is a place, at the other extreme the whole earth'.[2] A good starting point on the complex map of theatre environments in the eighteenth century is, perhaps, not the armchair, but the 'whole earth', which for the purposes of this chapter means the vast sociocultural space occupied by a defining architectural phenomenon of eighteenth-century Europe: the monumental public playhouse. If the equivalent of an armchair is the *fauteuil* a spectator occupies in the comfort of an intimate loge in a Parisian theatre, the 'whole earth' was that stony parade of proudly constructed playhouses that dotted the landscape of the continent from end to end, presenting to their citizen-spectators a symbol of cultural sophistication, rationalized urban space, municipal potency and nascent national unity.

'Nothing contributes to the magnificence of cities as much as public theatres', wrote the architect Jacques-François Blondel in the 1770s. 'These edifices must announce, by their grandeur and exterior arrangements, the importance of the cities in which they are constructed'.[3] This concept of the extreme importance of theatres echoed throughout the Enlightenment; it was promoted via a wave of architectural theory from such notable figures as the Chevalier de Chaumont, Charles Cochin, the Marquis de Marigny, A.-J. Roubo and Pierre Patte, who argued in their different manners that the urban environment – its beauty and salubrity as well as ordered, rationalized use of space – was a reflection of its people. In his vision of this new rationalized space, Voltaire writes that there must be 'public monuments of all kinds, to make Paris as magnificent as it is rich and populous, to one day equal Rome'.[4]

Voltaire's reference to Rome reflects the Enlightenment's abiding fascination with, and debt to, classicism, or the ideas and aesthetics of antiquity. The

eighteenth-century 'temple-theatres', as Daniel Rabreau calls them, fully
adopted the architectural features of ancient temples with majestic porticos,
gigantic columns and soaring pediments. They embodied the values we associate
with classic monumental architecture: impressive in size and grandeur,
distinguished by location, and constructed for permanence. These theatres
projected that 'monumental imperishability' that 'bears the stamp of the will to
power'.[5] They drew significance simultaneously from their proximity to
important structures like governmental buildings and yet standing apart and
not diminished by attachment to any other structure. Like all monuments, these
temple-theatres could 'call forth fear or wonder in the observer' and symbolize
'wealth, power, or truth'.[6] In sum, the construction of theatres as landmarks
was a phenomenon not seen since the ancient world. Prior to the eighteenth
century, the playhouses were any range of things – open to the air, slapdash,
courtly, temporary or inconspicuous – but not civic temples to theatrical art
modelled on the great architecture of the ancient world and taking pride of
place in the new urban hearts of civic topography. Such theatre buildings were
the product of a 'new vision of the possible relationship between a city and its
theatres' writes Marvin Carlson, 'which gradually brought the public theatre
from almost total obscurity to a prominence in the urban text rivalling that it
had enjoyed in classical times'.[7]

The prototype of this eighteenth-century innovation is found in Berlin with
the first free-standing theatre in Europe: the opera house commanded by
Prussian King Frederick II. Frederick acceded the throne in 1740, and soon
undertook 'major rebuilding of the capital in the modern manner with great
vistas, squares, and public buildings, including a new palace, an academy and an
opera house'.[8] The palatial opera house, designed by architect Georg Wenzeslaus
von Knobelsdorff with the intention of making the grandest theatre in Europe,
represented a monument to the ideals of state power and grandeur that the new
monarch strived to establish as he sought to elevate Prussia in the landscape of
European powers.[9] The opera house was a free-standing building prominently
located in the grand public square that eventually became known, in a nod to
Roman glory, as the Forum Fridericianum. The building conformed to classic
ideals with temple-like features, including an entrance faced by a staircase that
led to a raised portico lined with columns and topped with a classic triangular
pediment.[10] The Berlin opera house influenced theatre construction for several
subsequent decades in Europe. Examples of models following Knobelsdorff's
design include the Teatro Communale di Bologna (1763), La Scala (Milan,
1778), Royal Swedish Opera in Stockholm (1782), Stavovské (Prague, 1783);
and the Kamenny in St. Petersburg (1783).

While Berlin could claim anteriority in this movement, the full expression of
monumental theatre construction was nowhere more in evidence than in
France. 'Beginning in the mid-eighteenth century', writes Lauren Clay, 'the

FIGURE 4.1: *Berlin Opera House*, Jean-Laurent Legeay, *c.*1748. By permission of http://www.zeno.org – Contumax GmbH & Co. KG.

French playhouse was transformed into one of the most significant buildings in the urban landscape'.[11] The 'urban landscape' she is referring to here is not limited to Paris. In fact, in terms of theatre-building, Paris lagged behind France's provincial cities, a number of which saw the construction of outstanding monumental theatres in the decades after 1750. In Metz in 1751, for example, a new theatre was built in modified neoclassical fashion. The architect Soufflot designed a majestic theatre for the centre of Lyon (1754) facing the other signature monumental structure of municipal grandeur, the *Hôtel de Ville* (town hall).[12] In 1778, in the eastern city of Besançon, work began on a theatre designed by Claude-Nicolas Ledoux. The monumental entrance with portico topped by a rectangular pediment led to an innovative interior that included a partially hidden orchestra pit.[13] The most famous of the provincial theatres was the Grand Théâtre de Bordeaux, designed by Victor Louis. It was completed in 1780 at significant financial cost and following fierce power struggles between the crown and city council. With its unprecedented size, a grand interior staircase seen before only in palaces, and a long colonnade to accommodate the sheltered arrival of carriages, it garnered 'national and even international admiration as the largest and most elaborate theatre in France'.[14] Other cities followed suit: Amiens, Rheims and Nantes, most notably.

A significant feature of the monumental, free-standing theatres were new spaces of sociability made possible by these grand structures. They boasted of spacious vestibules, grand staircases, foyers and salons with windows overlooking the city. Social interaction began at the entrance, which in lieu of a single door now had entrances multiplied along the length of a majestic portico where audience members could arrive, mount stairs and mingle among the Doric columns as they entered the building. The grand staircase was both useful and significant as a symbol of the grandeur of the construction. 'This masterpiece of a staircase is a monument inside a monument' wrote the actor Fleury of the grand staircase in the theatre at Bordeaux.[15] A new use was found for these expanded foyers when female spectators began to mingle openly – an important shift in the presence of women in the playhouse that caused considerable consternation on the part of the more traditionally minded critics like Grimod de la Reynière.[16]

Such a boom in playhouse construction throughout France runs counter to commonplace ideas about the centrality of Paris versus the marginality of France's provincial cities, ideas which express a 'reductive duality imbued with the assumptions of Parisian cultural superiority and provincial immobility and backwardness'.[17] Like the monumental theatres that would soon crop up in the capital, these new French provincial theatres had the power to 'redefine the experience of dramatic and lyric entertainment, while celebrating civic pride and commercial success'.[18] The power of theatres to establish cultural capitals and realign the relationship between capital cities and provincial cities was not limited to the French example. Throughout Europe, the construction of theatres was one of the ways that cities established cultural purchase in an era of urban growth and change. On the whole, city populations grew markedly throughout Europe beginning in the sixteenth century and often in tandem with rural depopulation. This phenomenon was by no means uniform, but in general the number of cities with large populations (over 100,000) nearly doubled over the course of the eighteenth century.[19] This followed the momentum of sixteenth- and seventeenth-century growth. London may have grown from 80,000 in 1550 to half a million in 1700.[20] Paris had a somewhat larger population at the beginning of the eighteenth century. Estimates place it at 550,000, having more than doubled from about 220,000 just a hundred years before.[21] With this new urban strength came a clearer sense of civic identity and attention to the status of one's city in relative (and competing) terms to others within the larger spatial context – both intra-nationally and internationally. Still, while many provincial cities gained in importance, the spatialized idea of 'cultural capital' (a nation's privileged location for the production and consumption of culture) which had emerged in the seventeenth century, endured. 'Rapid growth, population concentration, and the development of large-scale, coordinated activities', writes Karen Newman in *Cultural Capitals*, 'fostered an unprecedented concentration of both financial and cultural capital and promoted distinctive urban behaviours, social geographies and new forms of sociability in the early modern city'.[22] Urbanization of eighteenth-century Europe was as much social (behavioural) as demographic.[23] For example, city experience inspired a new genre of literature about the urban experience. The London playwright John Gay came early in a century of writers obsessed with painting the portrait of city life with his *Trivia, or The Art of Walking the Streets of London* (1716). Later in the century and on the other side of the Channel the playwright Louis-Sébastien Mercier wrote volumes about Paris in *Tableau de Paris* (1781) and Nicholas Restif de la Bretonne crawled Paris in the dark in *Les Nuits de Paris* (1788–94). Eighteenth-century urbanization is a crucial context for understanding the significance of theatres: 'The role of theatres within city life is closely aligned with the rise of cities', particularly after 1740.[24]

Bordeaux's architect Victor Louis was also the architect for several important new theatres in Paris. From the end of the seventeenth century through the first half of the eighteenth, few new theatres were built in Paris, aside from small temporary theatres at the fairgrounds, private theatres and converted tennis courts. Parisian theatre construction was eventually made possible by the expanding contours of the city, evidenced by the addition of grand projects like the Champs-Elysées and the Place Louis-le-Grande.[25] Two theatres that opened within a year of each other in the 1780s mark the achievement of monumental theatres in Paris. A new theatre for the company of the Comédie-Française opened on the Left Bank on 9 April 1782 after twenty years of competing and revised plans. A year later, in 1783, on the opposite end of town on the Right Bank, a new theatre opened for the Opéra-Comique. Built by two different architects, the former Peyre and Wailly and the latter Heurtier, both are excellent examples of the reconceptualization of theatre architecture as classically inspired, temple-like, free-standing structures that, in spatial terms become part of the city's new urban self-presentation – its *mise en scène*. It is interesting to note that around this time the French word *théâtre* transforms from denoting the *scène* (stage) within a building, to the building itself.[26] This is significant insofar as it seems to resonate with the growing presence of a playhouse as a kind of stage on the urban landscape for the performance of civic identity. More than ten years in development through a succession of different designs, the new theatre finally built for the royal company, the Théâtre Français or, Comédie-Française, elevated the company's home from a façade theatre within city streets to the centrepiece of a newly planned urban quarter.[27] The plan of architects Peyre and Wailly followed the disposition laid out by André-Jacob Roubu *fils* in his 1777 treatise on theatre architecture. He called for theatres to be 'isolated on all sides and therefore situated in the middle of a square. . . . This square should be entered by several streets, the main ones aligned with the main lines of the edifice, so as to establish suitable vistas'.[28] In form, the exterior followed the neoclassical model with its temple columns on a raised portico; in emplacement and design, it manifested Voltaire's call that theatres should 'take up part of a public square, with the peristyle of a palace and the entrance of a temple'.[29] In its place of privilege on a small hill, at the orderly centre of a starburst of streets that led spectators to its portico as if inevitable, the new home of the Théâtre Français was emblematic of the shift in urban architecture that appealed to the Enlightenment-era's sense of order and clarity:

> The scheme of central place, circles or open squares, dominated by monuments, flanked symmetrically by public buildings, with avenues spreading out from such centres, profoundly altered every dimension of building. Unlike the medieval town, which one must slowly walk through to appreciate its never-ending transformation of mass and silhouette, its intricate and surprising details, one can take in a baroque town almost at a glance.[30]

That the monumental theatres were a much needed improvement over refashioned tennis courts does not in itself explain their existence nor completely capture their value for eighteenth-century urbanism. They were built through negotiation with, and as representation of, the growth and concentration of structural changes in governments and the coordination of municipal power, communication tools, markets, police, among other institutions of the urban environment. Their architectural features are the result, writes Rabreau, of the 'double function of theatres within the cities', which he explains as both practical and symbolic:

> The first, explicit function, was to be a place for spectacle that was endowed with a series of technical enhancements neglected during the period of touring troupes. But if the solidity of the edifice, if the security and comfort they assured, had become necessary, it was nonetheless insufficient for its representational function. The architecture must also respond to the need for visibility. Its public character would be better asserted if those commanding its construction were attentive to, not simply architecture, but the complex stakes involved in the urban programme and know how to resolve the difficult questions of location, financing, management or programming. This function was inscribed then, fully, within the context of urbanism.[31]

The monumental civic playhouses built from the 1740s to the end of the century are significant for what they reveal about theatre-going and eighteenth-century urbanization, about the role of identifiable symbols of cultural prominence, about the play of power between capitals and provincial cities and about how the eighteenth century continued to draw power from an appeal to antiquity's grandeur. They also speak to the widespread circulation of theories about and examples of theatre architecture around the continent from Rome to St. Petersburg. As a new and important addition to the theatrical environment of the Enlightenment, these landmark theatres reflect civic gratification – a kind of 'municipalism' – even as they presage theatre's role in nineteenth-century nationalism.

EXCLUSIVE SPACE

As a matter of theatre historiography, discovering details about performance environments – when they are not commercial playhouses or conspicuous monuments like those palaces of eighteenth-century theatrical glory that still figure in our tourist guidebooks – can be difficult. A database of more than 350 *théâtres de société* in eighteenth-century France, probably a fraction of the number that existed in that country alone, testifies to a widespread and defining theatrical phenomenon of Enlightenment Europe: private theatres.[32]

'Society theatre', if taken to mean merely the opposite of theatre by professionals for a paying public, is a term that can encompass a vast theatrical territory in the eighteenth century: from makeshift stages in rural barns to luxury theatres in city and country mansions; from the theatres in the palaces of kings and princes to the schools bearing their names; and featuring actors ranging from Marie Antoinette to a shy pupil at the College de Louis-le-Grand. With such variety, it is no surprise that the terms 'society theatre' or 'private theatre' are problematic descriptors. Scholars studying this significant but relatively unexplored area of eighteenth-century theatrical activity have by necessity tried to demarcate this vast arena of theatrical activity. David Trott uses *théâtres de société* to describe 'private spectacles, usually "chez soi" [at one's place], before a "circle" of friends and relatives, and executed by amateur actors'.[33] Antoine Lilti narrows the term perhaps more helpfully by noting that most theatres in the courts of monarchs and high nobility, which were typically the showcase for professional companies before an invited audience, were referred to by contemporaries as *théâtres particuliers* [private theatres] and thus were regarded as distinctly different from 'society theatres' in the homes of aristocrats and bourgeoisie.[34] But whether they were for and by aristocrats, magistrates, financiers or bourgeoisie, or in city or country homes, such theatres were ubiquitous in the landscape of eighteenth-century theatre. The creation of spectacles by individuals for enjoyment by a select audience of social equals was a phenomenon that grew in popularity throughout the Enlightenment. Indeed, the eighteenth century has been called the 'golden age of court and private theatres'.[35] In Paris, estimates are for 50 theatres in 1732, 160 by 1748 and possibly 200 by the end of the Old Regime – this not counting the theatres in French provincial and rural settings.[36] With France establishing the 'social fashion for the rest of Europe',[37] the phenomenon was multiplied in England

and Italy, Germany and Russia. The theatrical boom of the 1770s and 1780s in England is the subject of the 1787 parodic closet drama, *Private Theatricals*, by James Powell, for example. In Italy as in France, theatres were built in the country residences of princes as well as the urban mansions of the upper class.[38] Such was the passion for theatre-making that it extended to military regiments, where garrisons had theatres in which officers could be seen performing with professionals actors.[39]

Society theatres are not strictly an eighteenth-century phenomenon, but in all respects the period of the Enlightenment evidenced a remarkable passion for theatre at all levels of private investment of money and effort. It contributed to making 'thousands of theatre-lovers who since infancy acquired the passion to perform'.[40] The era saw the invention of 'theatremania', a term that encompassed the individual affliction (witness the 'theatrical calling' of Goethe's Wilhelm Meister) and the boom in the commercial theatre business (as discussed related to France in Lauren Clay's *Stagestruck*), but characterizes most precisely the widespread mania for making theatre on the part of anyone with the interest and means. 'A veritable frenzy for spectacles seized French society in the eighteenth century', writes Maurice Lever. 'The public houses not satisfying this widespread enthusiasm, private stages were created practically everywhere: at the court, army, in mansions and palaces, country homes, schools and seminaries, from the private residences in the hamlet of Saint-Germain, to the shop of one Monsieur Caron, the future Beaumarchais'.[41] That this passion for performing was also a part of Jesuit education is equally notable. Perhaps as many as 200 theatres existed in schools in France before the interdiction of 1762 prohibiting the Jesuit order and their formidable system of education. Performing texts in both Latin and French was used to teach 'a way of being of the world and in the world'.[42] The impact of scholastic activity was influential in the development of eighteenth-century theatre, for it 'expanded the taste for theatre, the lived *sense* of theatre, for thousands of youngsters every year',[43] ultimately shaping the enthusiasm of eighteenth-century spectators.

According to Marvin Carlson, the passion for private theatre was the result of 'the liberation of manners, a taste for intimacy, [and] a refinement of culture'.[44] It is this, but more. Martine de Rougemont suggests that for the members of the noble class, participating in private theatre-making, either as actor or audience, was a relief from the constant attention and restraints of comportment imposed on them by their stations: 'When "private life" is one long performance ruled by etiquette, it is liberating to change the mask, to disguise oneself, to play something else'. Moreover, as attendees at these activities, it was liberating for the aristocratic audiences to be 'nothing but spectators', since in the public theatres they were 'always a focal point'[45] of attention. For wealthy individuals, society theatre was an occasion to showcase both financial means and refinement; it was an exercise in the 'pleasure of spending'. Creating theatre was a privileged

FIGURE 4.2: *The Children's Theatre in the House of John Conduit*, William Hogarth, 1732.

means for demonstrating the acquisition of cultivation and savoir-vivre.[46] On the collective scale, the mania for making performance 'strengthened the bond of a social community'[47] and 'constituted one of the most stable foundations of modern life and social exchange'.[48]

The eighteenth century, historians have noted, was distinctly an era of 'unprecedented intensity and diversity of the associational impulse'.[49] In this context, society theatre belongs to the range of social activities of the period that allowed an exchange of opinions and ideas, creating an arena of shared and public discourse – a public sphere – that, following Jürgen Habermas, was quite different in form and effectiveness from prior regimes of social interaction. Society theatre, that is, was one activity among many in a new 'associational world' that emerged in the eighteenth century and that included salons, reading clubs, debating societies and Freemasonry. The emergent public sphere in the eighteenth century allowed interaction and communication among individuals to take place on an unprecedented scale, both in print and in person, and on a wide range of subjects – some that would soon foment political and social revolution.[50] Before continuing on this point, it would be useful to provide some illustrations of society theatres and how they constituted, spatially speaking, an environment.

The construction of society theatres reflected nested layers of social emulation that flowed from royalty to aristocrat to bourgeois. Theatres within royal courts such as those at Versailles and Fontainebleau became models for theatres in the homes of those aristocratic families capable of great expenditure, who constructed theatres in their city mansions and country châteaux, some designed by the leading architects of the day and containing sophisticated stage technology. This attribute of emulation is one of the few generalizations that can be made about society theatres, so varied as they were. As David Trott points out, 'there is not one single model' for society theatres.[51] Unfortunately, few have survived and primary source documentation remains to be fully explored.

Archives revealing architectural improvements made to the chateau of a prominent aristocratic family about eighty kilometres north-west of Paris, provide a rare look into an otherwise ordinary private theatre.[52] The daughter of Alexandre-Louis, the fifth duke of La Rochefoucauld, undertook renovation of a family chateau at La Roche-Guyon, commanding for it a small theatre of forty or fifty seats, inaugurated in 1768. Detailed invoices for painting, fabric, candles, decor and costumes reveal a sumptuous theatre that contained such details as expensive curtains and gilded decorations on cushioned armchairs. The designers were probably those associated with the family's sponsored art academy in Paris. As with many such theatres, the actors included members of the family. Scarce information about the repertory exists, but indications are of both musical and non-musical plays by recognized authors. While no exact records of spectators remains, the family associated with leading figures in science and politics of the day – Turgot, Lavoisier and Condorcet, to name but three – who could well have numbered among their spectators.

The description of a theatre owned by the dancer Marie-Madeleine Guimard at her residence on the rue Chaussée-d'Antin in Paris is similarly helpful. It was designed by Claude-Nicolas Ledoux and modelled on the theatre of the Petits Cabinets at Versailles. Her theatre was remarked as being a 'masterpiece of the genre', writes the historian Germain Bapst.

> It was decorated with great magnificence and exquisite taste; the curtain and the fabric of the loges were in pink silk, embroidered with silver; the seats were upholstered in the same material. The ceiling, in the form of a cupola, represented a sky with a myriad of cupids raining down. [. . .] This theatre quickly became the fashion. All the youthful folks of the time tried to get in, it was sometimes difficult. The seats were often occupied by the grandest of lords and the most serious of magistrates.[53]

An unpublished manuscript on country theatres is the source for information about performances in the 1760s by Madame de Maistre at her Chateau de Vaujours, near Paris. It describes a quite spectacular theatre event, with a hundred domestic servants attending to a crowd of a thousand people.[54] In France as elsewhere in Europe, theatres associated with working guilds emerged. These 'sociétés bourgeoises', imitating those above in the social hierarchy, created theatres for pleasure as well as for paying audiences.[55]

The passion to create theatre was bourgeois as well aristocratic and rural as well as urban, with spaces for society theatres ranging from improvised installations to purpose-built theatres for rich aristocrats and financiers.[56] Given the vast diversity of these places of performance, can they be considered collectively as a theatre environment? Theatre environments take shape in different ways. Architectural consistency and assigned locations, for example like the monumental playhouses discussed above, are only two of them. Society theatres cohere as an environment differently: through their similarity as social practice. As a theatrical environment, society theatres were linked rather like an organism, with theatre spaces multiplied by the hundreds, in effect creating a dispersed but still coherently recognizable spatial practice premised on social interaction. It was a tentacular environment or a web woven into the cultural fabric of the era.

The nature of this social interaction, however, and its significance in the context of the Enlightenment is complex. Society theatres, according to Rougemont, 'formed in the French theatre a public such as no theatre modern has very known, and for that reason, one can say that they gave it life'.[57] It is this *formation of a public* that seems to be one of the more puzzling questions for historians trying to understand society theatres beyond their important contribution to the development of news plays and actors. As a practice, making and attending society theatre was a deeply sociable activity, a way of reinforcing the bonds of a predetermined social community.[58] Society theatre 'was not a light or insignificant pastime, but a mode of expression fundamental to the manners of the time. It constituted a widespread system of communication for ideas, values, and way of being in the Enlightenment'.[59] But was this a formation in the new public sphere, engaged in the kinds of discourses that would foster critique and, eventually, resistance, to existing ideas and institutions? In an article that has become a point of reference on this subject, Antoine Lilti argues that this is not likely the case. Society theatres formed relationships between actors and audience, as well as between members of the audience, that were not at play in the regular theatres. In these private theatres, actors and spectators, hosts and guests, engaged in social code, a rapport of sociability that *inhibited* critical judgement. In society theatres, the audience was held together by the glue of 'agreement and good manners' and not as 'consumers of leisure' as in regular theatres, which included in the price of a ticket the right to criticize.[60]

His claim suggests that that society theatres were environments that cultivated a kind of exclusive sociability, bringing together attendees and participants in a shared exercise of social affirmation. If society theatres as realms of sociability in the eighteenth century are rather more reactionary than activist, this does not negate their significance, and helps prove theatre's importance in revealing the complexities in what we understand as the public sphere.

A telling event from the archives both complicates and reveals the nature of exclusive sociability we see at play in the space of society theatres. We know of the event because of police involvement and an investigation, which Jeffrey Ravel writes about in depth. In 1763, a performance of Rousseau's *Le Devin du village* was given in the private theatre of the chevalier Christophe-Louis Pajot de Villers. Following the performance, some domestic servants of de Villers started indulging in horse-play behind the curtain. Then, one of them raised the curtain while another of the pranksters – a coach driver – bared his buttocks to the audience members who were still filing out and gave it a hearty slap. This age-old insult speaks volumes about the occasion, repertory and audience of society theatre, as well as race (the servant raising the curtain was black) in the Old Regime. It reveals private theatres as environments inhabited not only by masters, but by servants, where the latter consumed the same theatrical culture to different effects. Ravels writes:

> What distinguishes this evening from thousands of other similar gatherings of the eighteenth century, in Paris or the provinces, are the contradictions that were so well revealed in that moment when the coachman undid his breeches, bent down and slapped his flesh with gusto. This visual and auditory demonstration undermines the fictions of sociability and equality girding the emerging idea of a thinking and rational public sphere, or egalitarian milieu. The actions of the coachman remind us first of all that these soldiers of the aristocracy and society women were never alone when they gathered amongst themselves; their valets, their servants and other domestics were there as well.[61]

While Villers' domestic servants engaged in their shared spectacle of eighteenth-century sociability, they were 'watched – usually in silence – by the domestics'.[62]

SPACES OF ALTERITY: FAIRGROUNDS, BOULEVARDS, FESTIVALS

'Above all, "official" and "non-official" theatres are differentiated in spatial terms', writes David Trott in a discussion contrasting eighteenth-century French alternative performance environments (the Parisian fairgrounds and boulevards) to the privileged venues of state supported and licensed theatres. Conceptually, we typically imagine theatre spaces organized vertically, he suggests, through metaphors of 'high' and 'low' venues. But there is a horizontal dimension to this official/non-official distinction, between the 'recognizable and the unusual, that is to say, between the "same" and "other"'.[63]

The final, overlapping environment I will examine in this chapter are some spaces of 'otherness' or alterity in Paris: first, the fairground, that legacy space of commerce and entertainment dating back centuries and which gained prominence in the eighteenth century as a venue of resistance, innovation and creativity; second, a new district known as the Boulevard, which challenged the protected repertory of the official theatres and eventually largely overtook their business; finally, the Palais-Royal, with its confluence of commerce and entertainment mapped onto an aristocratic space in proximity to the centre of French power. If monumental theatres were the manifestation of the growth of urban spaces and municipal power, and if society theatres tell us about the practices of eighteenth-century sociability, then fairground, boulevard and garden might be recognized as those alternative spaces in which we see both continuity and change, where marketplace and performance cohabit, different performance idioms compete and combine, and audiences across wide socio-economic gulfs comingle. Grouped together, the fairground, boulevard and leisure garden represent environments of alterity for the eighteenth-century theatrical scene that, in significant ways, becomes the new order of things.

While *théâtre de la foire* – fairground theatre – was certainly not exclusive to France,[64] it provides a salient example of the role of fairs in the landscape of eighteenth-century performance. Paris had two prominent ones: the three-month-long Saint-Germain fair in late winter/early spring, followed by the Saint-Laurent fair of the same length in summer. While these two leading fairs took place in different parts of the city, and differed somewhat in size, layout and architectural features, they featured common elements we still associate with fairground activities today: shopping, eating, gambling and entertainment. Both fairs could date their origins to the twelfth century and would fade by the Revolution. Purpose-built theatres became an important part of their physical layout in the eighteenth century and developed into premier environments for throngs of theatre-goers who came to enjoy semi-permanent, finely decorated and technologically advanced playhouses.[65]

Theatre of the fairground took place in a distinct environment, bound physically and limited temporally, where commerce existed side by side with myriad forms of popular entertainment.[66] As places of performance, the fairground offered an audacious mix of commerce with theatre and casual street performances by jugglers, magicians, acrobats and marionette masters, as well as mountebanks, displays of exotic animals, and scientific demonstrations.

FIGURE 4.3: A theatre at the Saint-Germain fair, late eighteenth century.

Audiences would be enticed into a theatre by skits or monologues performed for passers-by from doors and balconies. In response to the regulatory restrictions requiring them to avoid performing anything that would encroach on the exclusive rights held by the licensed theatres to specific plays, playwrights and genres, the fairground theatre in Paris developed unique and inventive genres, like pantomime and vaudeville, that were a triumph of creativity.

The variety and novelty of theatre at the fairground was due in part to the nature of these venues of performance. The seasonal spaces did not lend themselves to the strictures and controlled precepts of dramaturgical rules. Although many of these semi-permanent theatres evolved to become more elaborately decorated and with sophisticated stage technology, they were ultimately, by virtue of their place both within the city and in relation to the ludic space of the fairground, environments that were 'disarticulated, multiple, successive, illusionistic and marvellous, ephemeral'.[67] Fairground theatre and its repertory, simultaneously groundbreaking and carnivalesque, was very much an Enlightenment phenomenon in that it reflected the extent to which the eighteenth century made space for continuity with the past even while constructing a narrative of its own progressivism. Above all, fairgrounds reflected the growing comingling of socio-economic classes within performance environments. Robert Isherwood makes the case that fairgrounds were among those places in Paris that 'cracked the social stratification separating the highborn and lowborn' and where 'all ranks mingled openly and freely' in an unprecedented equality of 'pleasure, of taste'.[68] As an environment for the democratizing of taste, fairgrounds allowed for the convergence of popular and elite culture – indeed, it challenged those very categories. 'The fair entertainments were understood by most commentators of the age to be shows aimed at ordinary people, at the lower ranks of society', writes Isherwood. 'But it does not mean that *spectacles* intended to appeal to "le bas peuple" did not appeal to people of high rank, wealth, learning, and sophistication. It does not mean that we can blithely separate taste publics and draw distinctions between elite and popular culture'.[69] The development of a 'taste public' was ever more apparent on Paris's Right Bank boulevards, an environment for commerce, leisure and entertainment that popped up in middle of the eighteenth century and that, while not exactly duplicated in other cities, has similarities with districts like Covent Garden in London.

In the 1700s, an open stretch of land along the northern limits of Paris, in an area that once held a city wall, had developed by the mid-eighteenth century into a promenading district of street life, cafés and taverns, brothels and circuses, wax museums, music halls and theatres – especially theatres. This area known as the Boulevard, comprised a kind of permanent fair in the capital, a place where the aristocracy and high bourgeoisie could, for the first time, amuse themselves together while sharing the streets with the popular classes.[70] Between 1759 and the construction of the Théâtre des Grands-Danseurs du Roi by fairground theatre entrepreneur Jean-Baptiste Nicolet, and the end of the century, more than a dozen theatres were constructed along the Boulevard du

FIGURE 4.4: *Acrobats Outside the Théâtre des Variétés*, Jean-Marie Marlet, 1821.

Temple and nearby areas. The Boulevard became a place of permanence for one-time fairground companies and their entrepreneurs – especially after the Saint-Germain fair suffered a devastating fire in 1762. Inside these theatres, performances included such auxiliary entertainments as dancing, pantomimes and acrobatic interludes. These delights were interspersed among the presentation of contemporary plays. Because of legislated control over genre and the privileges of the royal theatres, drama of the Boulevard was required to stay within officially imposed regulations: no plays longer than three acts; no plays with characters of high social rank; no plays on serious or political themes; no plays with characters made famous on the great stage.[71] Outside the theatre, along the Boulevard promenades and in their exhibition halls, visitors found unlimited and unregulated entertaining pleasures. Indoors or out, the Boulevard represented an environment of leisure, commerce, entertainment and anarchy where 'marquises and lackeys, young pages and financiers, *robins* and tramps, all were engaged by the giddy gallimaufry of sights, sounds, and aromas'.[72]

In stark contrast to the staid and controlled focus of urban space and the gaze created by monumental theatres, the Boulevard was a visual jumble, resisting the singularity of focus and control of experience monumentalism implied. And unlike private theatres, with its sociability defined by likeness, agreement and codification, the boulevards were a place to exalt in revealing difference openness, critique and even a-sociability. While this cacophonous theatre culture on the edge of the city with its second-class repertory might suggest that the audience was of the lowest classes, 'who have need of amusement',[73] evidence suggests a mixed Boulevard crowd. Like the fairground, the Boulevard was an environment that provided alternative theatrical forms that resisted privileged theatres and their traditional classical values. But to recognize the alterity of the Boulevard does not mean assuming a concomitant class divide making up its public. The Boulevard theatres attracted spectators across typical class divisions. The 'Boulevard dramatic culture did not segment along the socio-economic barriers of society', writes Root-Bernstein. As an environment of 'interaction between dominant and shunned sectors of society', the Boulevard world speaks to 'a whole society moving toward dissolution and revolution'.[74] The Boulevard environment was a space shaped by a shared impulse toward towards invention and illogical juxtaposition, toward an alternate experience.

The Boulevard would soon have competition. In 1781, the architect Victor Louis was commissioned to turn the tree-filled public garden adjoining the Palais-Royal, the seventeenth-century city chateau belonging to the family of the Duke of Orleans, into a commercial and residential complex. The result was a garden enclosed on its formerly three open sides by a uniform block of sixty town homes, or pavilions, fronted with a continuous arcade on the western and eastern sides for boutiques at the ground and mezzanine levels. Into this new Palais-Royal garden, which opened to the public in 1784, were added two theatres: one in 1784 at the north-west corner of the complex (today's Théâtre du Palais-Royal) that featured a company of child actors, and one in 1791 at the south-west corner (today's Comédie-Française) that became the home of the Variétés-Amusantes, a former boulevard company. Added to this were a number of other performance spaces, including a circular tent where today's fountain stands.[75] To accommodate more paying merchants, further encroachment into the garden came in the form of long alleys of boutiques or stalls built out of wood and covered with a canopy – thus placing low-rent 'huts' selling cheap wares and offering paid attractions like human oddities side by side with the luxury goods being sold under the chandeliered archways of the townhouse arcades. With its theatres and popular entertainments, in addition to shopping, restaurants, hawkers, buskers, prostitutes, thieves and freak shows, the Palais-Royal might be best described as a seventeenth-century aristocratic garden transformed into an amalgam of shopping centre, theatre district and carnival midway.

Strolling in Paris today among the manicured trees and quiet elegance of the Palais-Royal, it is hard to imagine what a revolutionary space it had become by the late eighteenth century. It was not only that luxury goods and human oddities were displayed in unusually close proximity. Like strangers from

FIGURE 4.5: *View of the Garden of the Palais Royal*, Lespinasse and Le Coeur, 1791. By permission of the Bibliothèque nationale de France. Collection De Vinck, 1491.

different worlds forced to cohabit a new neighbourhood, the fairground, boulevard and high theatrical culture that had formerly claimed their distinct urban environments – both physically and symbolically – came together. The former palace where once Louis XIV resided with his mother had acquired boisterous neighbours when the Variétés-Amusantes moved into the elegant new theatre on the south-west corner, a space intended for the national opera, and when geeks were displayed in booths of wooden huts where once had been tree-lined alleys. Called the 'brain of the capital' by Restif de la Bretonne and the 'capital of Paris' by Louis-Sébastien Mercier, the Palais-Royal, in the heart of the city's Right Bank and steps from the Louvre, became the topographical manifestation of decades of converging environments, joining 'aristocratic Paris' to the 'marketplace culture of the boulevards and fair'.[76]

Civic monuments, private theatres, fairgrounds and commercial gardens – we might regard these as not merely contemporaneous throughout eighteenth-century Europe but more significantly, coexisting within a 'spatial economy', which Lefebvre describes as the social values that are assigned to places, the shared discourses they provoke, and the consensus of conventions about their uses that they generate.[77] Theatre environments of the Enlightenment were generative of new civic and national frameworks, provoking ways of thinking about theatrical spaces in resistant and combinative ways, and through their use shaping shared practices that would influence subsequent generations.

CHAPTER FIVE

Circulation

Emergent Modalities of Intercultural Performance

MITA CHOUDHURY

Frankfurt, Ellwangen in Württemberg, Rome, Regensburg and other pressure points of cultural effervescence in the eighteenth century were removed from London by geography; but, in fact, the artistic communities which circulated between and among these as well as other cities and principalities throughout Enlightenment Europe defied the limitations imposed by national borders and distance. Circulation of European theatrical talent, personnel, ideas and practices was thus stamped with the imprimatur of both cultural commerce and modernity. British theatre, the focus of this chapter, was no different from its modern European counterparts. Despite, and in sharp contradiction to, its nationalist pronouncements of distinctiveness and its self-possessed insularity, British culture and, by extension, British theatre took pride in its Graeco-Roman lineage and was shaped by assimilation, absorption and relentless infusion of foreign ideas and talent – making this the ideal site for a consideration in this chapter of circulation as a distinctly modern pan-European cultural phenomenon.

Theatre historian Bruce McConachie has described early American cultural commerce in terms of an 'ongoing circular process', one which produces not merely a bilateral exchange of ideas but, rather, a continuous and multifarious 'feedback loop',[1] one which facilitates the free flow of diverse technologies, ideas, personnel and influences. Likewise, in eighteenth-century Britain, the increasing value of theatre as global cultural capital created the impetus for, and was also the result of, multiple and ongoing circular processes and intercultural products. Ergo, the patterns of theatrical circulation in this period were analogous to the patterns of mercantilist exchange or the cross-fertilization of experiential knowledge or the flow of news and information between and among diverse cultural nodes. My analysis of circulation as it pertains to the eighteenth-century British theatre incorporates McConachie's useful definition of circulation and superimposes onto its time- and culture-specific parameters the element of space because both performance roster and company repertory must be understood as global (and expansive) rather than local (and contained) expressions of this culture. A narrative of the spatial dimension of circulation or circularity relies upon a global perspective, one which was in the eighteenth-century British entertainment industry infused with a sense of shared cultures and intercultural negotiations, confrontations and conflicts.[2]

Postmodern narratives of Enlightenment theatre relish as well as rely upon the legacy of the fine arts and particularly the extant visual images of the period (captured in oil on canvas, watercolour, etchings, drawings, sketches and mezzotints), which flourished in tandem with – as well as held the proverbial mirror up to – theatrical culture. The most powerful source of our ability to visualize the action on the eighteenth-century British stage and to understand how this theatre embodies the imprint of myriad modes of circulation is the German artist Johan Zoffany, whose name is synonymous with the golden age of British theatrical portraiture and, specifically, the 'conversation piece', or depictions of groups engaged in genteel conversation. Originally from Prague, Zoffany's father migrated to Germany and was a carpenter at the court of Prince Alexander Ferdinand von Thurn and Taxis in Frankfurt. Thus Zoffany spent his first fifteen impressionable years in and around Frankfurt where at first he studied in the same school as the son of the Prince.[3] At the age of thirteen he was transferred to Ellwangen in Württemberg, renowned for its craft industry, where Zoffany might have been trained in the art of sculpture. From there, and because of the transfer of his father's employment with the court of Prince Alexander Ferdinand, Zoffany went to Regensburg where his mother apprenticed him to a painter. While there is no extant evidence of how Zoffany absorbed and became interested in the baroque style of architecture (alongside his inherited interest in carpentry) during his formative years at Regensburg, Lady Mary Wortley Montagu's accounts (related to her 1716 visit) provide us with valuable vignettes of the cross-currents of continental culture which envoys from different states brought to this court of the Holy Roman Empire. Having acquired a wide range of artistic skills in this period, Zoffany was pressed upon to create designs and build 'elaborate temporary structures' for royal entertainment.[4] Diverse continental influences, grafted during his apprenticeship in Europe, thus came to be infused in Johan Zoffany's paintings of British theatre, which epitomize his distinctive style.[5] His paintings are powerful artefacts which postmodern historiographies borrow to narrate the story of eighteenth-century theatrical circulation. Grandiloquent and 'live',[6] Zoffany's paintings of theatrical scenes captured tense moments and embattled emotion on stage – moments of recognition, confrontation, revelation or revulsion – such that in each sample the 'live-ness' of the gestalt is both fluid and frozen in time, producing for posterity an archive emboldened by light and darkness, colour, shape, depth, dimension and movement. In Zoffany's theatrical representations, the specificities of acting styles, contemporary costume, stage lighting and the foreign artistic imprint on the native creative impulse were artfully integrated and naturalized into abiding pictures of British theatricality. So, for instance, in Zoffany's *Macbeth*, featuring David Garrick as the eponymous hero and Hannah Pritchard in her last known performance on the London stage as Lady Macbeth (Figure 5.1), the confluence of foreign and domestic elements is subsumed by the powerful rhetoric of theatricality.[7]

Since Zoffany provides one of the sharpest intercultural lenses through which we witness British theatrical practice, he is the appropriate launching pad for establishing the premise in this chapter that the eighteenth-century British theatre, with its distinctively European stamp, was a product of circulation and of intercultural exchanges which were essential elements of its identity. The

FIGURE 5.1: David Garrick and Hannah Pritchard in *Macbeth*, Johann Zoffany, oil on canvas, 1768. Courtesy of The Garrick Club, London.

narrative thread which shapes this chapter is necessarily selective and one which privileges the man who introduced Zoffany to the London theatre: David Garrick (1717–79). Playwright, editor, actor, manager and recruitment director extraordinaire, Garrick revealed his astute business sense when he introduced Zoffany to the British theatre and the theatre to this German émigré, creating an elaborate web of strategic pathways for cross-cultural circulations across the artistic communities in Britain and the Continent.[8]

In the story of theatrical circulation in the eighteenth century, geography is immanent: geography as cognitive landscape, geography as necessary corollary to self-fashioning, and geography as manifest destiny. Within this burgeoning consumer culture, the increasing awareness of national geography linked to British performance practice contributed to a heightened sense of collective national identity and cultural consciousness. Take, for instance, the strategy used by Tate Wilkinson to drive home what he perceived to be his sweeping influence on British theatre:

> I, Tate Wilkinson, whose various stage adventures and *sparrings* have been permitted, and favoured with acceptance, more or less, in almost every principal theatre in the three kingdoms, as Drury-Lane, Covent-Garden, Hay-Market, – Smock-Alley and Crow-Street, Dublin, – Bath, Edinburgh, Portsmouth, Winchester, Maidstone, Birmingham, Chester, Bristol, Norwich, York, Shrewsbury, Richmond in Surry, Exeter, Glasgow, Newcastle, Leeds, Lynn, Pontefract, Halifax, Doncaster, Hull, Wakefield, &c. – am the son of the late Rev John Wilkinson.[9]

Wilkinson was not just the patentee of the Theatres-Royal York and Hull;[10] indeed, as the *Memoirs of his Own Life* proudly postulates, his influence was national. His story, framed as it is by his sense of an expansive national geography, reflects his own as well as this culture's unwitting investment in the circulation of theatrical personnel and talent throughout 'almost every principal theatre in the three kingdoms'. From Wilkinson's perspective, the provincial theatres were no different from those in London: Drury Lane, Covent Garden and the Haymarket. Dismissing implicitly the hierarchy in any formulation of centre-periphery, Wilkinson may be seen here as arguing, like others of his generation, that circulation and the ease of lateral mobility of theatrical personnel had become the prime markers of the modern entertainment industry. Similarly invested in diversity and an expansive national geography, David Garrick created in his green room at Drury Lane an incubator, which became 'the school of British acting in the eighteenth century. Actor after actor trained in his Company went out to act in, manage, and build provincial theatres, sometimes doing all three in combination'.[11] Garrick's correspondence with the following protégés shows the extent of his influence and authority among young actors in London and the provinces: Mossop, Sparks, King (Dublin); Ross (Edinburgh); Arthur and Palmer (Bath); Yates (Birmingham); Love (Richmond); Aicken (Liverpool); and Willoughby Lacy, Murphy and Colman Jr (London). The circulation of acting styles as well as the uniformity of standards of the school of British acting in the eighteenth century may be attributed to David Garrick's unflinching efforts toward promoting and sustaining an efficient system of artistic cross-fertilization, which his protégés had been trained to sustain and spread across the theatres in Britain.[12]

Any historiography of the eighteenth-century British theatre would be incomplete without a consideration of circulation broadly construed and covering how continental theatrical cultures were imported and then affected British theatrical practice at home, which is the focus of the first segment of this chapter. Equally important in this story of circulation are those actors, actresses and other theatrical personnel who facilitated intercultural exchange, artistic dialogue and clashes of culture, which is the subject of the second segment of this chapter. But since circuitry is never unidirectional, a retrospective view must also consider how British plays travelled elsewhere, to the distant colonies where British political control was in the late eighteenth century either waxing or waning, either taking firm root or being relegated to the margins. The last segment of this chapter is thus a brief sketch of British theatrical practice along the Atlantic seaboard in America and in Calcutta, India, where the British first arrived right after Elizabeth I signed the charter for the establishment of the East India Company in 1600. The modernity of British theatrical praxis in the eighteenth century can best be explained in terms of a complex circuitry of ideas, products and personnel – and this modern culture industry was deeply and undeniably indebted to the vision and initiatives of David Garrick, as the discussion below demonstrates.

GARRICK IN FRANCE AND ITALY: THE INFUSION OF CONTINENTAL CULTURES AT HOME

Of particular importance to this segment on the pan-European circulation of neoclassical ideas is the way in which David Garrick introduced, sponsored and promoted cultural exchange. Well documented and publicized, Garrick's French excursions – one in the summer of 1751 and the other in 1763 – as well as his residency in Paris from November 1764 to April 1765, had an impact upon circulation as we understand the phenomenon. According to Garrick's biographer Thomas Davies,

> Mr. Garrick's residing for a considerable time in France and Italy afforded him an opportunity to compare the English stage with the theatres on the continent; and it cannot be doubted, that he noticed with accuracy the form

of their buildings, their several ornaments and decorations, the performance of the actors, and all the various compositions of the authors which were worthy of observation.[13]

Garrick's trips to Europe were only partly for pleasure; his brand of pleasure was an artful blend of revelling in his cultural immersion *and* establishing ties and strategic alliances with a vast array of entities connected to the world of theatre and culture. In this context, how important are his French roots? 'Although English biographers and French friends made much of Garrick's paternal Huguenot ancestry – the family name an Anglicization of *garrigues*, . . . Garrick himself, as far as can be discovered, never made an allusion to French origins, much less exploited them at home or abroad'.[14] Whether this was a strategy of denial designed to authenticate his British identity is irrelevant. Of importance to this discussion is the fact that despite his lack of fluency in French – a language he had learned and tried hard to practise – Garrick made many friends across the English Channel.

Among the leading members of the French literati whom Garrick met were Madame Clairon,[15] Jean le Rond d'Alembert,[16] historian Jean François Marmontel, Voltaire and probably Diderot and Grimm, but certainly Paul Henry d'Holbach in whose salon the Garricks met repeatedly novelist and actress Marie Jeanne Riccoboni.[17] Additionally, he got to know Claude-Pierre Patu, l'Abbé Bonnet, the actors La Noue and Henri-Louis LeKain and the manager Jean Monnet.[18] Fifteen years Garrick's senior and having plenty of clout in Paris, Monnet had introduced Garrick to the French author and theatre manager Charles Simon Favart (1710–92). It is not known when Garrick first met Monnet, whose Opéra-Comique was such a huge success in Paris that he crossed the Channel and, upon Garrick's suggestion, signed a contract to mount similar operas at the Little Theatre in the Haymarket. But Monnet's friendship with Garrick could not ward off the huge anti-Gallican riots which greeted his November 1748 opening at the Haymarket, forcing him to abandon this project after two nights.[19] Garrick biographers Stone and Kahrl note that Monnet 'scouted for and contracted with actors and dancers for Garrick; engaged artists, such as De Loutherbourg (designer); F.H. Barthélemon (musician, composer); and he sent new stage properties, such as the lycopodium torch'.[20] Made of lycopodium powder, this torch was used to produce fire, particularly on the operatic stage. Friendships such as the one Garrick had with Monnet thus paved the way for sharing technologies of stage productions, props and personnel. Paris also provided a platform for other astute continental recruitments for which Garrick has to be credited. Take, for instance, the example of Charles Denis, who was related to John Jacob Heidegger, and who proved to be a valuable asset for Garrick in Paris. A Swiss count known for his masquerades and for the elaborate show he put up for the coronation of George II (George

Frideric Handel wrote the coronation anthems), Heidegger was the manager of the Queen's Opera House in London and, later, in 1729, he was able to mount operas with Handel at the King's Theatre.

Discourses of the theatre and its sister arts resulted in further cross-disciplinary circulations, such as when architecture inspired the imagination of the travelling theatre manager or when painting influenced the contemporary modes of stage lighting. Relevant to this discussion is Garrick's developing tastes at this time for 'the study and influence of the Greek and Roman inheritance in the eighteenth century' and, more broadly, the artistic and intellectual allegiance to neoclassicism which Garrick was delighted to find deeply embedded in both the French and Italian cultures. When the Garricks visited Rome in 1763, they saw the Pantheon for the first time. In a letter to a friend, Garrick describes his experience thus:

> But my God, w^l was my Pleasure & Surprise! – I never felt so much in my life as when I Entered that glorious Structure; I gap'd, but could not speak for 5 Minutes – It is so very noble, that it has been in ye Power of Modern Frippery, or Popery (for it is a Church you know) to extinguish its grandeur & Elegance – Here I began to think myself in Old Rome, & when I saw the ruins of that famous amphitheatre . . . I then felt my own littleness[21]

As the leading aficionado of theatre arts and management, Garrick understood the interconnectedness of the arts and their impact on the theatre. For Garrick, this church dedicated to St Mary and the Martyrs is not only glorious, grand and elegant, but its Corinthian columns, rotunda and dome evoke deep emotions in him, making him speechless. Garrick's reaction, in other words, might be interpreted as a reaffirmation of not just one individual's but British culture's consciousness of its Graeco-Roman past, an inheritance inscribed very consciously in the Shakespeare Temple which adorned the gardens of his Hampton House villa. An extension of the main residence and sitting by River Thames, the Temple is a not-entirely modest homage to the very same ideas of grandeur captured in its Ionian columns, pediment and dome which Garrick witnessed first-hand in Rome in 1763. Zoffany memorialized in 1762 *The Shakespeare Temple at Hampton House, with Mr. and Mrs. David Garrick* (see Figure 5.2) while in residence there as Garrick's guest. This Temple, proclaiming as it does the martyrdom of Shakespeare, is also designed to flaunt Garrick's passionate avowal of a past which binds Britain to its Renaissance and Roman past.[22]

Soon thereafter, at the beginning of the new theatre season in London, Garrick commissioned Zoffany to work on a theatrical scene in *Venice Preserv'd*, which turned out to be an artistic snapshot of David Garrick as Jaffeir and Mrs Cibber as Belivera (1762). Penelope Treadwell's commentary on this oil-on-canvas painting is worth considering in this context and thus quoted in full here:

Zoffany's scene is lit by a street lamp in the left foreground, while the full moon rising behind a pillar in the top right-hand corner lights up the night sky over Venice. The buildings reflected in the canal on the opposite bank in the painting may have a particular significance because the dome and the campanile, placed so closely together (although their positions in reality are reversed), can be identified as the view of the Church of San Geremia as it is seen across the canal from La Riva di Biasio – a place with a notorious history. Biasio was the name of a butcher who, according to the chronicles of Venice, opened a shop selling human flesh as a substitute for pork, a crime for which he was beheaded between the two columns of the Piazetta. Zoffany, still fresh from his own experience of Venice, may well have had the story in mind when he painted the background, for it makes a fitting location for Otway's grim play, which ends in death for all the three principals.[23]

One generally assumes that the artist – Zoffany in this case – after having witnessed performances of a given play would reproduce the essence of a critical dramatic moment, capturing the dramatic tension and perhaps even highlighting it. This unidirectional pattern of representation, from the stage to the canvas, was in fact just one way in which theatrical paintings came into being. More often than not, there was cross-fertilization where the painting

FIGURE 5.2: *The Temple to Shakespeare at Hampton House with Mr. and Mrs. Garrick*, Johann Zoffany, oil on canvas, 1762. Courtesy of The Garrick Club, London.

FIGURE 5.3: David Garrick and Susanna Cibber in *Venice Preserv'd*, Johann Zoffany, oil on canvas, *c*.1763. Courtesy of The Garrick Club, London.

would influence stage properties and stage business as was the case with *Venice Preserv'd*. Ten years after Zoffany produced the now famous scene from the play, one which Treadwell has described with consummate skill, the technologies of stage lighting and scene design became even more sophisticated: Thus '[w]hen De Loutherbourg finally installed his stage lighting, scenic effects and other mechanical systems in 1773, he was seeking a similar kind of background for the players as Zoffany had provided in his paintings, in which the action was defined and enhanced by multi-faceted lighting and a stage set realistic enough to tell its own story'.[24] Zoffany's painting, in this example, shaped the future of stage lighting (more than ten years later, when the painting had achieved iconic status); therefore, one might argue that 'realism' on stage is produced here by a remarkably modern amalgamation of multicultural expression (German painter, French scene designer and British actors/subjects) strengthened by a number of allied arts whose fusion subsequently prompted a new way of engineering stage lighting, which led to innovation and progress. Zoffany's paintings were, therefore, not just about the theatre; they fuelled innovation and new production possibilities, so much so that it was on the canvas where the storyboard (to use anachronistically a concept associated with Alfred Hitchcock) was first conceived and then came to be perfected on stage, live. What has been described as the 'craft aspect of performance' with 'knowledge passed from master to protégé, generation after generation, as a lived experience'[25] was also in eighteenth-century Britain equally a product of intercultural and pan-European circulation.

GARRICK AS RECRUITMENT AGENT: THE PAN-EUROPEAN CIRCULATION OF ACTORS AND ACTRESSES

Under Garrick's leadership as well as Handel's close connections with continental artists, British theatre in the eighteenth century emerged as a bastion of progressive recruitment practices – facilitated by the circulation of actors, actresses, academicians and artists of all kinds – and the epitome of a modern entertainment industry. Equally, it was a place of chaos and contention, sparked more often than not by clashes of cultures and public outbursts of xenophobia. Attractive in theory, circulation often came at a great cost. On balance, however, any retrospective view based upon hard evidence reveals clearly the extent to which talent and the highest artistic standards were privileged in this culture (by Garrick, Handel, Heidegger and the spectators they served) even when the foreign presence fuelled foreign–domestic rivalry which, in turn, ignited controversy and heated public discourse. So, for instance, the Royal Academy of Music ruffled nationalist feathers as this diatribe against it and its theatrical personnel demonstrates:

> An academy, rightly understood, is a place for the propagation of science, by training up persons thereto from younger to riper years, under the instruction and inspection of proper artists: How can the *Italian Opera* properly be called an academy, when none are admitted but such as are, at least are thought, or ought to be, adepts in music? If that be an academy, so are the theatres of Drury-lane, and Lincolns-inn Fields: Nay, Punch's opera may pass for a lower kind of academy. Would it not be a glorious thing to have an opera of our own, in our own most noble tongue, in which the composer, singers, and orchestra, should be of our own growth? Not that we ought to disclaim all obligations to Italy, the mother of music, the nurse of Corelli, Handel, Bononcini, Geminiani; but then we ought not to be so stupidly partial to imagine ourselves too brutal a part of mankind to make any progress in the science: By the same reason that we love it, we may excel in it; love begets application, and application perfection. We have already had a Purcel, and no doubt there are now many latent geniuses, who only want proper instruction, application, and encouragement, to become great ornaments of the science, and make England emulate even Rome itself.[26]

Attributed to Daniel Defoe, the sentiments above were no different from those of John Gay, whose *Beggar's Opera* makes a strong case not only for the primacy of English culture but also its self-reflexive authority.

Movement, dynamism and volatility were inextricably linked to circulation. In this context consider, for instance, the most publicized case early in the century, that of the rivalry between two Italian opera singers, Faustina Bordoni and Francesca Cuzzoni. On 6 June 1727, at a performance of *Astianatte* (also referred to as *Astyanax*), when Cuzzoni appeared as Andromache and Bordoni as Hermione, an offstage fight broke out among the followers of each, triggering chaos and confusion in the theatre (the Haymarket).[27] The *British Journal* reported that 'a great Disturbance happened at the Opera, occasioned by the Partisans of the Two Celebrated Rival Ladies, Cuzzoni and Faustina. The Contention at first was only carried on by hissing on one Side, and Clapping on the other; but proceeded at length to Catcalls, and other great Indecencies'.[28] The onstage rivalry of these two singers was mimicked by the offstage clashes between the Countess of Pembroke (who was a supporter of Signora Cuzzoni) and the Countess of Burlington (who supported Signora Faustina).[29]

Who were these rival queens? Born in a noble family in Venice *c*.1700 and having received her training under Gasparini, Faustina made her debut performance (1716) at the Teatro Grimani di San Giovanni Grisostomo in Venice. She sang with the leading opera singers of Italy, including Cuzzoni, and 'by 1724 she could command a fee of 15,000 florins'. Her invitation to London came from George Frideric Handel and in May 1726 '[h]er splendid mezzo-soprano voice was first heard in the role of Rossana in Handel's *Alessandro* at the King's theatre in the Haymarket. The title role was taken by the eminent castrato Senesino, and Lisaura was sung by Faustina's chief rival, Signora Cuzzoni'.[30] Francesco Bernadi Senesino (1680–1759) was a castrato born in Siena, trained by Bernachi in Bologna, and recruited by Handel, who lured him to London with the exorbitant fee of £300 for an engagement.[31]

Francesca Cuzzoni was also born *c*.1700 in Parma. A soprano trained by Lanzi, Cuzzoni made her debut in the role of Dalinda in *Ariodante* in the autumn of 1718. Then came her invitation to London from Heidegger and Handel. Cuzzoni's first appearance in London was on 12 January 1723 when she acted in the role of Teofane in Handel's *Ottone*, which was performed at the Haymarket. '[W]hen *Ottone* was presented again on 15 January the ticket prices had jumped from half a guinea to four guineas, and for her benefit on 26 March 'some of the Nobility gave her 50 Guineas a Ticket', helping to bring her income in that performance to over £700'.[32] Of particular interest to theatre historians is the fact that all three of these Italian artists – Bordoni, Cuzzoni and Senesino – commanded a staggering salary of £2,000 a year – far above the highest salaries paid to British artists.[33] But these high salaries did not go unnoticed and the backlash was decisive. *The London Journal*, for instance, spoke out against the foreign invasion in no uncertain terms and a part of it goes as follows:

> Why Musick should be confined only to that Country is what we cannot perceive; since no person that ever came out of it equal'd the Harmony of our famous Purcell. As we delight so much in Italian Songs, we are likely to have enough of them, for as soon as Cuzzoni's Time is out, we are to have another over; for we are well assured Faustina, the fine Songstress at Venice, is invited.[34]

Indeed, the drama on- and offstage mirrored the charged theatrics of the streets outside, with audiences and the reading public weighing endlessly in on the effects of what many saw as foreign invasion of the cultural sphere. Predictably, pulp fiction became perversely punctilious and was happy to supply the public demand for dirt. In a sixpenny farcical tract titled *The Devil to Pay at St. James's*, for instance, the anonymous author presents a polemical series of questions about the fight: 'Which of the two is the Aggressor, I dare not determine. . . . Are you High Church or Low, Whig or Tory; are you for Court or Country, King George, or the Pretender: but are you for Faustina or Cuzzoni, Handel or Bononcini. There's the question'.[35] Satire veils the malevolence toward foreign artists even as the author describes the unprecedented nature of this skirmish. 'There was no such hurricane', this polemicist argues, between Pillotti and Isabella, Durastanti and Robinson, the artists of yesteryear:

> What therefore can be the Meaning! That these two ladies, and only them, should make such a rout is beyond my comprehension. God forbid I should judge amiss; yet I cannot but think there is more in this matter than people are afraid of; who knows but they are sent here to raise dissentions among true Protestants! There are too may shrewd causes of suspicion.

The tract goes on to legitimize the Popish Plot conjecture, one which would no doubt be popular at the time: George I is a protestant; the Italians pledge allegiance to the Pope; ergo, this is a Popish plot to undermine Protestantism and 'it is not safe to have Popish singers tolerated here, in England; but on the contrary it would be a great security to the Protestant Interest to have a Clause added to some Act of Parliament, obliging all Foreign Singers Dancers and Tumblers, to abjure the Devil, the Pope, and the Pretender, before they appear in Publick'.[36] This is not just an anti-theatrical sentiment but a protectionist one, written to ignite xenophobia and simultaneously to protect the interests of British actors and opera singers. For the price of a few pence or one shilling, the literate Londoner could procure various types of printed accounts of the warring queens.[37]

At the same time, audiences were always thirsting for new if not exotic forms of entertainment and Garrick understood that satiety would lead to boredom and boredom to plunging box-office receipts.[38] Therefore, '[i]n the summer of 1754, Mr. Garrick invited the celebrated Mr. Noverre to enter into an engagement with him for the ensuing winter, and to compose such dances as would surprise and captivate all the ranks of people'. The choreographer Jean Georges Noverre and his ballet-dancer wife Marguerite Louise (Sauveur) Noverre were well known in Europe, where his reputation rested upon the perception that 'he understood dancing scientifically' and that he had 'published a very learned and philosophical treatise upon that subject'. On Garrick's behest (in 1754), 'he composed that accumulation of multifarious figures, called the Chinese Festival'. Neither drama nor indeed just dance, this 'accumulation', launched in the autumn of 1755, was a spectacular extravaganza 'in which the dresses and customs of the Chinese were exhibited, in almost innumerable shapes and characters'. Garrick hired dancers from around the British Isles and Europe and the foreigners particularly, it was alleged, were hired 'at a considerable price'. At this inopportune time (November 1755) and against the backdrop of the Seven Years' War with France, nothing could impede the flow of negative attention to the theatre in general and to the Chinese Festival and Garrick in particular 'for employing such a large number Frenchmen in an English theatre, at a time of open war with their countrymen'.[39]

The London crowds were in uproar reflecting the anti-papal sentiments which had always simmered right below the surface. The spectacle on stage shifted to the spectacle in the theatre where angry crowds 'demolished the scenes, tore up the benches, broke the listres and girandoles, and did in a short time so much mischief to the inside of the theatre, that it scarce could be repaired in several days'. While those who occupied the boxes (the upper crust) supported Garrick, the pit and the galleries (where the plebeians sat) made their opposition felt. The clash of cultures was in this case trumped by the clash of class and the majority of the audience turned into a mob with 'ungovernable rage'. Garrick – or *Roscius Anglicanus* – became the chief target of their displeasure and he was thus made to cower before 'ungovernable rage of the people, who threatened to demolish his house'.[40] What did this episode reveal? The institutional authority of the eighteenth-century theatre was subject to the contingencies of the marketplace and the volatility of the streets outside. Garrick's Chinese festival also reveals in retrospect that the eighteenth-century stage was not ready for the kind of free artistic and aesthetic trade that Garrick envisioned for it. His initiative to sponsor and promote the circulation of domestic and foreign talent met with stolid obstacle and resistance. But to argue that there was no clearly discernible pattern of 'progress' would be to adopt a cynical view, one which would compromise the significance of encounter, interaction and exchange of talent and personnel. The eighteenth-century British entertainment industry was hugely invested in the change which circulation brings about and also able to absorb the volatility which such change and exchange engender – as the following section further demonstrates.

GARRICK'S DIASPORA: THE PLAY AS BOTH IMPERIAL PRODUCT AND BRITISH PROTOTYPE

The notion of Garrick's diaspora is used in this section to underscore the commonplace observation that culture is always eminently transportable. The circulation of British plays in Calcutta during the Age of Garrick followed a distinct pattern, and one which was different from the one in North America, for instance, for a variety of reasons. While the term 'colony' – mercantilist in essence and purportedly set up to advance the interests of trade and commerce – is used routinely to mark those foreign areas (of control or influence) where British, French or Spanish hegemony was first established, each colony had qualities which set it apart from others – which is especially the case with India and America in the eighteenth century. What were the main differences between British theatrical productions in America and in India? The distinctions between the two are seemingly minor but worth discussing even if with broad brushstrokes for here and now.

Western civilization established itself in North America by erasing or marginalizing the native populations and their cultures. The folk performances in North America – pre-encounter – ranged from storytelling and dancing to other rites, rituals and 'shamans', which were communal in nature and did not have any elements in common with the European traditions.[41] As the colonists established deep roots, English tradition became more pronounced in all leisure activities including but not limited to blood sports such as cockfighting and rites of passage that were boisterous and even destructive. The Puritans in New England, the Dutch Calvinists in New York and the Quakers in Pennsylvania favoured performances that fleshed out the principles of honour, humility and industry. Subtle differences between performances in New England and the Middle colonies and those in the South notwithstanding, the overwhelming impetus across the board was for using the theatre to drive home such morals as a work ethic and self-control, which would ward off individual sin. Meanwhile the social elites and the patriarchs in particular turned to traditional Western theatre so much so that in Virginia, around the Chesapeake Bay area, as well as up and down the Atlantic seaboard men of substance and leisure (including George Washington) went to the theatre to watch traditional British plays, plays which were written by British authors, performed on the stages of Drury Lane or Covent Garden, and then transported to America and performed by, for instance, The Hallam Company of Comedians from London, which also performed in Jamaica.[42] In 1758 David Douglass took over the management of this company which then came to be known as the Hallam-Douglass troupe.[43] Unsurprisingly, the plays of Shakespeare (*Richard III*, *King Lear*, *Macbeth*, *The Merchant of Venice*) were popular. Thomas Otway's *Venice Preserv'd*, Joseph Addison's *Cato* and John Dryden's *All for Love* were performed by actors who had been trained in London to emulate 'the genteel speech and body language' but they were, in fact, transferring the patriarchal values of the homeland to the newly acquired territories and domains of command and control.[44]

While populist republicanism manifested itself in the favourable reception of, for instance, *Cato* (prior to 1790), simultaneously, there were backlashes against the British, particularly against the actors while rioters often demanded patriotic subjects and tunes (which is only to be expected post-revolution). What distinguished 'western' American theatre from its British (or French) roots was the influence even late in the eighteenth century of the Puritans and their imprint in every facet of culture: 'For most Puritans, theatre was simply an elitist waste of time. . . . William Prynne's *Histriomastix* (1633), Jeremy Collier's *Short View of the Immorality and Profaneness of the English Stage* (1690), and William Penn's *No Cross, No Crown* (1699) undoubtedly hindered the development of theatre and drama in the colonies'.[45] In the *Sturm und Drang* of the English fledgling theatrical culture in America in the eighteenth century, we find clear evidence of the divide between the dominant culture and the one which had been marginalized into non-existence and pushed to the peripheries even as 'manifest destiny' was touted as the birthright of the imperialists.

In India, English play-going practice in the eighteenth century had at least two perceptible differences from its American counterpart. First, there was no religious intrusion or manoeuvre (by British Protestants or French Catholics) to control the various modes of leisure activities and to champion a particular sectarian interest or cause. Second, in the last few decades of the eighteenth century, America was Britain's past (and vice versa) while India was Britain's future. As the fairly extensive private correspondence, diaries and government records of Philip Francis, a member of the Colony Council, the then governor general of India Warren Hastings, and many other colonial administrators, visitors and East India Company operatives amply demonstrate, there was no need at this colonial end of the spectrum for the British to reject or resist their roots. Britain was thus nostalgically and enthusiastically recreated and celebrated in a number of ways in Calcutta and elsewhere on the Indian subcontinent under the unofficial auspices of the East India Company. The colonial capital, Calcutta, was segregated, with the 'Blackies of Calcutta' inhabiting one part and with the British concentration in and around Fort William – the command post occupied by colonial administrators and military personnel – and Chowringhree.[46] Evidence related to physical theatres and their structure or spatial configuration and their location in this divided city is limited at best. So, for instance, some records suggest that *c.*1778 Philip Francis lived behind the playhouse. 'The Playhouse referred to, known as the new one stood . . . behind (north of) Writer's Buildings'.[47] Of the formal and traditional theatrical settings, sketchy descriptions are as follows:

> Theatricals were in special favour amongst Calcutta pleasure-seekers, the subscription theatre (erected in 1775) being shut off from the southerly wind by Writer's Buildings, was furnished with wind-sails on the roof 'to promote coolness by a free circulation of air'. The auditorium consisted only of pit and boxes; the prices of admission were to the former eight rupees, and to the latter one gold mohur. The characters were all taken by gentlemen amateurs. Mrs. Fay saw *Venice Preserv'd* acted there in 1780, the part of Belvidera being taken by a Lieutenant Norfor. . . . [I]n addition to the most ambitious musical entertainments, such as the whole of Handel's 'Messiah', included anything from *Othello*, or *The Merchant of Venice*, down to the *Irish Widow* or the *Mock Doctor*.[48]

In addition to plays from the London repertoire, masquerades were also very popular forms of entertainment for which female costumes were ordered for the men (the unintended consequence of which was a throwback to the pre-Restoration era, when men acted in women's role in both masquerades and in plays).[49] A manuscript promptbook for Richard Brinsley Sheridan's *School for Scandal*, produced specifically for the Calcutta Theatre and dated 25 March 1782, provided the basis for my speculation[50] that David Garrick and the Drury Lane prompter William Hopkins were directly involved and instrumental in promoting British theatre in Calcutta. This promptbook includes, for instance, a detailed sketch of how the 'Picture Scene' was supposed to have been set up in the Calcutta Theatre (see Figure 5.4). Significantly, the diagrammatic representation of the Screen Scene in this Calcutta promptbook resembles closely the line-up on stage depicted in a theatrical painting by James Roberts (see Figures 5.5 and 5.6).

The cast list includes men who belonged to the inner circle of British colonial operatives stationed at Fort William, Calcutta. According to this list, while two well-known entities, Captain William Keasbury and Barnard Messink, played Charles Surface and Crabtree respectively, the female characters and the male actors who played them are listed as follows: Lady Teazle was played by Lieutenant Norfor; Maria by Mr Smith; Lady Sneerwell by Mr Wilkinson; Mrs Candour by Mr Ralph; and the Maid by Mr Cassey.[51] A cultural critique of the imperial modality of circulation, thus, must highlight the overlapping interests of British culture, literature and theatre and how these subtexts advanced the professional/financial prospects of imperial agents and, simultaneously, aggrandized British (or East India Company) coffers. Unlike their American counterparts, who relinquished their ties to the centre and carved out an

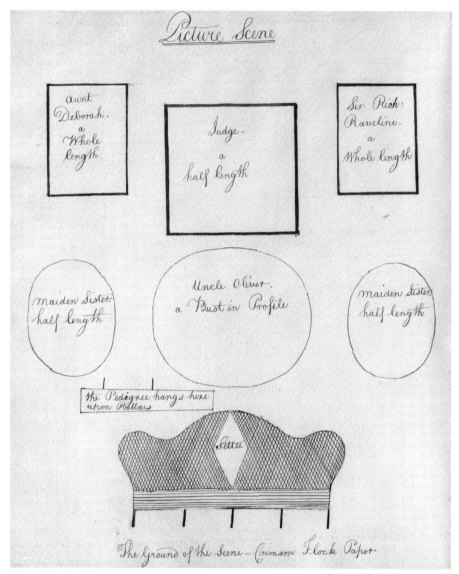

FIGURE 5.4: The Picture Scene in the Calcutta production of *The School for Scandal*, 1782. Folger Shelfmark MS W.a. 237. Used by permission of the Folger Shakespeare Library under a Creative Commons Attribution-ShareAlike 4.0 International Licence.

FIGURE 5.5: Frances Abington, Thomas King, John Palmer and William Smith in *The School for Scandal*, James Roberts, oil on canvas, 1779. Courtesy of The Garrick Club, London.

independent political and cultural trajectory, the colonists in India revelled in their newfound power and their sense of freedom from direct parliamentary intrusion, and, not surprisingly, they continued to simulate, mimic and replicate British culture in the distant colony.

IN SHORT: CIRCULATION AS CONTINGENCY AND COROLLARY TO PROGRESS

The Renaissance theatrical map, despite Shakespeare's successful experiments with the expansionist potential of global locations, remained anchored in Europe (Denmark, Venice, Wittenberg) with occasional detours through the Maghreb or the Ottoman Empire. After the Restoration and roughly a hundred years post-*The Merchant of Venice*, John Dryden's portrayal of Aureng-Zebe – to use just one example – presented a significant departure from the Eurocentrism of the Renaissance even though this dramatic rendition of the emperor of India[52] was designed more to press the right imperial buttons at home than to create a historically reliable dramatization of the Mughal empire at a specific point in time. Regarding Dryden's *Aureng-Zebe*, and writing a hundred or so years after the play's production on the London stage, Garrick biographer Thomas Davies noted that 'Charles II . . . pronounced it to be the best of all Dryden's tragedies'.[53] The play was, for Davies, 'Dryden's . . . most perfect

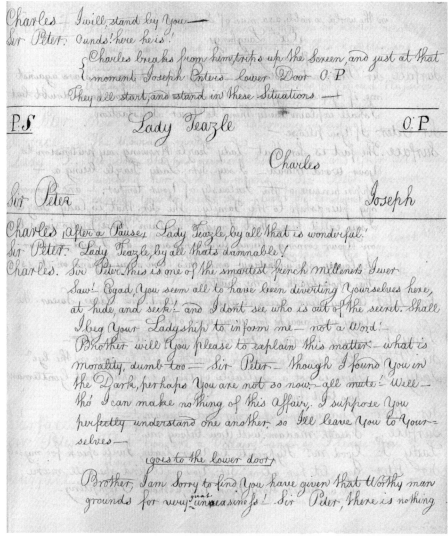

FIGURE 5.6: *The School for Scandal: A Comedy*, Richard Brinsley Sheridan, *c.*1782, Folger Shelfmark MS W.a. 237. Used by permission of the Folger Shakespeare Library under a Creative Commons Attribution-ShareAlike 4.0 International Licence.

tragedy in rhime'. What are the predominant features of this play which deserved praise more than a hundred years later? 'In this play, the passions are strongly depicted, the characters well discriminated, and the diction more familiar and dramatic, than in any of his preceding pieces'.[54] In retrospect, its technical perfection and its ability to capture the flavour of the times are the abiding features of the play. A symbol both foreign and domestic, a distant trope sufficiently homogenized and then appropriated and pressed into the demands of melodramatic British passion, the Mughal emperor Aureng-Zebe represents in Dryden's world *c.*1700 a limited model of circulation; but in Garrick's world *Aureng-Zebe* was a commendable period piece representing British tragedy and its slavish entanglements with statecraft at a time when monarchy was closely associated with the tragedy of regicide.

Toward the end of the eighteenth century, when culture, commerce, trade and taste became indistinguishable particles of progress, the circulation of talent and ideas found new and spectacular expression. So, for instance, George Frideric Handel's commemoration at Westminster Abbey in 1784, twenty-five years after his death, might be cited as an example of progress. In this grand performance, royalty and aristocracy as well as considerable artistic talent formed an alliance to drive home the point that national heritage could indeed be defined and upheld by the finest imports, by yet another German émigré. Neither Handel's origin (his country of birth, Germany, was the same as that of the then Queen Charlotte of Mecklenburg-Strelitz) nor indeed his rocky record as the man at the helm of the Haymarket Theatre stood in the way of one of the finest and most artfully choreographed tributes to his talent. In this instance, even as the sound of music reverberated within the institutional framework of Westminster Abbey, the foreign–domestic bifurcation was made irrelevant and inconsequential. Meanwhile, Richard Brinsley Sheridan's plays – marvellous expressions of British imperial humour – found easy access to stages in the British colonies in, among other locations, Kingston and Calcutta. The late eighteenth-century theatre, in other words, could no longer be circumscribed by the conventional borders of nation or obscurantist ideas of national heritage when the nation itself was poised for global supremacy on the eve of full-blown empire. Garrick's wide-ranging impact – particularly his innovative approach to circulation – came at a time when Britain could not afford to just look back; it had to forge a new future and a modern cultural heritage infused with the contingencies of its ever-widening global presence.

CHAPTER SIX

Interpretations

From Theatrephobia *to a Theatrical 'Science of Man'*

LOGAN J. CONNORS

In his 1796 speech to members of the *Institut de France*, Pierre Jean George Cabanis claimed that 'physiology, the study of ideas, and morality are nothing but three branches of one and identical science, which can be called without hesitation, the science of man'.[1] Cabanis, a physiologist, doctor and strict materialist, is credited for applying Enlightenment ideals of religious doubt and the scientific method to the emerging field of psychology. Cabanis broke with previous explanations of the mind and its processes by postulating that behavioural disorders were diseases of the brain rather than 'moral *dérèglements*', 'disturbances of the *âme*' or '*maladies de l'esprit*'.[2]

Cabanis's thesis was a final chapter of an effort to explain humankind after more than thirty years of materialist physiological research in France. Cabanis's desire to attach psychological causality to internal, biological processes was a reassessment of human understanding by a researcher whose avowed interest was the *science of man* – a wide- and far-reaching set of theories about humankind that sought, perhaps most famously in David Hume's *Treatise of Human Nature* (1739), to ground moral and psychological aspects of life to the mind/body's sympathetic response rather than to theology. But Cabanis's effort was, in another way, the first chapter of a new project; for unlike Hume and other 'sympathetic philosophers', Cabanis was focused on the interior rather than the exterior, relegating stimuli to internal, physiological (and to a certain extent genetic) functions of brain activity. Not unlike several scientific theories of psychology today, Cabanis sought to explain psychological principles through chemistry and endocrinology; what the brain was focused upon, in love with, or empathetic to was of lesser concern.

The Enlightenment existed in between and fully engaged with two psychosocial viewpoints: a metaphysical and often religious model of explaining individual and social behaviour; and an emerging scientific discourse typified by Cabanis's work on physiology, which would eventually dominate the modern sciences. The Enlightenment 'science of man' placed a thinking, socializing and political human being at the centre of reflection in all domains from history to economics to medicine.[3] As far as literature and the arts are concerned, this 'science of man', with its 'importance accorded to knowledge of the self',[4] provided a theoretical scaffold for fictional and non-fictional genres that focused on individual experiences and detailed the complex interiority of human cognition and emotion, as evidenced in travel narratives, autobiography, the libertine novel and the coming-of-age story. Although scholars have evinced what is called the 'psychological turn' of the Enlightenment with studies of the rich production of novels and other forms of literature from the period, theatre has not garnered the same critical attention. Yet the theatre of the Enlightenment, particularly in France, was the premiere theoretical venue for both conceptualizing and expressing this new 'science of man'.

For many scholars both past and present, French theatre of the Enlightenment was little more than a stale waiting room, lodged awkwardly between the palace of seventeenth-century neoclassicism and the Romantic renovations to the stage in post-Revolutionary France. This interpretation of Enlightenment theatre, however, fails to account for the wild popularity of dramatic literature and theatrical performances at the time and ignores the essential role that theatre and drama played in defining and disseminating a 'science of man' – perhaps the Enlightenment's most important intellectual contribution to the history of ideas.

Theatre, with its unique ability to portray human interaction against a malleable backdrop of fiction, was an efficient venue to develop new theories about both the individual and society. The drive to learn more about humankind during the European Enlightenment led to dramatic theories and genres that attempted to understand, explain, inspire and transform the men and women who attended and read plays. The French *drame* (or *drame bourgeois*) emerged at the height of Enlightenment France and was lauded by some of France's most rigorous 'scientists of man'. It was the most explicit attempt to represent the relationships between the self, the other and the institutions that governed a range of French social classes.

Drawing from a host of sources, including works by George Lillo, Richard Steele and other English playwrights, the *drame* in France was conceptualized and disseminated by Denis Diderot, Louis-Caron de Beaumarchais, Louis-Sébastien Mercier and, to a certain extent, Voltaire. Contrary to serious comedies and bourgeois tragedies from other European traditions, *drames* were part of a concerted social mission on the part of French *philosophes*. They were often accompanied by lengthy theoretical treatises and prefaces that were intended to present the genre as a social, aesthetic and psychological experiment, designed to help spectators and readers learn more about themselves as members of a tangible and improvable world.[5] *Drames* sought to boost the emotional responses of readers and spectators through a host of dramaturgical and sentimental strategies. Playwrights of the *drame* argued that learning and pleasure operated in tandem and through a specific code of sensibility – an emotional regime of affectivity – that existed at the intersection of mind and body, and that attached heightened emotional states to learning, personal benefit and social improvement.[6]

Yet this optimistic interpretation of theatre's benefits was not shared by all; the intellectual road to Diderot and the *philosophes* was at times treacherous. Theatre, 'because of its immensely social and collective nature', 'has often been viewed with suspicion, particularly by political and religious partisans. An integral part of theatre's cultural history is therefore its place in philosophical, theological, and artistic debates where its status oscillates between outright rejection . . . and pedagogical affirmation'.[7] One goal of this chapter is thus to show how this 'oscillation' in the interpretation of theatre's merits operated against a backdrop of social and philosophical discourses both before and during the Enlightenment.

During early modernity, discourses about theatre mapped on to philosophies of art and the emotions, and more specifically, to the value of the emotions felt during an experience with art. The period, I argue, was witness to a shift in both the history of the emotions and the history of interpretation. During the Enlightenment, the way by which theatre was defined became increasingly relational – a model for aesthetic judgement that retains value today.

First, I will detail a few characteristics of the *drame* – the Enlightenment's most important theoretical contribution to the history of theatre – before presenting an alternative and surprising genealogy of the project: virulent, religious, anti-theatrical discourse. Fundamentally different in intent but with the same focus on affect and change, anti-theatrical writers previewed Enlightenment renovations to the stage by defining theatre in terms of the somatic, psychological and social response of spectators to the stage. As we shall see, religious anti-theatrical writers played a vital role in the development of the anthropological theatre criticism that the *philosophes* would later adopt and change. This investigation of drama's pessimistic underbelly emerges as necessary in order to better understand the Enlightenment's contribution to the cultural history of theatre. In the final part of this chapter, I show how Enlightenment writers – and particularly Jean-Baptiste (the abbé) Dubos – accomplished a shift in the histories of psychology and theatre by devising a new theory of the types of emotions endured by the spectator during the theatrical event. Following the authors of my study, I refuse to conceptualize theatre as mere dramatic literature and as one genre in the history of poetry. Instead, I will insist on the essential role of drama and dramatic theory in the political, social and emotional lives of readers and audiences during a cataclysmic time in the history of Europe.

DIDEROT'S RELATIONAL DRAMA

Diderot's *drame* conceptualizes human interaction as the central feature of a representable universe. In his theoretical texts and in his plays from the late 1750s and early 1760s, Diderot alters classical traditions in an effort to affect spectators with a host of dramaturgical and emotional strategies. In his most famous *drame*, The Natural Son (*Le Fils naturel*, 1757), Diderot charts the moral courses of several characters who overcome conflict to achieve personal, familial and social improvement. Blending fiction and dramatic criticism into one work, Diderot included three *Dialogues* (*Les Entretiens sur Le Fils naturel*) as an addendum to his play text. In the *Dialogues*, the play's protagonist, Dorval, discusses dramatic norms against the backdrop of his family life after the end of the play's narrative (a happy conclusion during which each character reasons through his or her conflicts before the father figure returns to confirm a virtuous ending). Dorval and the narrator ('Moi') debate typical dramatic issues, including the unities of time, place and action, as well as the visual separation of the stage from the public (the 'fourth wall'). Dorval and his interlocutor, particularly in the 'Second Dialogue', delve into the details of stage movement, acting techniques and costuming. By including both the play and a fictionalized rendering of a community's response to the play, Diderot presents his readers with an overall assessment of theatre as a moral, emotional and social force. Judgement of whether a play is good or bad is based on how dramatic elements affect spectator-actor-critics like Dorval, the lead character of both the play and the accompanying *Dialogues*.[8]

To summarize a complex – and at times contradictory – theoretical text, one could say that Diderot's overall goal is to introduce and justify his new dramatic genre as a sort of theatrical 'science of man' – a means to learn more about humankind through the theatre. Like Cabanis's attempt to remove psychology from the moral and theological registers, Diderot shows a similar scepticism for external narratives of human behaviour. The characters Dorval, Constance, Rosalie and Clairville possess the ability to overcome social conflict in the play without the help of classical theatrical ruses and strategies such as rich uncles, meddling valets or a benevolent king. At the conclusion of The Natural Son, Dorval, with Constance's help, has come to the realization that a romantic relationship with Rosalie would damage the group's social fabric because Clairville, Dorval's best friend, is in love with her. The happy ending occurs in

FIGURE 6.1: Portrait of Denis Diderot, Louis-Michel van Loo, 1767. Paris, Musée du Louvre, Getty Images.

the dramatic narrative before the arrival of the father figure, who confirms that, in fact, Rosalie and Dorval are long-lost siblings.[9] The father and, with him, the past, are superannuated: an interpersonal and sentimental decision-making process based on the current needs of the community replaces the abrupt absolution or revelation of the *rex / pater / deus ex machina* – a dramaturgical device in classical and neoclassical plays during which a king, father or god-figure arrives at the end of the play to resolve a conflict that the main characters are unable to overcome themselves.[10]

Diderot's *drame* reflects on humankind both on stage and after the theatrical event: the *Dialogues* follow the spectators and actors of *The Natural Son* into the period after the narrative events have already taken place, showing readers how dramatic affect operates in fiction and in the world. *The Natural Son* creates this affect through the actions and dialogues of the characters; then, the *Dialogues* describe that affect – and how others could achieve it with their own *drames* – through the testimony of the now character-spectator-critic, Dorval.

According to Diderot, a dramatic *tableau* was the 'true portrayal' of the characters on stage by the playwright so that the spectacle would appear as 'faithful to nature' as a painting.[11] The aesthetic novelty of Diderot's project is difficult to dispute; Diderot's invention of the *tableau* – the heart of the *drame* – broke with previous traditions to emerge as the quintessential Enlightenment effect in theatre. The *tableau* inaugurated a new conception of illusion by excluding, 'as much as possible, the spectator from the spectacle; even though it is in order to touch his/her heart, to affect him/her violently, and to stir his/her imagination so forcefully that it invades the spectacle'.[12] The spectator's imagination invades the stage as meaning-making occurs on a relational level of interdependence among the playwright, actors and spectators. This aesthetic system is predicated on both a new social order in theatrical representation and a heightened significance placed by theorists in the power of emotional response; never before had France seen a closer proximity between the characters of fiction on the stage and the real conditions of spectators in the theatre.[13] Knowledge or 'science of man' – the comprehendible character, the absorbed spectator, the socially engaged playwright – defined the theatrical genre supported by France's *encyclopédistes* and *philosophes*; it stands to reason that some of the most prolific writers of *drames* were also engaged in research in the emerging domain of a 'science of man'.[14]

Diderot expanded his theory of the *tableau* with his 1773 work, *The Paradox of the Actor*. In this dialogical treatise on acting, the *philosophe* argues that excellent actors (those who successfully execute the *tableau*) maintain an internal cold-bloodedness during a theatrical performance; mediocre actors, by contrast, actually feel the heightened emotional states of their characters. Spurning a vocabulary of enthusiasm for a rhetoric of reason and calculation, Diderot shows a 'change of heart' from the *Dialogues* to the *Paradox* that has led many scholars to view the latter as a departure from the author's praise of sensibility during 1750s and 1760s.[15] After all, Diderot seems unequivocal about theatrical emotions in the *Paradox*; he writes in the conclusion that 'perfectly imitated passion enables that which passion itself couldn't accomplish'.[16]

Diderot's treatise on acting, however, is as much an extension of a theatrical 'science of man' as a break from previous theorization on the emotions. By focusing on how the actor engages with his or her own emotions during performances and rehearsals, Diderot furthers the theoretical mission of explaining human sentiments through the analysis of theatrical practices. In the *Paradox*, he details the emotional processes of the theatrical event that he had developed in his earlier works. He continues in the vein of his 1757 *Dialogues on The Natural Son* by arguing that actors can and should boost the emotional charge of theatrical performances.[17] Grounded in new materialist scientific discourses of the 1760s, Diderot's *Paradox* interrogates the relationships between affect and cognition; it 'takes the body as a central theme', explaining it through 'practical physiology, speculative biology, and the aesthetics of theatrical creation and expression'.[18]

Diderot's notion of *raison* is not characterized by a detached Cartesian cogito, but rather by a learned corporeal state, developed by a rigorous actor through physical and mental repetition. As Joseph Roach argues, in Diderot's work, 'mind and body are inextricably interwoven in the same web of nervous fibers'.[19] While the *Paradox* manifests a different type of emotional theorization – a deeper look into the precise mechanisms of acting and a more exacting recognition of the links between cognition and the physical mechanism – at no time does the *philosophe* question the overall value of spectator emotion. The *Paradox* is the next logical step in Diderot's concurrent analysis of theatre and human physiology. Diderot's *Paradox* and his *Dialogues* thus achieve similar goals: they focus the reader's attention on the intricacies of emotional processes; underline spectator enthusiasm as the goal of theatrical performance; and bolster the theatrical event as a theoretically serious experience for philosophical investigation.

Diderot's *Dialogues on The Natural Son*, however, remain the *philosophe*'s most spectator-focused theoretical text. Published as an addendum to his play, *The Natural Son*, the *Dialogues* serve as the theoretical frame to Diderot's most innovative dramatic creation: the *drame*. In the critical milieu, the *drame* broke with prescribed theatrical rules as the spectator, both as character in (Dorval) and consumer of (the narrator of the *Dialogues*) the dramatic fiction, moves the critical locus of the play from rule-making critics, who are exterior to the experience (i.e. classical academicians or *doctes*), to the actual (or imagined) responses of theatre-going consumers – members of a community, who are present during the event. The avowed goals of *philosophe* theatre had thus become fully anthropological: real men and women – writers, actors, spectators and readers – determined theatre's value based on the perception of how plays affected, explained and improved participants in the event. This new theatrical 'science of man' – the quest to study, represent and perfect humankind through a lived dramatic experience – flowed from a radical reassessment of the spectator's relationship to theatrical performance.

For Diderot, this meant addressing some of the most famous theoretical texts and plays of the French neoclassical period. In order to understand the paramount changes to the interpretation of theatre and its effects during the Enlightenment, it is important first to gain a clear picture of the theoretical landscape in place before Diderot. Many recent and not-so-recent studies place Diderot's *drame*, and Enlightenment theatre in general, in dialogue with France's long-standing tradition of dramatic rule making and theatrical theorization. Scholars, quite logically, read the *philosophe*'s project as a result of or a response to France's neoclassical drama of the seventeenth century – a period often considered the heyday of rule-based comedy and tragedy. New scholarship on the seventeenth century, however, has undone the myth that theatre from this period was little more than a competition among institutionally established critics and playwrights to prove who could follow (and who could enforce) classical rules with the most accuracy.

Recent scholars – John Lyons, Georges Forestier and Joseph Harris, for example – have uncovered innovative theories about both dramatic literature and theatrical performance in treatises by François Hédelin, abbé d'Aubignac, Jules de La Mesnardière, Pierre Corneille, Jean Racine, René Rapin and Molière. These scholars, and others,[20] have shown that the seventeenth century did not demonstrate 'a very tidy, formulaic, and static vision of a highly regulated stage', but rather a diverse network of competing discourses about theatre.[21] Moreover, with a cursory glance at the works of Diderot, Voltaire, Beaumarchais and Mercier – France's famous proponents of the stage one century later – it is clear that seventeenth-century theorists and playwrights were the models of writers and dramatists of the Enlightenment. But despite the similarities between neoclassical and Enlightenment interpretations of theatre, the overall goal of seventeenth-century dramatists was inherently different from the goal of Enlightenment playwrights and theorists. Classical theorists, for the most part, made 'no reference to actual spectators'.[22] Instead, they theorized about a unified spectator with an ideal, and ultimately, impossible response to theatrical works. This difference between classical and Enlightenment dramatic theory hinges upon diverging ideas about the importance of theatre publics as salient sources of judgement as well as the means by which playwrights should engage the emotions of spectators and readers.

Tragic dramatists of the French neoclassical period, with their larger-than-life characters and temporally and culturally distant settings, sought to affect spectators through schemes of magnification rather than proximity. Neoclassical playwrights – Corneille and Racine alike – represented the grandiose or the exaggerated to provide a powerful example of a common emotion. In doing so, the seventeenth-century stage 'is able to represent actions far more brutal than its spectators are capable of committing . . . thus articulating on an exaggerated and fictional level certain unrecognized psychological impulses shared by the spectators'.[23]

Neoclassical theatre was certainly concerned with the 'Spectator' – an amalgamated, theoretical figure. What separates eighteenth-century Enlightenment theatre from seventeenth-century theatre is the reduction of magnification and 'passion-typing' (horror, terror, jealousy, etc.) in favour of granular detail deployed by playwrights during the Enlightenment to increase the emotional engulfment of the spectator and cause (what writers perceived as) a post-performance response of personal and social improvement.[24] The difference is thus a question of subject: neoclassical theatre, despite its rich poetic diversity and passionate moments, concentrates on the complex psychology of the fictional character and not necessarily on the spectators in the playhouse seats or the actual readers of the play. During the eighteenth century, the psychological distinction between dramatic character and actual spectator begins to scale down. But an important question emerges: where does this 'anthropological' assessment of the theatre's merits come from?

Establishing a genealogy of Diderot's *drame* is arduous, owing to the novelty of his theatrical mission. The *philosophe* was an avid reader of French classical theatre; he was also indebted to more recent, sentimental genres such as *comédies larmoyantes* (tearful comedies) and bourgeois tragedy – genres that garnered a significant number of performances and readers during the 1730s and 1740s.[25] Moreover, given the importance of visual *tableaux* in Diderot's work, an interrogation of the *philosophe*'s pictorial sources, from Antoine Watteau to Jean-Baptiste Greuze, is also paramount.[26] These roads to the *drame* are well travelled; yet they do not fully explicate the relationship between Enlightenment theatre and a concurrent mission to study humankind – the 'science of man'. My goal in the rest of this chapter is to show an alternate route to Diderot's project – a quintessential theatrical project of the Enlightenment – by focusing less on his plot themes, socio-economic considerations and character compositions, and more on the *philosophe*'s overall interpretation of theatre as a venue of affect, knowledge and change. Tracing this turn towards the real effects of theatre takes us in a very different direction.

Diderot's praise of theatre as a fundamental agent of change seems like a far cry from the opinions of the religious anti-theatrical writers who were intent on destroying the theatre one century earlier during the pinnacle of Louis XIV's reign. Nevertheless, this force, whether protestant, Jansenist, or Oratorian in confession, reflected with vigour on the lived moment of spectating or reading drama – on what we might call today the transformative power of theatre.[27] Like in theories of the *drame*, dramatic literature and performance in anti-theatrical discourse are holistic: reading and attending plays affects the body, the heart (and emotional life) and the soul. Theatre is interpersonal in both traditions: it affects our relationships with others and influences the trajectory of society as a whole. Or, returning to Cabanis's desire to combine the *sciences* into one, we can assert that both the anti-theatrical and Diderotian traditions combine the moral with the aesthetic in an attempt to evaluate the scope and the goals of the theatrical experience – a positive experience of Enlightenment for Diderot and the *philosophes*; a nefarious, but nevertheless life-altering moment for those against theatre.

The obvious difference between religious anti-theatrical tracts of the seventeenth century and Diderot's theatrical 'science of man' is axiomatic, not ontological: theatre is valued or not valued anthropologically, and not for its ability or not to conform to previous poetic examples or abstract rules (no matter how varied or rich those rules may be). Both traditions impart a desire to explain human nature and detail the complex processes involved in psychology and human relations through a discussion of theatrical performance and reading; also, and perhaps most importantly, both traditions believe that theatre causes this profound change to the self and to society through emotional processes.

Pierre Nicole's 1667 *Treatise on the Theatre* [*Traité de la comédie*], examined in the following section, is a masterful attack against theatre as a human experience. It is indicative of the emotionally charged rhetoric of anti-theatricality in seventeenth-century France. Nicole laments the theatre because of its negative consequences on personal health, family relationships and society – the very same entities that Diderot and other Enlightenment writers argued were ameliorated by one's experience with drama. Nicole's vitriol against the stage has already elicited a variety of studies. Rather than reading the *Treatise* against his other writings, comparing its themes and rhetorical strategies to the cleric Jacques-Bénigne Bossuet's more famous *Maxims on the Theatre* [*Maximes sur la comédie*] (1694), or analysing the work against the backdrop of *all* religious writing against the stage during the seventeenth century,[28] I demonstrate how the definition of theatre (or *la comédie*) proposed by Nicole ultimately previewed the conceptions of theatre during the Enlightenment. In doing so, I underline the pertinence of contrarian, religious anti-theatrical conceptions of the theatrical experience and thus integrate these narratives into a more general history of theatre.

PIERRE NICOLE AND THE
CONTAGION OF THE STAGE

Nicole wrote his *Treatise on the Theatre* at an important moment in the history of French theatre. The second half of the seventeenth century was a golden era of dramatic output (Pierre and Thomas Corneille, Jean Racine, Jean de Rotrou, Molière) and theorization (François Hédelin, abbé d'Aubignac, Charles de Saint-Évremond, Jules de La Mesnardière, René Rapin, etc.). Nicole's treatise against the stage appeared in the context of an increasing amount of pro- and anti-theatrical tracts, and in the wake of Corneille's debates with members of the Académie française in the 1630s and early 1640s. This polemical environment changed the way writers talked about judgement and theatrical quality, inaugurating a new conception of a judging theatre public, whose evolution and importance would accelerate during the Enlightenment.[29]

Although the religious case against dramatic literature and performance in France started as early as the sixteenth century,[30] Nicole's particular condemnation of the stage warrants attention. The cleric's detailed analysis of

FIGURE 6.2: Portrait of Pierre Nicole, theologian and philosopher, seventeenth century. Paris, Bibliothèque nationale de France, Getty Images.

the intensities, mechanisms and types of emotions endured by spectators previews the Enlightenment's relational and emotional aesthetics of theatre. In addition to rehashing the historical arguments against spectacles often employed by Church officials in their *Treatises* and *Dissertations*, Nicole, informed by Cartesian mechanics and definitions of the passions,[31] changes the nature of the discussion by focusing more on the phenomenon of spectating than on the opinions of patristic moralists or on the history of Church decisions related to actors, spectacles and writers.

Nicole and other fierce enemies of the spectating experience argue that the sensations felt by spectators are very real.[32] In addition to moral arguments grounded in Church history, ecclesiastical writers had the scientific 'evidence' that 'sensibility and passion are stirred in the psyche by a force, matter in motion, that impresses itself on the body and initiates a chain of causal physiological action and reaction'.[33] For Nicole, this chain of reactions continues beyond ephemeral feelings during the performance; spectators actually learn from the experience. Theatre emerges as relational and dangerous because emotions are passed interpersonally through processes that are independent of the mind's control.

In his detailed assessment of emotion and spectating, Nicole concentrates first on actors, whom he claims are responsible for provoking dangerous affect during the theatrical performance:

> It [acting] is a job where the goal is to please others and where men and women represent the passions of hate, anger, ambition, revenge and, mostly, love. Actors have to demonstrate [these passions] in the most natural and the most lively way as possible. They would never be able to do so if they didn't incite these passions in themselves and if their souls weren't imprinted by them in order to show them on the outside through gesture and speech. Those who represent the passion of love are necessarily affected by this passion while they represent it. It is impossible that they could erase this desired impression from their minds or that this passion wouldn't leave a strong disposition [to love] that they had so willingly wanted to feel.[34]

The emotions are fully embodied by the actor before they are passed to the spectators. According to the Jansenist cleric, the actor commits a sin and enchants spectators into committing sins that are then impossible to 'erase', becoming repeatable, emotionally learned acts after the performance. In fact, Nicole condemns actors for multiple reasons: their goal of entertainment is not 'Christian'; they are paid to appear as something they are not; they have a special capacity to feel and express emotions; and they cannot control themselves offstage because of their constant embodiment of evil passions onstage. While Nicole is certainly no friend to actors, his intense focus on how they affect spectators and his analysis of their social interactions beyond the stage show the origins of a 'serious interest in the psychology of acting'.[35]

For Nicole, the lines between being and appearing are muddled, even absent. Unlike in Diderot's *Paradox*, actors really do live the part. They feel and exhibit the same passions, then, spectators feel and learn those same (evil) passions. Nicole, anticipating Jean-Jacques Rousseau's critique of the theatre approximately a hundred years later,[36] negates the possibility of an emotional purging or intellectual clearing through catharsis. In fact, it is the emotional response to drama after the event – the emotional durability of performance – that is most alarming.

The way the emotions operate in theatre is dangerous, according to Nicole, because of a pedagogy that evades metaphysical regulators such as the soul, the conscience, the mind or the heart. Nicole writes that theatre performances only teach us half the lesson: we revel in the pleasurable moment but fail to understand any potential drawbacks, which are, for Nicole, the guilt and anguish of sin – for 'when plays excite this passion, they do not imprint at the same time the love that regulates it'.[37] With performance, spectators get the carrot without the stick; the luscious poison without sobering antidote.[38]

Rather than assuming its role as what Enlightenment *philosophes* would later call a 'School of Virtue', the experience of spectating, without a cognitive part to the passions, emerges as an overwhelming outlet for the emotions from which the Church sought to provide a means of respite and defence:

> As such, the theatre, by its own nature, is a school and lesson in vice, because it is an art during which one excites vicious passions in oneself . . . What makes the danger in theatre even greater, however, is that it banishes all of the possible remedies that might stop its evil impressions. The heart is softened by pleasure. The mind is occupied by exterior objects and it is completely intoxicated by the insanity before it. By consequence, [the mind] is outside of the state of Christian vigilance that is necessary to avoid temptation.[39]

Theatrical performance is too powerful an experience for spectators. Pleasure fills the heart, 'foreign objects' overwhelm the soul, and emotions, such as lust, fear and sadness, replace the normative calm of 'Christian vigilance'. According to Nicole, this lack of reason – or vigilance – allows the devil to enter our minds surreptitiously to whisper dangerous lessons – in a 'special language' – into our ears.[40] Once that happens, our entire way of communicating with others changes as we adopt this new language of sin: plays 'do not only excite the passions, but they also teach the language of passions, meaning, the art of displaying them and making them appear in a delightful and ingenious manner; this is no small evil'.[41]

The theatre is powerful because it involves sight and sound. Spectators cannot help themselves; the dramatic text is dangerous enough but then rendered even more pernicious by the actor, who brings the passions literally *to life*. 'This loss of control', writes Henry Phillips, 'is further stressed in the moralists' examination of drama's aural and visual qualities, which are seen as contributing factors in the nature of drama as deceit'.[42] Nicole creates an alternative poetics that includes both narrative (the play's story) and performance-based criteria, thus showing that he and other anti-theatrical writers 'are aware of the attraction of a performance and of the way in which a text is given life by the actor'.[43] Nicole, like Diderot, argues that a successful (or dangerous) theatrical performance hinges upon the actor's craft.

In what we might call a conceptual preview to the *philosophes* of Enlightenment France, Nicole defines theatre relationally, based on how the event affects spectators psychologically, morally and socially. Nicole's argument is that good people can be steered in the wrong direction by performance. Theatre is a visual,[44] lived experience, and not merely a type of poetry; no dramatic rule can steer the spectator back into moral good. Unlike neoclassical theorists at the time, Nicole doubts the existence of a cathartic process, arguing, like the *philosophes*, that theatre should be assessed based on its post-production response – by the durability of the lessons learned and the emotions felt during the performance.

Like Nicole, the *philosophes* of Enlightenment France locate the essence of the performance in a period of introspection and personal change – both during and after the theatrical event. Using the same strategies as the *theatrephobic* cleric, Enlightenment writers detail the actual emotions felt by spectators during a real theatrical event. Both of these seemingly disparate traditions thus avoid the theoretical or ideal emotional responses prescribed in literary treatises and *poétiques*. Of course, for Nicole, the personal transformation of the spectator or actor is inherently bad; theatre overwhelms the body, the mind and ultimately, society. During the Enlightenment, emotions emerge as capable of inspiring decision-making processes that result in personal happiness and social improvement. This major shift of values was only possible, as we shall see in this final section, through a fundamental reassessment of the emotions in theatre.

RESPONDING TO ATTACK: TOWARDS A MINDFUL AND EMOTIONAL THEATRICAL EVENT

Nicole's attack against the theatre on moral, social and emotional grounds provoked several direct responses during the last half of the seventeenth century. None of these rebuttals, however, engaged fundamentally with Nicole's innovative theories on the emotional processes of spectating or reading drama. For example, a young upstart, Jean Racine, wrote a riposte to Nicole in which the dramatist compares plays to Church writings, arguing that even a serious religious cleric like Blaise Pascal 'introduces on the stage, at times Dominicans, at times doctors, and always Jesuits' in his *Provincial Letters* [*Lettres provinciales*].[45] Racine's defence of the theatre was bold: he gestures to the similarities between the writings of a moralist and the texts of dramatic authors. Racine goes on to say that he 'could say just as much about novels',[46] once again brazenly connecting both traditions, but ultimately sidestepping Nicole's arguments about the effects of theatrical performance. Racine, like many seventeenth-century critics, relegates any definition of the theatre, at least de facto, to dramatic scripts and universalizing *poétiques*.

Nicole's attack was just as much against the experience of spectatorship as against the character compositions, situations and plot twists of dramatic writing. Two decades later, a Theatine priest, Francesco Caffaro, attempted to defend theatre through historical arguments (e.g. the fathers of the Church such as St Thomas and St Cyprian were not entirely against visual spectacles) and a sociological perspective (Caffaro stated that he knew plenty of upstanding people who go to the theatre). These arguments met formidable opposition. The famous bishop and close adviser to Louis XIV, Jacques-Bénigne Bossuet, dismantled every biblical argument and condemned Caffaro's theatre-going friends to hell in his *Maxims and Reflections on Theatre* (*Maximes et réflexions sur la comédie*, 1694). Bossuet also picked up where Nicole left off by relegating, once again, the emotions felt during a performance to the body[47] and by conflating the various positive emotions deployed in drama into the categories of vice and lust.

At the end of the seventeenth century, the Church was a main source of theorization about a relational aesthetic that judges theatre according to how it affects spectators and readers. While proponents of theatre are often inclined to argue that the stage has historical precedents, that dramatic literature is good pedagogy or that performances are merely harmless pleasures, it is often the virulent anti-theatricalists who go to great lengths to describe the theatre's real consequences. Religious anti-theatrical writers viewed drama with suspicion; they nonetheless located the essence of the dramatic arts in the theatrical experience, judging plays on their ability to affect spectators and readers. Otherwise stated: writers like Nicole, through their harsh criticism of the theatre and its effects, gestured to what would later develop during the Enlightenment as a more optimistic theatrical 'science of man'. But first, proponents of theatre had to adumbrate a new theory of the emotions in order to rehabilitate the phenomenological moment of reading or viewing a play.

The Enlightenment defence of the emotions in theatre did not emerge overnight. Several theoreticians avoided the emotional question entirely, choosing instead to downplay the passionate moments of acting and spectating in their treatises and pamphlets. For example, in his *Treatise on the Recitative*

(*Traité du récitatif*, 1707), Jean-Léonor de Grimarest eschews an emotional vocabulary in his work on acting, favouring a technical description of declamation and oral rhetoric. Grimarest writes that 'the actor must carefully study himself in order to make the best gestures and attitudes: in order to satisfy the spectators, he must cultivate his pronunciation by paying attention to the utmost details of his voice'.[48] Grimarest's *Treatise* underlines the mechanisms an actor ought to employ in order to satisfy a spectator; the author refuses, however, to provide any further information about the nature of that satisfaction or the mindset of the actor while onstage. A reader is left wondering: is satisfaction an intellectual appreciation of or a visceral reaction to the stage? Yet even a *technicien* like Grimarest is unable to escape the ambiguous emotional language of the passions; as Jeffrey Leichman argues in a recent study, Grimarest concludes his opus by admitting that, when onstage, a good actor is always moved by a mysterious inner force that Grimarest calls 'fire'.[49]

A few years later, however, the French critical milieu saw what was nothing short of a paradigm shift in theories of the emotions in theatre when the abbé Dubos published his *Critical Reflections on Poetry and on Painting* (*Réflexions critiques sur la poésie et sur la peinture*, 1719), a diverse project describing virtually all forms of visual art.

About the type of emotion experienced by a spectator, Dubos writes:

> Painters and poets excite these artificial passions by presenting imitations of objects capable of exciting true passions in us. Because the impression that these imitations make on us is of the same nature as the object's impression imitated by the painter or the poet would be on us; because the impression made by the imitation is only different from the imitated object's impression in that it is weaker, it must therefore excite in our mind a passion that resembles that which the imitated object could have excited. The copy of the object must thus excite in us a copy of the passion that the object would have excited.[50]

Dubos proposes a radically different interpretation of the theatrical event by adding layers and phases to a now very mindful *and* emotional act of spectating. The immediate or overwhelming aspects of the emotions in either classical dramatic theory or anti-theatrical tracts against the stage are subdued or sequenced by Dubos into a cognitive event that includes both sensory perception and information processing. Dubos is not trying to rationalize or downplay the emotions during a performance; these emotions are not the same emotions that characterize our everyday lives, but he is quick to point out that they certainly feel like real emotions. But because we are attending a play, the emotions in theatre are categorically different and it is safe to take pleasure in the performance – even if this pleasure feels the same as pleasure by another source.

FIGURE 6.3: *Actors of the Comédie-Française*, Jean-Antoine Watteau, 1712. State
Hermitage, St. Petersburg, Getty Images.

To use Nicole's lexicon, because these emotions do not affect us *réellement* (i.e.
in our soul) our 'Christian vigilance' remains unscathed.[51]

Continuing to describe this emotional process, Dubos writes that 'we enjoy
our emotion without being alarmed by the terror that it might last too long . . .
the affliction, one might say, is only on the surface of our heart and we feel
without difficulty that our tears will end with the performance of the ingenious
fiction that caused them to flow'.[52] It is possible that Dubos's take on the
emotions is a legitimate epistemology of the theatrical event – an attempt to
locate and parse the emotions felt during a performance on what he called the
'surface' of our heart, or what we might conceptualize now as a crossroads
between cognition and somatic affect. Or, perhaps Dubos's theory was just a
slippery trick in order to salvage pleasure (and theatre) from the grasp of the
Church. Authorial intent does not matter as much as the effects of the *Reflections*
– a text that influenced a host of more famous Enlightenment writers, including
Voltaire, Diderot and Rousseau. Dubos essentially returned dramatic theory to
the performance and to the emotional experiences of spectators by strengthening

the value of affectivity while at the same time adding a safety net (and a serious thought process) to the act of spectating. Critics could now evaluate a play using relational criteria assessed during the spectator-critic's subjective experience during the event, for this experience was now conceptualized as both mindful *and* emotional.

Dubos breaks with previous theories by moulding the thinking, feeling subject into a centrepiece of aesthetic judgement. As Harris points out, contrary to 'predecessors [who] had typically hypothesized audience responses in order to ratify pre-existing dramatic precepts, Dubos explicitly derives the rules he proposes from reflections on human psychology that stretch far beyond the theatre'.[53] These combinations – theatre and psychology; theatre and learning; emotional response and social amelioration – were the theoretical undergirding for many of the most important theatrical projects of the Enlightenment. During the decades following the publication of Dubos's *Reflections*, a host of dramatic authors employed an aesthetic that they termed *le pathétique*, or *l'effet* or *l'intérêt*.[54] This new dramatic current emerged as a more holistic, more diverse and even more accurate means to treat the emotions. Where there was once an attempt to depict a universally constructed emotion like terror – with its (paradoxically) specific class and poetic requirements – there was now a new emphasis on real spectator affect to dramatic subjects that were thought to resonate more with the public. During the Enlightenment, dramatic authors recognized and sought to influence the public's life that stretched 'far beyond the theatre'.

Authors of tearful comedies, *drames* and other Enlightenment theatrical projects demonstrated heightened concern for the audiovisual event of performance and for the quotidian experiences of real spectators, as opposed to the poetic norms of dramatic tradition. Many productions conceptualized the emotions as relational conduits of learning and pleasure among real subjects, not a mere means to entertain the theoretical, unified public of neoclassical discourse or overwhelm the theatre-going 'sinners' in *theatrephobic* tracts.

Dubos's mindful and pleasurable take on the emotions was thus a theoretical framework for authors to conduct psychological and social experiments with their plays – psychosocial dramatic projects in which new types of characters negotiated new emotional situations, like nostalgia, patriotism and friendship. This emotional regime change helped inaugurate some of the most famous theatrical works of 1720s and 1730s, including Marivaux's experiments on the function of love in society, Houdar de La Motte's sentimental tragedies, Nivelle de La Chaussée's *comédies larmoyantes*, and more. These dramatic works represented the complexities of specific emotional valences and intensities through, among other strategies, increasingly identificatory plots and visual considerations to draw attention to the stage.

This 'psychological turn' witnessed in French theatre during the early Enlightenment set the stage for the French *drame* of the 1750s and 1760s.

Diderot and other Enlightenment writers of the *drame* reinterpreted the role of theatre and the emotions in society. French *philosophes* offered the *drame* as a dramaturgical and social mission which would in turn influence a variety of European theatrical projects, from the theatre of the French Revolution to

FIGURE 6.4: Madame Favart in Pierre de Marivaux's *La Fausse suivante*.
Bibliothèque des arts décoratifs, Paris, Getty Images.

Lessing's bourgeois dramas and experiments in *Sturm und Drang*, Goethe's prose and translation works and Schiller's aesthetic projects, as well as other German publications during late eighteenth and early nineteenth centuries.[55]

More generally, the Enlightenment interpretation of theatre as a venue for emotional learning emerges as an interesting case study in a broader history of affectivity, sentiment and the arts. In his work on the history of emotions,

FIGURE 6.5: Portrait of Jean-Jacques Rousseau, Édouard Lacretelle, 1843. Versailles, Château de Versailles, Getty Images.

William Reddy cautions literary scholars who analyse the representation of emotions from before the advent of modern psychology. Reddy writes that literary historians 'tend to regard ideas about emotions from the past as interesting, even fascinating, configurations to be understood as part of their own time. They have not asked themselves what relation such past ideas have to the "reality" of emotions'.[56] The 'reality' of emotions is certainly a tricky construction, which is why Reddy puts the term in scare quotes. But perhaps the theatre is an experience where we can turn to find moments when a specific culture like France's during the Enlightenment began to conceptualize its discursive limits and uncover processes in which something like a scientific 'nature', rather than religion, superstition or morality, plays a role.

Early-modern writers – *theatrephobes* and *philosophes* alike – reflected on both the innateness of emotional response in theatre as well as on the fact that these powerful moments of affectivity were part of a culturing process. For anti-theatricalists like Nicole and Rousseau, the culture of the stage was harmful to the self, 'useless' to society and even 'dangerous' to the State.[57] For the majority of Enlightenment *philosophes*, however, the theatre was a powerful venue to learn about humankind. Like Cabanis in the late eighteenth century and psychologists, anthropologists and philosophers today, French *philosophes* were attempting to tease out the 'commerce' (to use Locke's term) between nature and nurture. Early-modern 'scientists of man' used theatre to interrogate and describe the complexity of our psyche, and mainly that it includes, just like a theatre performance, both the ephemeral and the planned. This new interpretation of theatre as a place of discovery resulted from a rich debate over affect, cognition and performance; only in this period and place of *theatromania* – the French Enlightenment – could the dramatic arts play such a vital role in the histories of philosophy and psychology.

CHAPTER SEVEN

Communities of Production

Eighteenth-Century Acting Companies

DEBORAH C. PAYNE

Theatre by its very nature is communal: actors, designers, dramatists and stagehands work collectively to mount a play in real time before an audience. Other artistic forms also require mutual effort but their goal is to present a *finished* product to the consumer, not to make collaboration an integral part of the aesthetic experience. Indeed, many forms of art attempt to erase traces of communal endeavour, just as they repress the labour of invention. As we know from the scholarship of Svetlana Alpers, for instance, Rembrandt's studio was a veritable assembly line, with pupils painting specialized bits of the canvas (hands, clouds, drapery).[1] Buyers, however, paid for the completed painting, one supposedly created by the master himself, not to see apprentices churning out their specialization. For Rembrandt's customers, the pleasure inhered in the aesthetically finished product, as is often true of the plastic arts, literature and film. We want to read *Mrs Dalloway*, not watch Virginia Woolf bent over pen and paper, working through successive drafts. We want to hear John Williams' soaring brass anthem for *Star Wars* in its full orchestration, not endure the tedium of sound mixing.

Theatre offers a very different aesthetic experience, the opportunity to see a community of artistic production – as this chapter explores, actors – work collectively towards the creation of an embodied fiction. Actors thus function simultaneously as process and product, as labouring subject and aesthetic object, a complex relationship that requires delicate, ongoing calibration between these different functions. Actors do not mould materials external to themselves; moreover, the all too human bodies that constitute their medium are fragile, motile and emotional, subject to ageing and accidents, outbursts and lapses. Admittedly, paint can fade, marble can chip and film stock dissolve, but these are the effects of time or cataclysms, not an inherent property of the medium itself. Mutability, however, is inherent to acting, a guarantee that every performance will be unique. The wayward performing body makes absolute reproducibility impossible, its glory and its curse. On the one hand, theatre has a purchase on authenticity, unlike, say, Roman knock-offs of Greek statues. A performance might be good, bad or indifferent, but it cannot be forged or reproduced. On the other hand, so common to theatre is the unexpected that we even have a word – improvise – that designates the actor's need to grapple spontaneously with contingencies, such as falling scenery or feckless colleagues. Actors can arrive drunk, forget lines or miss cues. They sometimes run into sets or mishandle props. If bored, they might fall back upon mere recitation, failing to connect emotionally with their dramatic character or the audience. If amused at their own antics, they laugh uncontrollably, breaking the dramatic illusion.

From the early modern period until the Enlightenment, acting companies devised rehearsal techniques and imposed rules intended to harness these structural attributes, especially the fact of the all too volatile and therefore unpredictable human body. Companies sought to inculcate the physical and vocal technique that ensured consistent performances while still allowing for the unexpected brilliant turn. To these ends, fledgling performers were often apprenticed to the company for several years.[2] The English experimented briefly in the late seventeenth century with a 'nursery', a training and performance venue for junior actors.[3] Rehearsals for short plays, afterpieces and farces ran between a week and a fortnight, usually taking place in the mid-morning while actors were still freshly rested. More demanding scripts were accorded a month.[4] An actor usually 'owned' a part until retirement, at which point the successor would be taught the vocal inflections, blocking and stage business associated with the role. Like other joint stock ventures, such as the East India Company, the acting troupe paid shareholders by shares, essentially the division of profits after operating expenses. In France, senior actors received one share, with *débutantes* earning half a share and managers two shares, sometimes more. Apprentices normally received only room and board.[5] Shareholding encouraged collegiality and high standards: if a poor performance ruined the show, then no one was paid. And finally, in an attempt to maintain quality, companies chastised errant actors that showed up late, behaved badly or failed to memorize their lines.

The eighteenth century, nevertheless, ushered in several important changes for this community of production. An overriding belief in humanism, the notion that Europeans shared a core morality that warranted protection through basic freedoms and rights, made for improved conditions for actors. Accordingly, women acquired more authority as managers and star performers, while performers in general, including the infirm and aged, received guarantees beyond the actor's benefit. The period also maintained that *common* [emphasis mine] sense and the impartial voice of reason, both in principle available to every right-minded citizen, would check arbitrary rule and make possible self-governance (this is, after all, the century that ushered in the French and American Revolutions). Thus it should not surprise that, detached from aristocratic patronage, acting companies functioned increasingly as independent entities, both in Europe and in the expanding colonies. Additionally, Jürgen Habermas famously demonstrated how the Enlightenment project depended upon the social spaces and burgeoning print culture that helped citizens not only navigate the tempests of parochialism but also disembark safely on the shores of egalitarianism.[6] Along with coffee houses, salons, galleries and museums, the theatre emerged as one of several spaces of sociability where spectators could acquire the *politesse* essential to an informed, enlightened citizenry. As a consequence, actors were no longer looked upon as vagabonds, servants or artisans, as they had been in the sixteenth and early seventeenth centuries, but as producers of important cultural knowledge, a new social standing that acting companies were eager to exploit.

Nevertheless, as Michel Foucault observes, Enlightenment humanism was not merely the alembic for the distillation of human rights: it also exacted a cost by subjecting people to the hegemonic regimen of a single, universal code of behaviour and imposing various technologies of social control.[7] Like other emergent professions in the period, acting companies increasingly regulated their members with an eye towards producing consistent, professional results. Acting schools, a late eighteenth-century creation, were thought to inculcate in performers a standard of predictability and uniformity that surpassed earlier training techniques. The invention of new positions within the company, such as directors and dramaturgs, points to the perceived need for experts that could reinforce this new sense of professionalization. At the same time, Enlightenment preoccupation with singularity, as seen in the figure of the celebrity, countered the desire for a reproducible, disciplined product. Acting companies responded accordingly, accommodating the demands of stars for higher pay and flexible working conditions while banking on their desirability at the box-office. Thus while acting companies grappled, as always, with the tectonic attributes of their art form, they did so in a way that differed significantly from earlier periods.

SELF-GOVERNANCE AND RIGHTS

Commercial theatre – whereby one paid for the pleasure of seeing actors perform scripted and improvisational plays – is largely a sixteenth-century invention across Western Europe. Frequently likened to prostitutes, also purveyors of pleasure, companies of actors were subjected to various social controls by governments and religious authorities. In an effort to escape ongoing harassment by the city fathers, Shakespeare's company, for instance, moved to the Bankside, out of their legal reach. In their quest for performance space, commercial French companies clashed with the *Confrérie* (or Brotherhood) *de la Passion*, which from 1578 onwards controlled the *Hôtel de Bourgogne*, one of the few available playhouses in Paris. Frequently the *Confrérie* made it impossible for companies to rent alternative venues.[8] Specific legal instruments directed against actors catalysed companies into seeking safeguards; for instance, the 1572 'Acte for the punishment of Vagabonds' reduced players in England to the status of beggars and therefore subject to whipping and branding. Only by turning to powerful aristocrats who lent their name and livery could companies of actors rebrand themselves as 'servants' rather than 'vagabonds'.[9] The possessive case underscores the custodial relationship: acting companies were known as Queen Henrietta's Men, the Lord Chamberlain's Men or Lady Elizabeth's Men, names that signalled the legal protection conferred by influential patrons.

Government regulations also limited the number of acting companies in capitals across Europe and curtailed regional performances. By 1660, for instance, only two companies were licensed to perform in London, while in Paris no more than two or three troupes of actors normally performed at any given time. Travelling players frequently had to apply to regional authorities for a licence that would sanction performance in the local jurisdiction. Regulated too was the composition of the companies. In Protestant countries, actresses – thought to inflame male desire – were kept from the boards until 1655 in Amsterdam and 1660 in London, thus forcing companies to employ boys in female roles. To mitigate allegations of licentiousness, Spanish laws compelled actresses to be married, but the same was true of actors, who were required to have their wives present, even on tour.[10] Families constituted the bulk of performers in Italian *commedia dell'arte* troupes, while in France actors frequently intermarried, a practice that helped to offset allegations of licentiousness by religious and civic authorities.

By the eighteenth century, English companies no longer needed to display their protection by nobility, a change that began in England in 1682 when the King's Company and the Duke's Company combined to form the United Company. From that point onward, acting companies were increasingly associated with place, not patronage, a shift in signification pointing to their gradual detachment from courtly protection and overt government interference. For instance, the company managed by David Garrick from 1747 until 1776 was simply known as Drury Lane, the name of the playhouse and the neighbourhood. The same shift occurred in Italy, as companies of actors once sponsored by learned academies, such as the Sienese *Intronati*, became self-sustaining commercial entities in cities like Milan and Venice. The banishment of well-heeled (and often noble) spectators from the stage and the green room trumpeted another call to independence by companies that sought to exercise more control over performance and rehearsal spaces. Seated on stools in full view of the audience, these spectators occupied the periphery of the stage picture, leaving little room for actors to manoeuvre as they entered and exited. French companies finally succeeded in petitioning the government for their removal in 1759, with English companies following suit in 1762. And no longer did religious and civic authorities have the power to ban companies, forbid actresses or compel employment. English actors in the late seventeenth century, for instance, had to petition the court for permission to leave or change companies, a prohibition that would have been unthinkable a century later.[11] And while both the Comédie-Française and the Comédie-Italienne as state-sponsored companies were technically under the supervision of the Gentlemen of the Chamber, they met weekly to decide upon scripts, assign roles and manage finances without overt government interference. After 1759 weekly deliberations even included *pensionnaires*, yet another indication of gradual democratization.[12]

Nonetheless those very attributes of live performance purveyed by acting companies – sensuality, uniqueness and spontaneity – continued to give governments pause. Perhaps most threatening of all was the capacity of theatre to produce what emotion theorists call 'affect contagion': the catching of feelings as affect leaps from one body to another or, in the case of performance, from actor to spectators. Certainly, the Enlightenment was profoundly interested in the transmission of feeling: the philosopher David Hume, for instance, described how 'others enter into the same humour, and catch the sentiment, by a contagion or natural sympathy'.[13] Revolutionary zeal could potentially prove as 'contagious' as moral uplift among audience members, and various legal instruments, ranging from the English 1737 Licensing Act to the 1752 Act for Regulating Places of Public Entertainment (25 Geo II, c. xxxvi) attempted to curtail the number and ownership of companies to prevent the emotional 'contamination' of spectators. Their juridical reach, however, proved feeble, especially outside London. With backing from the local business community, theatres and acting companies flourished in small cities throughout England, especially in the second half of the century. Only if a witness were willing to bring a complaint could the 1737 Act be enforced; in actuality, the popularity of the acting companies and an incipient sense of provincial rights meant that few were willing to do so.[14] In England nine royal patents alone were granted between 1768 and 1778 to companies in Bath, Norwich, York, Hull, Liverpool, Manchester, Chester, Bristol and Newcastle.[15] In Paris the number of playhouses swelled from three in 1750 to seven by 1789 to accommodate the uptick in acting troupes; over that same period, twenty-seven theatre buildings were constructed in the regions.[16]

The growth in regional companies created management opportunities for women, especially in England. During the Restoration, opportunities were few: Mary Davenant appears to have had some say in the operations of the Duke's Company after her husband William died in 1668, and while the actresses Elizabeth Barry and Anne Bracegirdle helped to establish a new company at Lincoln's Inn Fields in 1695, management largely fell to Thomas Betterton. By contrast, women in the second half of the eighteenth century exercised far more authority in the establishment and running of companies. Tryphosa Butler (née Brockell) established a touring circuit in Yorkshire, eventually co-founding with her husband the Richmond Theatre in 1788, a historical moment when, according to Thomas C. Crochunis, 'new legislation had strengthened the conditions for investment in provincial theatres'.[17] Sarah Baker built the Kentish theatre circuit, travelling the coastal towns of Dover, Canterbury, Rochester and Faversham in the 1770s.[18] Both women used their positions to employ members of their extended families. Outside England as well, women established and managed playhouses: the actress Mrs Ward, for instance, used subscriptions to fund the first purpose-built theatre in Edinburgh in 1746. Even though the West End of London was, according to Tracy C. Davis, 'the toughest market to break into', Frances Brook and her husband John, in concert with Mary Ann and Richard Yates, managed the Haymarket from 1773 to 1778.[19]

Historical change was less pronounced in continental countries such as France, where there was indeed precedent for female management; for instance, in 1643 Madeleine Béjart co-founded with Molière the Illustre Théâtre, the basis for the Comédie-Française, and she appears to have exercised significant control over daily operations. Even in France, however, women could be excluded from having a say in company affairs, especially in the capital. The formal agreement of 1716 drawn up between the actor-manager Luigi Riccoboni and the Comédie-Italienne stipulates that women will 'never have a vote in the assembly and can never make proposals or complaints'.[20] By the mid-century more republican attitudes in keeping with an Enlightenment embrace of self-governance swept away these vestiges of paternalism. Both the Comédie-Française and the Comédie-Italienne moved towards a cooperative, profit-sharing model whereby *all* members of the acting company shared the burden of debt as well as the benefit of profit. Regulations after the 1720s pointedly use the conjunction 'and' in referring to obligations and privileges shared by both sexes.[21]

Perhaps nowhere is the increased autonomy of the Enlightenment acting company more evident than in the troupes that traversed colonies from Jamaica to America. These companies, according to Douglas McDermott, emulated 'the model of social organization with which the United States began: an autonomous group of adults contracting to cooperate for their common good in creating a better version of the culture they had left behind'.[22] Between 1752 and 1776, actors in these colonial troupes were given seasonal contracts to play specific lines of business. The manager, normally the leading actor, was responsible for hiring personnel, determining the repertory, providing scenery, selecting performance spaces and arranging tours. They moved freely from one territory to another, decamping for the Caribbean when economic downturns limited demand for their product in the American colonies. They were, by earlier European standards, utterly independent, answerable only to the contingencies of the local environment. Conditions after the Revolution found expression in additional changes to the colonial acting company. With continental expansion, so did the need arise for additional companies of actors to travel these new circuits. As settlers dispersed over vast territories, 'local interests invariably took precedence over national ones', a change that in turn encouraged the development of specialized acting companies intended to appeal to burgeoning class and regional differences.[23] Demand, however, soon outstripped supply, which in turn meant that the most popular actors were no longer tethered to a single company. Functioning as free agents, these 'stars' now had the clout to demand perquisites and high salaries, a shift in status paralleling the new nation's gradual transition from 'autonomous, self-governing communities in the eighteenth century to industrial entrepreneurship' in the nineteenth.[24]

If Enlightenment notions of self-determination underwrote the gradual detachment of the acting company from courts and learned academies, the humanist principle of rights guaranteed additional protections for performers. In the previous century, actors sometimes received the proceeds of a benefit performance just prior to retirement; they could also be awarded compensation for work-related injuries. The prompter John Downes, for instance, reports how the actor Philip Cademan was '[u]nfortunately, with a sharp Foil pierc'd near the Eye, which so Maim'd both his Hand and his Speech, that he can make little use of either; for which Mischance, he has receiv'd a Pension ever since 1673, being 35 Years a goe'.[25] Compensation, however, appears to be largely ad hoc in the early modern period, with the acting company deciding individual cases on the basis of merit or available resources. By the mid-eighteenth century, benefit performances for actors became much more frequent; additionally, reformers in England – following the precedent of the Decay'd Musicians Fund – devised in 1759 a 'scheme to relieve infirm players' along with a proposed home for indigent actors.

Initially deemed 'too grandiose for prospective subscribers', the scheme eventually came to fruition in December of 1765 'when Drury Lane and Covent Garden both founded, within ten days of each other, funds intent on meeting similar objectives'.[26] The actor Robert Baddeley deeded a country house to the fund that would become a 'Theatrical Asylum' for infirm and elderly actors.[27]

Similar charitable projects soon followed in Bath and Norwich. Seven years of work entitled actors to an annuity for life if enfeebled by age or illness, an extraordinarily generous benefit by modern standards. The fund also covered medical expenses, drugs, annuities for widows and children, and even funeral expenses. By 1776 the Covent Garden Fund was incorporated by Royal Charter, while the Drury Lane Fund was promulgated as an Act of Parliament, locating, as David Worrall observes, 'both of these institutions among the beginnings of modern British workplace welfare legislation'.[28] In France, the 'act of association' drawn up in 1758 by the Comédie-Française guaranteed actors an income of 1,000 *livres* annually after twenty years of service. If, however, they were judged 'indispensable' to the company, actors were required to serve for another ten years; in return, they would enjoy an increased yearly pension of 1,500 *livres*.[29]

THE THEATRE AND SOCIABILITY

Jürgen Habermas's enormously influential theory of the 'public sphere' has drawn attention to the coffee houses, newspapers, Masonic lodges, salons and academic societies that functioned as real and virtual spaces for the discussion of civic issues, thereby allowing citizens to fashion themselves as rational Enlightenment subjects.

The same was true of the Enlightenment playhouse, a highly charged public space in which acting companies could stage embodied stories that allowed spectators to 'try on', emotionally and intellectually, the exciting new ideas bubbling up from the deep springs of Enlightenment thought. Tragedies such as Joseph Addison's *Cato* (1712) questioned absolutist politics, while Voltaire's *Le fanatisme, ou Mahomet le Prophète* (1736) interrogated religious fanaticism. Comedies such as John Gay's *The Beggar's Opera* (1728) satirized class divisions, while Pierre Beaumarchais's *Le Mariage de Figaro* (1781–4) extolled the virtues of companionate over aristocratic marriage, a thinly veiled allegory for republicanism trumping monarchy. Audiences reacted to new works with whistles, applause, cheers, catcalls and loud interruptions, and acting companies responded accordingly in this dynamic, volatile space. Violent disapproval could force companies to modify or even eliminate a play from the repertory. The infamous *Chinese Festival* riots of 1755 at Drury Lane, for instance, reveal the extent to which the London theatre, according to Heather McPherson, 'had become a highly politicized cultural battlefield, which was implicated in broader struggles over national identity and the imperialist project'.[30] Class warfare erupted when members of the nobility leapt into the pit to seize the lower-class ringleaders that had organized opposition to this imported chinoiserie-style balletic extravaganza. As Figure 7.1 illustrates, spectators even rioted over admission prices, climbing onto the stage to stop the performance. In the French playhouse, the *parterre*, the space immediately in front of the stage,

Riot at Covent Garden Theatre, in 1763, in consequence of the Managers refusing to admit half-price in the Opera of Artaxerxes.

FIGURE 7.1: *Riot at Covent Garden Theatre*, 1763. Harry R. Beard Collection, given by Isobel Beard © Victoria and Albert Museum, London.

was renowned for loud, often boisterous public criticism, as well as vocal exchange between actors and spectators. Indeed, the word came to designate both the space and the people who occupied it.

Theatrical spaces like the *parterre* not only played an important role in fashioning a national identity but also in educating people 'how to refine their opinions and insert them into a public discourse critical of the artistic endeavours they witnessed'.[31] The acting companies, of course, facilitated this ongoing public discourse, sometimes to their detriment when audience disapproval halted the production. Above all else, the *parterre* represents the quintessentially Enlightenment belief that aesthetic judgement was available to anyone, performer and spectator alike, willing to submit the vagaries of personal taste to the test of reason. No longer were aesthetic distinctions the exclusive purview of intellectual, landed and moneyed elites; rather, as Jean-Baptiste Dubos observed in 1733, '[w]ith the help of their internal instincts, all men can tell, without knowing the rules, whether artistic works are good or bad . . . Without knowing the rules, the *parterre* judges a theatrical work just as well as those in the business of the theatre'.[32] Moreover, unlike reading – increasingly by the eighteenth century a solitary endeavour – the ability of the acting company to present a collaborative aesthetic experience that was both finished product and ongoing process encouraged an immediate emotional response from the audience. Hans Ulrich Gumbrecht argues that performance surpasses reading in teaching people how to exercise judgement 'because the theatrical experience much more closely approximates everyday experience than does the act of reading alone'.[33]

The acting company was instrumental to replicating 'everyday experience' in the playhouse and therefore productive of the new Enlightenment citizen. No longer mere vagabonds or servants to the crown, actors participated in civic discourse, literally giving voice to characters that challenged the *Ancien Régime* or openly satirized religious hypocrisy. Moreover, the very structural attributes of performance once eyed nervously by governments – sensuality, immediacy and unpredictability – transformed playhouse space into an especially potent site for the mutual exploration of daring ideas and subversive opinions by actors and audiences alike. As Tiffany Stern notes, spectators by mid-century were 'involved more in "dramatic collusion" than dramatic illusion'.[34] Actors accordingly reacted visibly to boisterous commentary from the *parterre*, the pit or the upper galleries, sometimes favouring certain segments of the audience. The English actor Richard Yates, for instance, leaned over the orchestra to declaim his speeches directly to the pit, even in scenes involving dialogue with other characters.[35] Moreover, the practice of treating the first performance as a rehearsal – and therefore subject to revision – intensified an already emotionally fraught relationship between the acting company and the audience. The theatre manager and playwright Richard Brinsley Sheridan described in the preface to his 1778 comedy, *The Rivals*, his habit of treating 'a First Night's Audience, as a candid and judicious friend attending, in behalf of the Public, at his last Rehearsal'.[36] Friends, however, are liable to level criticism as well as approval, and spectators sometimes treated players with a familiarity that seems astonishing by modern standards, an intimacy the actors readily reciprocated. The audience, for instance, insisted upon an onstage apology from the actor Samuel Reddish, when he forgot to show up one evening for a performance; finally, satisfied with his 'truly pitiable' looks, they forgave him. By the same token, the actress Mrs Bellamy stopped her performance as Juliet to demand an apology from an audience member that had laughed just as she was about to swallow poison.[37]

If the acting company by dint of the inherent dynamism of eighteenth-century performance space shaped civic discourse to an unparalleled degree, so did individual actors mould social change offstage as well. The actor Jean-Marie Collot d'Herbois supported the French Revolution, contributing to the first constitution written for the new republic; Sheridan became a member of parliament; the American Revolutionary War commander John Paul Jones performed with the David Douglass company in Jamaica during his youth; and Guillaume-Antoine Nourry (known by his stage name of 'Grammont') served in the National Guard during the first two years of the Revolution while simultaneously performing at the Théâtre Français. By 1793 he would serve as adjutant-general on the staff of Charles-Philippe Ronsin, the newly appointed Brigadier General. So closely associated was the Comédie-Française troupe with insurgency that pamphlets printed just after the outbreak of the Revolution 'defended the troupe by representing the Comédiens as the true revolutionaries under attack by self-interested, entrepreneurial theatre managers and a self-serving *corps* of authors'.[38]

That unprecedented social fluidity, whereby actors were able to move between the theatre and other spaces of the public sphere, also showed in the intellectual networks of the 'Republic of Letters', an Enlightenment concept that not only encompassed formal institutions but also the informal meeting of minds, whether in print or in person. David Garrick, for instance, numbered among the literary luminaries, such as Samuel Johnson and James Boswell, that formed the Royal Society of Arts in 1754. The extraordinary reach of his correspondence reveals access to artistic and intellectual circles that expanded steadily over his lifetime. Indeed, by the time Garrick and his wife embarked upon a two-year grand tour in 1763 (Figure 7.2), he was lionized abroad by expat English aristocrats; Italian and French actors, including the famous *La Clairon*, the dramatist Burette de Belloy; the internationally renowned

FIGURE 7.2: *A Caricature Group in Florence*, Thomas Patch, 1765/6. This oil on canvas depicts the actor David Garrick on his Grand Tour of 1763–4. By permission of the Royal Albert Memorial Museum, Exeter, Devon, UK/Bridgeman Images.

philosopher and *encyclopédiste* Denis Diderot; and the respected historian Jean-François Marmontel, also a member of the *encyclopédiste* movement. Despite his grave misgivings about English tragedy, Voltaire regretted never meeting the actor who was arguably the paramount interpreter of Shakespeare in the eighteenth century. As a point of comparison, early modern philosophers, such as Michel de Montaigne and Francis Bacon never to our knowledge expressed the desire to know actors; indeed, one is hard-pressed to imagine either man deigning to make the acquaintance of a mere 'player'. Even the emergent discipline of the natural sciences welcomed performers, who contributed to print publications, scientific societies and nascent museum collections. The German actor and playwright Ferdinand Ochsenheimer developed a keen interest in lepidopterology at the close of the eighteenth century, publishing studies while actively performing in Berlin and Vienna. His collection of 3,772 specimens went to the Hungarian National Museum. The career of Karl Ludwig Giesecke is especially exemplary of the social fluidity of the Enlightenment actor: a performer, a translator (he translated the libretti of *Le Nozze de Figaro* and *Cosi fan Tutte* into German), a poet and a stage manager, he joined Mozart's Masonic lodge, ultimately leaving the stage to become a well-known mineralogist.

STATUS AND CELEBRITY

Nowhere is the change in the status of the acting company more evident than in their apotheosis from suspect outlaws to arbiters of good taste, which, like aesthetic judgement, was no longer the domain of the aristocracy. Ambitious merchants and citizens' wives could read novels and peruse instruction manuals with an eye towards acquiring the manners that distinguished the arriviste from old money, but the acting company's ability to mimic, in the words of Gumbrecht, 'everyday experience' rendered it an especially powerful site for modelling suitable speech and deportment. As recent social history has documented, the eighteenth century was a period of rising consumption, and anyone with enough money could acquire luxury goods like fine porcelain or a silk dress.[39] Proper use of these expensive objects, however, had to be learned. Companies painstakingly trained actors in the subtle gestures and vocal intonations that marked class distinctions. During performance actors showed audiences how to take snuff correctly, how to handle a fan and how to make polite conversation. The desire to see acting companies model good taste was especially keen in colonial outposts, where most people did not have access to the traditional European spaces of sociability, such as the salons, drawing rooms or academies that taught gentility. Most colonials looked instead to playhouses in Charleston, Dublin or Williamsburg to learn comportment and speech, a social desire that acting companies were quick to exploit. According to Odai

Johnson, the American theatre manager David Douglass 'strategically positioned his theatres as finishing schools for acquiring gentility'.[40]

Perhaps it should not surprise that one of the leading elocutionists of the period, Thomas Sheridan (and father of Richard Brinsley, the playwright), was himself a colonial and a man of the theatre. Hailing originally from Dublin, where he managed the Smock Alley playhouse, Sheridan would subsequently earn good money teaching Scots and Irish merchants how to speak like their English betters, an endeavour that bespoke egalitarian ends well beyond the commonplace desire for upward mobility. His influential *A Course of Lectures on Elocution* (1762) linked the state of the English language to the state of the culture; for Sheridan, as Dana Harrington argues, a corrupt language 'reflects a less democratic, less "civil" society'.[41] To acquire the proper British speech conducive to democracy, Sheridan especially advocated observing actors, 'whose profession it is, to speak from memory, the sentiments of others, and yet to deliver them, as if they were the result of their own immediate feelings'.[42] John Rutledge, who would become the second Chief Justice of the American Supreme Court, concurred with Sheridan's recommendation: 'I know of nothing more entertaining and more likely to give you a graceful manner of speaking than seeing a good play well acted'.[43] Thus in the colonies especially can be detected the evolution of acting companies from dangerous entities to bastions of culture. Tellingly, between 1758 and 1775 nineteen new theatres were built in America and the anglophone Caribbean. Most colonial outposts had playhouses long before they had hospitals, and citizens that balked at paying taxes for roads were more than happy to support a resident or touring company.[44]

The very sites of sociability that gave rise to the status of the acting company also made possible the creation of the celebrity, largely an eighteenth-century invention. Star actors have always been idolized for the ineffable quality – what Joseph Roach calls 'it' – that allowed them to display 'the power of apparently effortless embodiment of contradictory qualities simultaneously: strength *and* vulnerability, innocence *and* experience, and singularity *and* typicality among them'.[45] Accordingly, acting companies accommodated star performers that could transmute these idiosyncratic qualities into a box-office draw. The Enlightenment fascination with 'genius', however, fetishized star performers like Sarah Siddons or *La Clairon* to an unprecedented degree, putting them on par with poets and painters. Originally signifying a protective spirit that ruled over men or places, 'genius' by the mid-century designated, according to Samuel Johnson's *Dictionary* (1755), 'a man endowed with superior faculties'. Geniuses by definition were extraordinary: men and women possessed of an original turn of mind or an inspired, unique artistic ability. That these phenomenal individuals would captivate audiences in a culture that increasingly extolled singularity goes without saying. The public sphere of print, especially the burgeoning realm of 'cheap print', such as newspapers and magazines, also made possible an unprecedented degree of obsessive devotion. Unmoored from the dynamism of the playhouse, static images of actors now peered out from book illustrations and engraved prints. Affordable commodities, such as fans, playing cards and china, also contributed to the circulation of celebrity images, with actors forever memorialized in silk, glossy paper or Meissen porcelain, this last seen in the figurine of the actor Kitty Clive (Figure 7.3). If illustrations and material objects provided consumers with access to an idealized exterior of actors, magazine

FIGURE 7.3: Bow porcelain factory figure of the actress Kitty Clive as 'Mrs Riot' in David Garrick's farce, *Lethe*, *c.*1750. Digital image by permission of the Fitzwilliam Museum, Cambridge.

articles and biographies held forth the prospect of understanding an interiority that might explain the exceptionality of the star performer.

The advent of the celebrity also signals a change in economic relations within the acting company: functioning as free agents, star performers could command top-tier fees and move freely between troupes. An uptick in benefit performances also increased their financial worth significantly: one benefit yielded the equivalent of at least one month's salary, if not two. David Garrick's estate was valued at £100,000 at his death, well over £12 million in modern terms. Audiences were ambivalent, however, about the earning power of celebrities. Newspapers ran five to ten notices a day of upcoming benefits; they also reported box-office receipts. Advertised locations for the sale of benefit tickets 'typically included the actor's home address and various shops and coffee houses'.[46] Audiences thus knew about the most intimate details of the lives of celebrities, such as their earnings and residence; indeed, the very mechanism of print that disseminated their presence beyond the playhouse also blurred the lines between their public and private personas, sometimes with uncomfortable results. On the one hand, audiences wanted celebrities to be aloof, superior and altogether deserving of their stardom. On the other hand, the publication of personal information and the circulation of their images promoted an illusion of familiarity – of social equity – upon which spectators could project their own fantasies of upward mobility.

As Joseph Roach points out, the circulation of these celebrity images 'in the absence of their persons . . . came at the price of an equally inflated notoriety'.[47] Celebrity actresses especially struggled to negotiate these tensions, and they were often subject to hypersexualized representations in the popular press. Even society portrait painters like Joshua Reynolds mapped an eroticized intimacy onto his thespian subjects, as seen in his canvas of 'Frances Abington as "Miss Prue" in Congreve's *Love for Love*' (Figure 7.4). Abington boldly returns the viewer's gaze, her eyes knowing and her left thumb resting suggestively on slightly parted lips. Seated on a chair turned backwards, she leans into the space with ease, her lap dog snuggled amorously at her waist. The portrait at once evinces familiarity and distance, the promise of sexual access countered by the sitter's social authority as indicated by her expensive dress and the moody, overcast sky over her left shoulder, a backdrop more in keeping with a religious hermit than an eighteenth-century actress. Celebrities such as Abington capitalized on the inherent ambiguity in their social status, vacillating from onstage tease (she originated the role of Lady Teazle in Sheridan's *The School for Scandal*) to fashion trendsetter. The 'Abington cap' was much copied by female spectators, as were her flowing gowns, gossamer confections dangerously close to *negligées*.[48] Other actresses, such as Sarah Siddons, fashioned themselves as domesticated wives and mothers in an attempt to shape the public discourse surrounding female celebrity.[49] For most performers, however, the technologies of reproduction that enabled prominence also

FIGURE 7.4: The actress Frances Abington as 'Miss Prue' in William Congreve's *Love for Love*, 1770.

functioned paradoxically to reduce them to the frozen albeit singular image at odds with the inherent dynamism of their craft.

FROM CRAFT TO PROFESSION

The Enlightenment, as the philosopher Michel Foucault has shown, saw the emergence of the natural sciences and modern medicine, and while these disciplines are usually extolled for representing advances in human thought, their deployment of scientific 'neutrality' also functioned as a technology of social control, a theme he was to explore in successive works.[50] The shift, for instance, from midwifery to obstetrics excluded women from assisting in childbirth and imposed on physicians strict standards that combined observation with normalization. Acting companies underwent a similar transformation as they evolved from the scrappy guilds of the early modern period to large, highly regulated modern entities. Training shifted from the individualized apprenticeship system that had dominated English training or the in-house coaching that had typified the continental company. Increasingly deemed insufficient, these methods were by mid-century replaced by schools where pupils could be observed, corrected and examined in accordance with standardized principles. The actor Conrad Ekhof founded an acting academy in Schwerin, Germany in 1753, while Catherine II ('the Great') established the Imperial Theatre School in St. Petersburg for the training of Russian actors, dancers and singers.[51] The Comédie-Française established a Royal Dramatic School soon after, in 1786 (renamed the Conservatoire after the Revolution), with other Western European countries soon following suit.

Acting companies have always used training to encourage consistent performances; by the mid-eighteenth century, they additionally used coercive discipline, fines and punishment to standardize acceptable behaviour. This shift away from external oversight (i.e. royal or civic injunctions) to self-regulation bespeaks another Foucauldian theme, namely how the early modern exercise of power by 'law, rule, or sovereign will' was replaced by 'the mechanics of the coercive forces whose exercise takes a disciplinary form'.[52] The constitution for the acting academy founded by Ekhof, for instance, stipulated meetings every two weeks; 'rational' research into 'the characters and roles' of plays under consideration, and 'critical observations on the plays and their performance . . . as well as ideas as to how various errors have occurred [which] can be eradicated or corrected'. Intoxication was prohibited, as was 'unbalanced reason'.[53] The detailed instructions issued by the Board of Directors for the Danish Royal Theatre in 1754 demanded that actors uphold 'decency' and alert the Director if they detect in a play 'expressions offensive to modesty and good manners'. Further stipulated were length and frequency of rehearsals, time frames for memorizing parts, and even permissible moments for loitering in the green room.[54] Regulations for the Royal Dramatic Company of Sweden were even more stringent, fining actors 'for failure to learn half one's part by the first rehearsal, and one's whole part by the second'.[55] The regulations laid down in 1766 by Tadeusz Lipski for the National Theatre of Poland were perhaps the most comprehensive of all, levelling fines for every conceivable infraction, ranging from picking a quarrel with a fellow actor (four red zlotys) to improvisation (one red zloty) to contradicting the director (arrest or loss of half a month's salary) to participating 'in a drinking bout in town' (punished by 'a fine or arrest according to the gravity of his delinquency').[56]

The invention of specialists, such as the director and the dramaturg, within the company also spoke to the perceived need to transform actors from idiosyncratic individuals into social subjects requiring oversight and training. As occurred in other fields, experts emerged as part of an ensemble of discursive practices, which included regulation and knowledge, that could not only control but also render predictable large numbers of people. By the 1770s, the Comédie-Française had expanded to fifty actors and the Comédie-Italienne to seventy. In England, companies more than doubled, going from thirty-five to forty actors in 1660 to eighty by 1800.[57] Also swelling enormously in ranks were the support staff, the stagehands, dressers, laundresses, ticket takers, dancers, musicians, prompters, scene painters and even candle snuffers that in turn necessitated the specialists that would bring order to these burgeoning organizations. Additionally, the invention of the director and the dramaturg were essential to constituting acting as a disciplinary field of specialized knowledge that now required experts to complete tasks that were once commonly shared amongst actors. Prior to the Enlightenment, plays were produced without directors. Instead, a stage manager or a lead actor (often the same person) supervised rehearsals, and actors learnt their roles without directors giving line readings or providing interpretations of the script. While it would be another 150 years before the director functioned as the *auteur* now common in companies such as the National Theatre of Great Britain, figures such as David Garrick in England and Johann Wolfgang von Goethe in Germany certainly worked towards an unprecedented coherence of style and effect. Goethe, for instance, instituted longer rehearsals, emphasized the proper speaking of verse and inaugurated ensemble acting. No longer would actors simply play their accustomed 'lines' as in the early modern period; instead, even leading performers at the Weimar Court Theatre were expected to subordinate their desire for star roles to the larger interest of achieving a harmonious whole.[58] And, finally, the invention of specialists and the normalization of company behaviour ensured the sanctity of the theatre as a bourgeois space, a respectable forum for the interrogation of middle-class ideas. When Gotthold Ephraim Lessing was engaged as adviser, critic and dramaturg to the newly inaugurated Hamburg National Theatre in 1767, his mission in large part, as the opening night prologue states, was 'to succor the state to transform the angry, wild man / Into a human being, citizen, friend and patriot'.[59]

Manuals and acting theory were also constitutive of the specialized knowledge now shoring up the newly professionalized company. Prior to 1700, one is hard-pressed (in the West, at any rate) to find any meaningful study of acting, one of the reasons we know so little about early modern performance practices other than the odd comment. So desperate for information are Shakespeareans, for instance, that Hamlet's famous Speech to the Players is frequently taken uncritically as evidence of Elizabethan acting technique.[60] Even mid-seventeenth century commentators on the theatre, such as François Hédelin, abbé d'Aubignac, and John Dryden, concerned themselves largely with questions of dramatic form, not acting. By the mid-eighteenth century, however, treatises on acting flood bookshops and fill the pages of journals, treating this erstwhile craft as a 'science'. Accordingly, commentators such as Aaron Hill, who assembled the pieces he wrote for the *Prompter* into a single volume, *Essay on the Art of Acting* (1753), explore at length the psychology of acting rather than simply describing technique, an approach also taken up by Diderot in his famous *Le Paradoxe sur le comédien* (*The Paradox of Acting*), written between 1773 and 1777. These theorists attempt to explain the dynamics of performance: did actors move audiences by imitation or experience? Did an actor playing Hamlet have to feel the prince's melancholy himself – or was it sufficient to have witnessed instances of melancholy, which could then be reproduced in performance? According to Diderot, the actor managed to be the character while still remaining in control of technique, the 'paradox' of his title. Actors even theorized themselves and their practice, as did other artists increasingly in the eighteenth century: the great French actress *La Clairon* published her reflections in *Mémoires d'Hyppolite Clairon et réflexions sur l'art dramatique* (1798). She reminds readers of the fallibility of the medium – the actor's body and voice – as well as the exhausting effects of performance. *La Clairon*, as Jeffrey M. Leichman points out, rejected the study of nature, preferring instead the examination of historical, cultural and personal circumstances when creating a dramatic character: 'A true Enlightenment actress, Clairon's belief in the perfectibility of her craft reflects broader trends in the history of performance'.[61]

No longer defined by the caste system that had dominated every aspect of European life, an illegitimate girl like *La Clairon*, 'by dint of study, observation, determination – and acting', was welcomed into royal courts and analysed by philosophers.[62] As a point of contrast, the skill of early modern actresses such as Nell Gwyn (another performer of illegitimate origins) may have caught the eye of nobility, but sexual availability, not self-invention, ultimately secured their upward mobility. *La Clairon* exercised control over her career, moving between the provinces and Paris and between autonomous performance and company membership. Her memoir additionally captures the intellectual fluidity of the late eighteenth-century actor: a mainstay of the Comédie-Française, she nonetheless corresponded with Diderot, Marmontel and Voltaire and frequented the salons of Mmes Geoffrin and Necker.[63] Perhaps, above all else, we can glimpse in *La Clairon*'s observations on her art the transformation of the acting company from a guild protective of its trade secrets to a profession openly examined, weighed and dissected in the public sphere. The late seventeenth-century actor Thomas Betterton learned the role of Hamlet in a manner that typifies artisanal craft: from the theatre manager William Davenant, who had 'seen Mr. *Taylor* of the *Black-Fryars* Company Act it, who being Instructed by the Author Mr. *Shakespear*'.[64] *La Clairon*, however, opens to public scrutiny every aspect of her art, putting on display her finely honed technique and emphasizing throughout the 'superhuman force to *act well* in tragedy for more than ten years'.[65] Her memoir, published at the close of the century, incarnates the transformation of the acting company and its members from artisans purveying forbidden pleasure to producers of the specialized knowledge that increasingly came to typify the Enlightenment project.

CHAPTER EIGHT

Repertoire and Genres

Cultural Logics and the Trick of Theatrical Longevity

LISA A. FREEMAN

On her very first night in London and much to her youthful delight, the eponymous heroine of Frances Burney's *Evelina* (1778) finds herself at the Theatre Royal Drury Lane where she witnesses a performance of Benjamin Hoadly's *The Suspicious Husband* featuring the greatest actor of the age, David Garrick, in one of his signature roles as Ranger.[1] Much of Burney's novel is given over to Evelina's first encounters with, and gradual acculturation to, the many 'gaieties of London life' and amidst the swirl of balls, ridottos, operas and puppet shows, promenades on the Mall in St James during the day and visits to Marylebone and Ranelagh Gardens in the evenings, we come to understand that the playhouses of London were embedded in an extraordinarily competitive, commercial marketplace devoted to supplying public diversions.[2]

Burney's decision to send Evelina to the theatre on her first night in London, rather than to one of the many other places of public amusement, signals the pre-eminent status of the playhouse as a cultural and social site. Perhaps even more conspicuously, Evelina's confusion over the other roles in the play and her 'raptures' over Garrick's performance – 'Such ease! such vivacity in his manner! such grace in his motions! such fire and meaning in his eyes . . . every look *speaks*!'[3] – make it clear to us that it was Garrick himself rather than the comedy in question that was the main attraction of the extended evening. New as she was to the London scene, Evelina had not yet had the chance either to form a developed sense of the repertory or to cultivate a concomitant storehouse of theatrical memories; but other playgoers – both fictional and real – not only would have had the expectation that they would see their favourite actors in their signature roles year after year but would also take great pleasure and sometimes experience great dismay when they compared current performances to the memories of performances past. Their knowledge of the stage business and their anticipation of the dramaturgical vocabularies enacted played a major role in shaping the repertory and in securing its reception.[4]

Evelina's other featured venture to the playhouse to see William Congreve's *Love for Love* marks a different aspect of the repertory and the cultural salience of its various genres over the course of the long eighteenth century. First produced at Lincoln's Inn Fields in 1695, and more successful in its time than *The Way of the World* for which Congreve is now better known, this witty comedy of intrigue and manners features such plot elements as seduction, cuckoldry and marriage under false pretences, all of which would have been considered risqué content by the more respectable among the middling sort by the mid-eighteenth century. Thus, in her remarks on *Love for Love* for the British Theatre series, actress, playwright and novelist Elizabeth Inchbald somewhat prudishly observed,

> Were the characters in "Love for Love" as natural, and as edifying as they are witty, it would be a perfect composition: but the conversation of so many of the persons of this drama is either so immoral, or so tinctured with their occupations and propensities, that no such people now exist, and it is to be supposed, never, at any period, existed.[5]

Such admonishments speak to the ideals of female modesty that reigned in this period, and Evelina's mortified reaction to what she terms the 'extremely indelicate' action is meant to be read as an index of her feminine attainments and innocent virtue. That Evelina and her female companion Miss Mirvan were 'perpetually out of countenance, and could neither make any observations [them]selves, nor venture to listen to those of others', and that the brutish Captain Mirvan mocks them for not finding the comedy 'sentimental enough'[6] illustrates not only the relative constrictions on female conduct that had been instituted by this time but also captures for us the extent to which, while theatrical tastes and fashions changed over time, plays of an earlier age nevertheless persisted in the repertory, providing occasions for deep excursions into theatrical memory and reflecting lingering or emergent cultural sensibilities, as each new generation encountered and responded to dramatic productions of the past. Thus, even Inchbald concedes that, 'when all the imperfections of "Love for Love" are summed up, there still remains a balance of entertainment so delectable, that it pleases at the present era as it did at the past, and will continue its attractions as long as wit, or a theatre shall charm'.[7]

In this chapter, I explore the cultural work performed by the eighteenth-century repertoire both in its retention and adaptation of past 'delectations', and as it grew to accommodate new genres, new works and new tastes. For this endeavour, the English playhouse of the long eighteenth century provides us with a unique set of conditions for mapping how a repertory might be formed and transformed, as the Restoration in 1660 marked not just the reinstauration of the Stuart monarchy but also the reopening of the London playhouses after their closure in 1642 as England descended into Civil War. The eighteen-year public hiatus in dramatic productions meant that theatre practitioners of the late seventeenth century had not only to grapple with a dramaturgical past whose social and political preoccupations stood at an unevenly disjoint distance from the present but also to begin to shape a repertory that would address contemporary concerns and generate a new vision of theatrical posterity. A commercial as well as an artistic endeavour, the London repertory in this period is thus marked both by a desire to innovate and by an interest in articulating a dramatic genealogy, especially evident in the elevation of Shakespeare as the premiere English playwright, that would underwrite a sense of the theatre's essential role in the formation and maintenance of a distinctively English national identity. As much as we might be tempted, then, to organize a cultural history of Enlightenment theatre with an eye toward a steady progression into the future, the repertoire and the generic structures of which it is comprised teach us to look backwards for the recursive influences of dramatic lineages and performance genealogies. To illustrate this point over the course of this chapter, I will look repeatedly to the following critical questions in the English case, though they are equally applicable to the development of theatre on the continent: How was the repertoire at once both sustained over time through the persistence and perseverance of particular works and transformed over time by generic and structural innovations? And how did the business practices of the acting companies shape the repertoire experience of actors and audiences to produce a keen sense of theatrical culture and an indelible awareness of theatrical history? By approaching the London stage as an exemplar for these practices and by attending to the particular cultural interests that shape these developments, we will find our way to a more dynamic and enlivened understanding of the history of the theatre in this period.

REPERTORY AND THE BUSINESS OF THE STAGE

To reopen the playhouses in 1660, Charles II issued royal patents to perform plays to two holdovers from the pre-Civil War theatrical scene: Thomas Killigrew, who was to preside over the King's Company; and Sir William Davenant who was to hold sway over the Duke's Company. To set the playhouses in motion, the king simply divided the pre-war repertory, which had remained popular in print despite the closure of the theatres, and gave each company the exclusive right to produce the plays that were in their grant.[8] The dramatic repertoire for 1660/1 was thus made up entirely of plays from the pre-Civil War era and was dominated in particular by the plays of Beaumont and Fletcher, whose works had been published in a folio edition in 1647.[9] Killigrew and Davenant, however, both understood the potential commercial value of novelty, and they were quite eager to introduce new plays to the stage that would reflect their close ties to the monarch and his court, celebrating the libertine ethos of Cavalier life abroad in comedies and delving in heroic dramas into the fraught political concerns of the day including the status of sovereignty, the locus of authority and the right to rule.[10] In the 1661/2 season, fifty-four of the plays produced came from the pre-Restoration period and four were entirely new, but by the 1667/8 season, more momentum had been gained, with only thirty-three plays from the pre-Restoration period and twenty from the contemporary era, twelve of which were entirely new for that season.[11] Still, even as new playwrights such as John Dryden, George Etherege, Aphra Behn, William Congreve, George Farquhar, Nicholas Rowe and Susannah Centlivre came to prominence, the London stages continued to be dominated by works of authors from the earlier periods. Of the 192 nights that made up the 1740/1 season at Drury Lane, for instance, eighty-five of those nights were devoted to a mainpiece performance of one of Shakespeare's plays.[12]

The business interests and practices of the playhouse managers exerted a tremendous influence over the repertoire and its variety. When falling revenues compelled the King's Company to merge with the Duke's Company to form the United Company in 1682, innovation came almost to a standstill, as without competition there was nothing to motivate the development and production of new plays. When Thomas Betterton led a revolt against manager Christopher Rich in 1695 and convinced many of the best players to join him in forming a new company at Lincoln's Inn Fields, the need to compete suddenly became quite high. Thus where the 1683/4 season saw only four new plays, the 1695/6 season saw an explosion of new works with no fewer than twenty-five.[13] Similarly, in the politically and theatrically raucous years leading up to the passage of the 1737 Stage Licensing Act, when competition among the many large and small theatre companies was fierce, there was a dramatic increase in the number of new plays. Once the theatre scene was limited again by that legislative act to the two patent houses, the number of new plays in a season was greatly reduced and there was a pronounced shift to the relative safety of stock plays in the repertory.[14]

Betterton's initial success in forming a new company suggests the power that an actor of great prominence could wield on the stages of the long eighteenth century. Indeed many critics have deemed the period the age of the actor, with playwrights playing a much less significant artistic and economic role. Actors were hired into companies in accordance with their line of business – first tragic actor, second tragic actor, first comic actress, etc. – and once they took on a role, it was considered their property until they chose to resign the part. Given these arrangements, playwrights could tailor their plays to the strengths of particular actors in a company and expect those star players to appear in those roles for years to come. Audience members who were familiar with the workings of each theatre and its repertoire could confidently guess at the type of the play they would witness based on the actors listed in a playbill, and managers or actors who frustrated those expectations, either by flouting generic expectations or by playing against type, did so at their peril.

Over the course of a season, a leading or supporting actor or actress might perform in as many as forty to fifty different parts. Except in the case of an extraordinary hit, audiences expected a different play to be mounted every night; and managers rotated the stock productions in and out of the repertory that would play best to the histrionic talents of their company. A play might appear once in the first weeks of the season and then a few weeks later or not again until the last few weeks of the season; indeed, it might not appear again at all. As a result of this practice, 'ranking performers face[d] a nightly change of bill which obligated them to retain innumerable stock parts, learn their lines in forthcoming new or revived plays, [and] rehearse in the morning the play for that night as well as a forthcoming drama'.[15] Their resilience under this regimen was remarkable and far surpasses anything we would expect of actors in our own age.

London seasons generally ran from September to May or early June, and managers usually opened the season with stock plays that not only would draw audiences back to the theatres after a summer hiatus but would also require the return to London of a large number of their company members, who would have dispersed to the provincial and fairground acting circuits over the summer.[16] New plays were rarely offered before November, so the first months of the season would consist almost entirely of stock favourites and revivals of plays that may have fallen out of fashion but that managers thought might inspire new interest. By December, the theatrical and social season was in full swing, with managers offering the largest number of new plays in January and February. March marked the beginning of what was known as benefit season, performances of plays that were especially selected by actors or actresses in the company who received a share of the house proceeds for that evening. Benefits for actors and for other members of the company would run on select nights through the rest of the season and along with command performances – performances of plays offered at the particular importunity of a member of the royal family – could have a remarkable impact on the content of the repertory. To draw the largest possible audience and thus increase their income, star actors usually chose one of their signature roles, thus ensuring the retention of certain plays in the stock repertory. New and ambitious actors in pursuit of a breakthrough performance that would elevate their status on the boards might select a role in a play in which the reigning stars had made their marks.

Over the years, audiences would develop a fine-tuned sense of an actor and the particular combination of gestures and intonations he or she might employ in a particular role and in the performance of what were known as 'points', set pieces in a play whose enactment by star actors was intensely studied for the precision with which the actor or actress reproduced the same lines and gestures that they had offered in the same part so many times before. It was particular sport, moreover, not only for audiences to compare one actor's or actress's performance in a point to that of another but also to compare an actor's or actress's performance in the same part year after year. Thus the great tragic actress Sarah Siddons scored a particular éclat in her debut performance of Lady Macbeth when she departed from the revered practice of Hannah Pritchard *by setting down* the candle to make the motion of hand-washing in the sleepwalking scene, yet suffered in critical reviews of her performance of that same part in her later years, as spectators noted the decline of her extraordinary vivacity and reflected mournfully on what they experienced as a painful loss.[17] Similarly, when Charles Macklin chose in 1741 to forego the popular, comic portrayal of Shylock that had been originated in 1701 by Thomas Doggett to stage Shylock instead as a tragic villain, his performance was met with thunderous applause at least in part because audiences were so startled by the stark contrast in representations.[18] Audiences thrilled, moreover, to the duelling productions of *Romeo and Juliet* that marked the 1750/1 season as Garrick and George Ann Bellamy at Drury Lane vied for the laurels with Spranger Barry and Susannah Cibber at Covent Garden over the course of twelve nights running. Taking advantage of the proximity of the two theatres, audience members 'preferring Barry's seductive scenes in the first three acts at Covent Garden nipped over to see Garrick's more tragic presentation of the star-crossed lovers in the last two acts at Drury Lane'.[19] While the two houses profited greatly from the immediate event, individual audience members garnered bragging rights as witnesses to an extraordinary episode in national cultural memory.

GENERIC PREOCCUPATIONS: CONTINUITY AND INNOVATION

Not only did actors often develop a specialization in one genre or another – Siddons in tragedy, Ned Shuter in comedy, for instance – but so, too, did playwrights and audiences look to genre, respectively, to provide the scaffolding and cultural logics for their tales. Genres are not rigid, however; rather, they are transformed over time. How a writer responds to, reflects upon or resists the supposed strictures of genre and how an audience responds to aesthetic conservatism and innovation can tell us a great deal about a particular cultural moment and its ideological and political interests. When we look to the repertory, we can find, then, not just a chronicle of dramatic and performance histories but also a record of ideological change and generic transformation.

In order to illustrate both the deep investment in dramatic genealogies and the generic interests that underwrote those investments, I turn to a discussion of two interrelated plays, one from the pre-Restoration era, Richard Brome's *A Jovial Crew* (1641/2), which persisted in the repertory in various incarnations to the end of the eighteenth century, and a new work in an entirely new genre, John Gay's *The Beggar's Opera* (1728), which was one of the most successful plays in the eighteenth-century repertory, a blockbuster with sixty-two performances in its debut season and an influence on musical drama to the present day. Each of these plays relies heavily on a meta-dramatic apparatus that foregrounds generic conventions, and both plays reference contemporary politics and deploy genre to reflect on the particular class hierarchies that regulate social and political intercourse. Linked to one another through their longevity and influence upon one another in the repertory, they are both also deeply intertwined with English theatrical history, its dramatic and performance lineages, and its role in producing quintessential ideas about a theatrically inflected English national identity.

Richard Brome's *A Jovial Crew, Or The Merry Beggars* was not only the very last play to be performed before the theatres were closed in 1642, but was also one of the very first plays to be revived when the theatres reopened. With its first Restoration production staged at Gibbon's Tennis Court in Vere Street on 25 July 1661 by the King's Company, it represented a return to the boards of a playhouse prodigy, whose theatrical lineage could be traced back to Ben Jonson, under whom Brome had served as a playwriting apprentice.[20] Drawing on themes and motifs from earlier plays by Jonson and Beaumont and Fletcher, Brome's play features the tale of a benevolent landowner named Oldrents, who has become so unnerved by a fortune teller's prophecy that his daughters will become beggars that he has fallen into a state of deep melancholy.[21] His old friend Hearty who takes particular pleasure in double meanings, however, cautions Oldrents, and by implication us, not to place too much stock in the prediction, reasoning that prophecies arc as likely to come true as not and that in any case, 'You'll never find their meaning until the event'.[22] Following hard on Brome's prologue, which describes his reluctance to submit to the contemporary taste for romances, Hearty's observation raises the question of what meaning we should assign to a play until we know its 'event' or ending. To what extent, we are asked to consider, do generic conventions – comedies and romances generally end in marriage and tragedy in death, for instance – determine or indeed overdetermine the meanings we attribute to a text? How are our expectations either fulfilled or frustrated, and what impact does that have on what we take to be the meaning of the play?

These questions and their potential ideological implications are a central concern of *A Jovial Crew*, and they become all the more palpable when Oldrents's daughters fulfil the prognostication but only, as Hearty anticipates, in a certain fashion. Oppressed by their father's despondency and bored with the usual urbane entertainments that might otherwise distract persons of their class standing, Meriel and Rachel convince their lovers Vincent and Hilliard to run off with them to join the beggar nation. They become beggars but only insofar as they take on the role of beggar, much the way an actor might take on the role of king, a point dramatized when the foursome tries and fails both to learn the beggar way of speaking and to follow the begging script prepared for them by their beggar mentor Springlove. While they thus play at being beggars, they are never truly reduced to that state.

This distinction is underlined even further by Brome's contravening approach to romance conventions. At first glance, he appears to fulfil the conventional requirements of a romance plot – young lovers, oppressed by the strictures and demands of their social position, run off to the countryside in search of the freedoms to be had in the more natural state of a pastoral idyll. Yet as Tiffany Stern points out, Brome allows too many elements of the real to intrude upon this idyll; he 'appears to be creating a non-romance out of the very romance features he is apparently adopting'.[23] In short, every plot element in Brome's drama not only produces a double meaning but acts in what John Gay will term in *The Beggar's Opera* 'a double capacity'.[24] It is no accident, for instance, that when Rachel clarifies what it means to be a 'downright beggar', she stipulates that she wishes to be 'without equivocation, statute beggars',[25] unwittingly making it clear that the status of a beggar is not free but rather quite specifically governed by law. What appears to be a flight to freedom, then, turns out to be only a flight to an order of persons just as stringently regulated by the state as is the courtier's fealty to the court. The fantasy that they are escaping to a place where the subjects are

> Free above scot-free – that observe no law,
> Obey no governor, use no religion
> But what they draw from their own ancient custom
> Or constitute themselves

is belied by the qualifying clause that ends the last line that they would 'yet [be] no rebels'.[26] This locution, of course, had particular resonance during the years of unrest leading up to the Civil War when the play was first presented on the stages of London. The fact that the monarchy had been restored when Killigrew revived the play makes these words all the more poignant and carries that history forward into the Restoration and eighteenth-century repertory. Either way, we are to understand that the beggar nation does not constitute an alternative commonwealth. Rather, as Martin Butler keenly observes, the supposed privileges and liberties exercised by the beggars are precisely those 'of the politically unfree, the disenfranchised, who are subject to whatever "liberties" the enfranchised . . . may freely take with them and against which they have no redress'.[27]

Soon enough, indeed, and again at odds with the fanciful conventions of romance, Meriel and Rachel and their consorts Vincent and Hilliard discover that the beggar life is one not only of deprivation and hardship but also of constant contention with the law. The vagabond life they have romanticized is not actually a thing of choice but rather is necessitated by the threat of arrest for lingering in one place too long and risking the capricious judgements of those in authority like the ill-humoured Justice Clack whose 'own rule . . . is to punish before [he] examine[s]'.[28] The plot reaches a climax, then, when the foursome is rounded up with the rest of the beggars and pressed into performing a play to entertain Justice Clack's guests, who include Oldrents.

In this climactic scene, Oldrents is presented with a bill of plays from which he is to choose the entertainment for the evening; but they all seem too closely to resemble his life: *The Two Lost Daughters*, *The Vagrant Steward*, *The Old Squire and the Fortune-Teller* and *The Beggar's Prophecy*.[29] 'All of these titles', as he exclaims, 'may serve to one play of a story that I know too well'.[30] Refusing all of them, he alights instead on *The Merry Beggars*, unaware, of course, that this is the alternative title of the play we, as audience members, have been watching unfold all along. When the players proceed to enact versions of scenes that we have already witnessed, the lines between the real world and the play world begin to blur. While within the frame of the play we watch Meriel and Rachel play versions of themselves, from a broader perspective we watch as those characters are themselves played by players who play at acting gentlewomen who play at acting beggars who play at acting players who play at acting gentlewomen. The multiple layers of mirroring and playing beg the question of where we ought to situate ourselves in the play to distil its meaning. From Oldrents's perspective, Meriel and Rachel have, in the capacity of players, turned themselves pleasingly into beggars or supplicants, a transformation of status that he had dreaded and lamented earlier in the play. Recognizing his daughters, he observes, 'The purpose of their play is but to work my friendship or their peace with me, and they have it'.[31] In reaching such a conclusion, however, Oldrents contradicts his own dictum that, 'True stories and true jests do seldom thrive on stage',[32] and we find that the real of the representation trumps its fictions. In this fashion, Brome not only completely overturns the usual operations of romance where the fanciful transforms the real; he mocks and parodies them. If we have come to the play in the hope that it will satisfy our taste for comedic romance, moreover, we are bound to walk away with a slightly funny taste in our mouths. While the play ends with the marriages we have been trained to expect, for instance, we never actually know which suitor is designed for which daughter; indeed, as characters they all seem rather interchangeable. Further, the recursive climax in which the events of the play that we have been witnessing are rehearsed makes it difficult for us to locate the 'event' of the romance, as the many meta-dramatic layers of representation complicate rather than fulfil our expectations. In this manner, Brome both appeases popular tastes and resists them, suggesting perhaps that at a time of political crisis those who fantasize about an escape into romance might be better served by a dose of the real.[33] As a genre, he suggests, romance only ever seems to motivate unmotivated action, that is, it only ever plays at the real.

Among many other thematic influences, including the use of song to locate the heart of England in its countryside, Gay's *The Beggar's Opera* also took on *A Jovial Crew*'s preoccupations with the problem of generic overdetermination, with romance as an emptied-out aesthetic category, and with audience tastes as a burden on playwrights. Amidst the rampant energy of commodification and commercialization that marked the eighteenth century, however, Gay was even more concerned than Brome about the devaluation of aesthetics and the surrender of art to commerce. To dramatize these concerns, he situates *The Beggar's Opera* literally as an operatic production written by a beggar and in the 'Introduction' to the play, we find the beggar ingratiating himself with one of the actors by assuring him that he has taken care to stock his opera with all of the elements that were driving London audiences at Italian operas so wild with pleasure. Thus the Beggar expounds:

> I have introduced similes that are in all your celebrated operas: the swallow, the moth, the bee, the ship, the flower, etc. Besides I have a prison scene, which the ladies always reckon charmingly pathetic . . . I hope I may be forgiven, that I have not made my opera throughout unnatural, like those in vogue; for I have no recitative. Excepting this, as I have consented to have neither prologue nor epilogue, it must be allowed an opera in all its forms.[34]

With this preamble Gay dramatizes his concern that literary hierarchies and generic forms had been debased to such an extent that they had become dissociated from any sound cultural logic. As far as the Beggar is concerned, all he needed to do to make his composition an 'opera' is to provide for the assemblage of elements that audiences had come to value so highly and, in Gay's view, so unthinkingly. By framing his play in this manner and by offering an innovative play featuring a satiric amalgam of multiple genres including heroic drama, criminal biography, pastoral and romance, Gay prompts his audience, as did Brome, to take a critical perspective on the action, that is, to recognize the incorporation of generic conventions as such, to develop an awareness of the extent to which those conventions shape our understanding, and to experience the crisis of meaning precipitated when conventional understandings are confounded.

In inventing the English ballad opera form, Gay was taking specific aim, moreover, at the growth and popularity of Italian Opera on the London stage, producing a parody of many of its most coveted elements, even as he substituted traditional English and Scottish ballads for the usual operatic compositions. With a total of sixty-nine different airs inserted into the fabric of the play, many of whose melodies were drawn from urban broadsides and country folk songs that were deeply rooted in popular culture, Gay deliberately stoked English national pride and cultivated his audience's patriotic desire to form a bulwark against any type of foreign invasion – whether cultural or political.

While the play tantalizes us with elements picked from a variety of genres, it works especially hard, both dramatically and musically, to draw us into the romance plot. At the centre of The Beggar's Opera we find the heroine Polly Peachum, daughter of Peachum, an underworld ringleader of thieves who provides for the warehousing and fencing of the goods they steal. Living up to his name, each month Peachum weighs how much each thief brings in in goods against how much he might gain by impeaching the thief to the authorities. Much to her parents' dismay, Polly has fallen in love with and secretly married Macheath, a charismatic highwayman and the putative hero of our play. The plot revolves around her parents' concern that Macheath will be too much of a liability for their business and that as a member of the family he would gain access to information that could impeach them before they could impeach him. They urge Polly to turn him in, but, avouching her true love, she remains impervious to their pleas and helps Macheath flee from the authorities. Defying a ubiquitous culture of individual financial interest where gentlemen are thieves and thieves gentlemen, which Gay attributes through a variety of satiric, topical references to the example set by the corrupt administration of Prime Minister Robert Walpole, Polly remains stalwart and true; but there are a number of warning signs that suggest we ought to be wary of the romance plot or at least sceptical of Polly's romantic attachment to Macheath.

First, as much as the affecting ballad he had shared with Polly on parting may have drawn us in to the romance plot, once on his own Macheath quickly disabuses us of any romantic notions: 'What a fool is a fond wench. Polly is most confoundedly bit. I love the sex. And a man who loves money might as well be contented with one guinea as I with one woman'.[35] A cross between a rake and a rogue, Macheath functions here both as a mock figure of chivalric romance and as the degraded protagonist in a heroic drama, torn between the duelling impulses of love and honour but truly attached to neither. After fleeing the Peachum warehouse, he indulges in drinking and womanizing – 'I must have women', he exclaims, 'There is nothing unbends the mind like them'[36] – until he is betrayed by a prostitute named Jenny Diver and taken to Newgate prison. As it turns out, there are any number of women, including Lucy Lockit, the daughter of Peachum's business partner, who not only claim Macheath as their husband but who have also borne children by him. As Macheath prepares for the gallows, he is besieged not only by the quarrelling rivals Lucy and Polly, in a cruel satire of the infamously feuding Italian opera stars Cuzzoni and Faustina, but also by, 'Four women more . . . with a child apiece'.[37] Rather than face those women, the fantastically potent Macheath urges the Sherriff's officers to lead him out to the scaffold.

If Macheath proves faithless but entertaining in his ability to adapt the generic conventions he thinks most effective in the moment, Polly proves not only naive but also a kind of generic dead end. For all of her passion, we learn early on that Polly is motivated not by some set of intrinsic characteristics but rather by the plots of the romance fictions that Macheath, by way of seduction, has encouraged her to read. 'Nay, my dear', she blithely avouches before he flees, 'I have no reason to doubt you, for I find in the romance you lent me, none of the great heroes were ever false in love'.[38] If, as a number of critics have claimed, Gay has situated Polly as the moral paragon of the play – even going so far, if Hogarth's famous painting of the prison scene is to be believed, as to dress her in pure white while the other characters appear in golds, reds, greens and blacks (Figure 8.1) – her status is eroded to the extent that romance is itself laid open as an empty form that motivates arbitrary desires. Even more significantly, despite her resistance to the culture of commodity, Polly herself turns out to be no more than the effect of one of the more compelling and popular narrative commodities on the market.

Indeed, any misplaced confidence in the independent impulse of romance is conspicuously mocked by the final turn of the play. As Macheath is being marched to the scaffold to be hanged, the Beggar and the Player step forward again. Cowed by the Player's insistence that the play cannot possibly be an opera if it ends tragically, the Beggar gives up his pretensions to 'strict poetical justice' and instead concedes, 'Your objection, sir, is very just, and is easily removed. For you must allow that in this kind of drama 'tis no matter how absurdly things are brought about. – So, you rabble there, run and cry a reprieve. Let the prisoner be brought back to his wives in triumph'.[39] Here we witness the arbitrariness of the ending, the 'event' determined as the Player notes 'to comply with the taste of the town'.[40] This might explain why audiences even today gasp in horror when in a film version of *The Beggar's Opera* featuring the rock star Roger Daltrey as Macheath, the Player's gesture of reprieve is mistaken at a distance for a sign to proceed with the execution.[41] As Macheath drops through the scaffold to his death, we are deprived of the conspicuously unrealistic ending that the generic conventions of romance have taught us to

FIGURE 8.1: John Gay's *The Beggar's Opera*, Act III, 1731. Harry R. Beard Collection, given by Isobel Beard © Victoria and Albert Museum, London.

desire most. Rather than heed the words of Macheath's final song in which he reflects on his burning 'inconstancy' and laments the fact that he can retire with but one woman, we prefer, as did eighteenth-century London audiences, to accept the reprieve and to enter into the romantic illusion that he will happily commit himself solely to Polly 'for life'.[42] In this manner, Gay both satisfies audience tastes and makes a mockery of them.

As did Brome before him, then, Gay deploys a set of well-known generic conventions to comment not only on romance but also on the unrealistic cultural logics that such forms were designed to sustain. Further, just as the portrait of the beggar's commonwealth provided Brome with the opportunity to comment on the stratified politics in the years leading up to the English Civil War, so too did Gay's depiction of a criminal underclass create an opportunity to satirize the craven politics of the supposedly legitimate classes in the era of Walpole. While *A Jovial Crew* was a steady component of the repertory, playing at least once or more every year between 1704 and 1724, *The Beggar's Opera* proved an immediate sensation and a long-term commercial success as one of the most performed plays of the eighteenth century. Often occupying the season-opening spot, the play also became a favourite vehicle for highlighting the talents of female artists and provided the occasion for a number of spectacular rivalries over the parts of Polly Peachum and Lucy Lockit.[43] The introduction of a new Polly to the stage was always a notable event and attracted great audiences. Theatrical genealogies were built, moreover, not just around the part of Polly but also around the part of Macheath, with the latter becoming a favourite transvestite role for some of the leading actresses of the age.[44]

Just as the reliance on song and folk culture in *A Jovial Crew* was said to have influenced *The Beggar's Opera*, so, too, did *The Beggar's Opera*, in turn, influence the stage history of *A Jovial Crew*. Following Gay's success, Brome's play was transformed in 1731 into a comic opera with fifty-three new songs and retitled *The Jovial Crew*. Not insignificantly, moreover, given the intertwined history of these two plays, Susannah Cibber, Kitty Clive (née Raftor), and a cross-dressed Charlotte Charke who all feature so famously in the performance history of *The Beggar's Opera*, all took up roles in this new production as Meriel, Amie and Hilliard respectively. Indeed, as Tiffany Stern has noted, the two plays could often be found juxtaposed with one another in the repertory.[45] Performed as both a mainpiece and as a one-act afterpiece, *The Jovial Crew* was adapted further into an immensely popular new mainpiece in 1760 with Miss Brent and later Miss Catley, both also of Polly fame, playing Rachel (Figures 8.2 and 8.3). Finally, in 1770 *The Jovial Crew* was again adapted into a two-act afterpiece, featuring a 'Crutch Dance' and retitled *The Ladies Frolick*, and in this malleable fashion the play persisted in the repertory along with *The Beggar's Opera* almost to the end of the century. Together, they pulled the dramatic past into the repertory and extended its future. In the historical relationship between *A Jovial Crew* and *The Beggar's Opera*, we can thus see how the repertory itself was a recursive enterprise, signifying a movement forward even as it circled back repetitively to prior practices.

TRAGIC POSTERITY AND COMIC FUTURITY

While both Brome and then Gay deployed romance as a means to comment on the social and political conditions of the day, the repertory's engagement with tragedy and comedy was driven by a proleptic investment, respectively, in posterity and futurity. As the British Empire expanded and the heterogeneous middling classes began to take a much more central role in both the economic and political settlements of the nation, tragedy and comedy were adapted both to reflect those imperial and mercantile aspirations and to assuage the anxieties to which they gave rise. Where tragedy was thus devoted to imagining the various conditions that might pose a threat to the nation's posterity, comedy was engaged in modelling the social relations that could ensure its futurity. Following the settlements of the Glorious Revolution, moreover, the drama of the late seventeenth century moved rather conspicuously to focus on the plight

The Beggars Opera.

J: Robert ad viv: delt

Miss Catley in the Character of Polly.

FIGURE 8.2: Miss Catley as 'Polly' from John Gay's *The Beggar's Opera*, 1768–1793.
By permission of the Trustees of the British Museum.

FIGURE 8.3: Miss Catley as 'Rachel' from Richard Brome's *The Jovial Crew*, *c.*1781. Harry R. Beard Collection, given by Isobel Beard © Victoria and Albert Museum, London.

of individuals among the less exalted ranks and to explore the sentiments and sensibilities that would ultimately inform middle-class ideology. Two subgenres would emerge in the eighteenth-century repertory to give focus to these concerns: bourgeois or domestic tragedy and sentimental comedy or *comédie larmoyante*. Both took their point of departure from and subsequently grew out of the affective and emotive pulse of the pathetic tragedies that dominated the playhouses of the late seventeenth and early eighteenth centuries and both increasingly charted gendered dichotomies of masculinity and femininity.

Emergent in the 1680s and exemplified by the works of Thomas Otway and John Banks, pathetic tragedies, 'deriv[ed] their power', as Jean Marsden has observed, 'not from their potential to shock, but from their ability to thrill with scenes of suffering innocence', that is, in their ability to generate pathos.[46] Their predominance in the repertory throughout the eighteenth century was attributable in large part, moreover, to the strong roles they provided for actresses, with the subgenre known as she-tragedies, focused, in particular, on innocent female suffering. With plays such as Thomas Southerne's *The Fatal Marriage; or, The Innocent Adultery* (1694), William Congreve's *The Mourning Bride* (1697), and Nicholas Rowe's *The Fair Penitent* (1703) and *The Tragedy of Jane Shore* (1714), she-tragedy reached its zenith between 1690 and 1714 and became known especially for its evocative exhibitions of female sexuality.[47] As I have suggested elsewhere, however, the main tension in the performance of she-tragedy was, 'the tension between the spectacle of women in emotionally compelling roles and the narratives that were devoted to taming the characters they portrayed'.[48] In a brief review of the performance history of Southerne's *The Fatal Marriage*, I want to illustrate, then, not just how the original play situated female sexuality within the scope of tragedy but also how the effects of this tragedy were modulated in performance over time, transforming the play into a domestic tragedy – a tragedy focused on the private woes of private individuals – to suit the changing tastes of the emergent middling classes.

Southerne adapted the plot of his play from Aphra Behn's novella, *The History of the Nun; or, The Fair Vow-Breaker* (1689). In Behn's narrative, the protagonist Isabella breaks her vow of chastity and leaves the convent to marry Henault, who is subsequently disinherited by his father. To recover financial ground and to redeem himself in his father's good graces, Henault decides to become a soldier, at the first thought of which Isabella is so overwhelmed with grief that she miscarries. Henault goes off to war, where he meets and becomes fast friends with Villenoys, a former suitor to Isabella. When Henault falls in battle and his body is not recovered, he is presumed dead. Villenoys returns to Isabella and after two years convinces her that it is in her best financial interest to marry him. After five years of marriage, Isabella finds herself in love with her new husband. When Henault, who had actually been enslaved for seven years, suddenly appears very much alive, Isabella resolves to murder him. Claiming that Henault had died naturally from the shock of the news that she had remarried, she convinces Villenoys to save her honour by disposing of the body. Mistrusting Villenoys, however, she not only sews Henault into a sack for disposal but also stitches the full sack to Villenoys, so that when he throws the body into the river, he too will drown. In an eroticized scene on the scaffold, in which she appears so 'very majestic and charming' that she 'set all hearts a flaming even in that mortifying minute of preparation for death', Isabella is beheaded for her crimes – but only, that is, after she holds forth at length against the sins of vow-breakers.[49]

Behn's approach to this narrative is distinctly Tory if not Jacobite, as following the objections of these political factions to the deposition of James II, the main crime emphasized in the tale is that of vow-breaking. In the wake of the Glorious Revolution in which not just oaths of loyalty to James II were broken, but so too were sacred oaths in support of the indefeasible right of hereditary succession, Behn's moralistic condemnation of vow-breakers would have resonated loudly. In this tale, moreover, Isabella is no innocent but rather a calculating young woman who constantly seeks her advantage. In chilling detail, the story traces her progress from eager novitiate to murderer, all the while noting her vanity and inherent aptitude for deceit and manipulation.

In adapting this tale for the stage, Southerne not only diminishes Isabella's guilt in any crimes but also her sense of agency, transforming her in accordance with the increasingly powerful, gendered dictates of domestic ideology from active perpetrator to passive victim. When asked, for instance, what she will do to hold off the creditors who have come to the door, she replies emblematically: 'Do! Nothing, no, for I am born to suffer'.[50] Indeed, Isabella's suffering and her precarious mental state take centre stage in Southerne's adaptation. When the play opens, Isabella is not only the almost seven-year, but still utterly grief-stricken, presumed widow of Biron, but also the mother of his child, an alteration that immediately resituates Isabella less as sexual siren than as solicitous mother. Her first appearance on stage is in the company of her young son, and her interest in his future well-being becomes one of the main reasons she finally agrees to marry the wealthy Villeroy – 'I live', she exclaims, 'but in my Child'.[51] No sooner has the marriage been consummated then her first husband Biron arrives on the scene, throwing Isabella into a distracted frenzy. Soon, however, Biron learns the cause of Isabella's distraction and resolves, rather than allow her to suffer further, to kill himself. Before he can do so, he is set upon by a murderous gang hired by his brother Carlos, who knew all along that Biron was still alive but who wanted to retain the privileged place of heir to their father. Biron dies of his injuries and Isabella soon follows him with a self-inflicted wound, leaving a 'Mothers Legacy' behind in the form of her frightened and traumatized child.[52]

Where Behn's shrewd and calculating heroine is one of the drivers of the action, Southerne's Isabella is almost entirely passive, reacting to circumstances as they arise. Theatrically, her passion for suffering and her failing mental state hold the stage in almost every scene, but they also consistently mark the frailty of the female mind and body. While Isabella's departure from the convent is noted, moreover, it is not the main focus of recrimination. That burden, reflecting Southerne's more Whiggish interests, falls on the father, Count Baldwin, for failing to rule wisely and for sowing the seeds of dissent and rebellion among his sons. The threat to posterity here is represented in the failure to attend properly to patriarchal responsibilities, but in the form of Biron's orphaned child, Count Baldwin will have a chance to redeem himself and his posterity. To the extent that the private woes of individuals now stood in for the woes of the nation, the tragedy thus both looked back at the patriarchal failings of the past and tried to prognosticate a new patriarchal way forward.

Although Susan Staves has argued that with *The Fatal Marriage*, 'it is really Southerne . . . who invents bourgeois domestic tragedy', it would take a further revision by Garrick and the heightened emotive powers of Sarah Siddons to bring the transformation of Behn's amatory fiction into a domestic tragedy to its fullest realization.[53] Following its first appearance on the stage in 1694, *The Fatal Marriage* had become a steady staple of the repertory, with two or three performances at the patent playhouses almost every season. In 1757, however, Garrick decided to revise Southerne's play, eliminating the comic subplot that Southerne had added and heightening the focus both on Carlos's villainy and on Isabella's physical vulnerability and mental deterioration.[54] With Garrick playing Biron to Susannah Cibber's Isabella, this new rendition, retitled *Isabella; Or, The Fatal Marriage*, enjoyed renewed success with a long run of fourteen performances in its first season.

It was not, however, until Sarah Siddons took the stage as Isabella in her sensational 1782 return debut on the London stage that the play became a full-blown hit, with audiences returning over and over again to witness Siddons' electrifying representations of the dual pangs of motherhood and madness. Southerne's original production had featured Elizabeth Barry in the role of Isabella, and he paid knowing tribute both to her extraordinary acting powers and to the ways in which an embodied performance could transform a dramatic text when he wrote: 'I made the Play for her part, and her part has made the Play for me . . . I gave it just motion enough to crawl into the World, but by her power, and spirit of playing, she has breathe'd a soul into it, that may keep it alive'.[55] Still, as powerful as Barry's performances were said to be on the stage, her portrait of a maternal and innocent Isabella would have clashed with her own notoriety off the stage as mistress to any number of powerful men, including the libertine Earl of Rochester. Siddons, in contrast, deliberately cultivated a public persona and celebrity in which the projection of motherhood was central, and her appearance in the role of Isabella followed her well-publicized retirement from the Bath stage in which she displayed her three children on stage as the 'THREE REASONS' why she had to pursue a more lucrative career on the London stage.[56] These claims were made all the more resonant when she appeared as Isabella with her own eight-year-old son Henry playing the part of her young son (Figure 8.4). When the young child turns in the opening scene to express his sadness at his mother's distress, the effects could not have been more astonishing, and Isabella's impulse to provide for her child by marrying Villeroy would have been that much more palpable as an act of self-sacrifice. In this manner, Siddons embodied an evolution in acting style and audience taste to shape a repertory that was attuned not just to expression of sentiment but even more so to the display of sensibility.

Where Southerne alerts playgoers to the threat of patriarchal failure but only hints at the remedy going forward at the end of *The Fatal Marriage*, sentimental comedies took great care to map that futurity. Deferring from the traditional course of comedies of manner, humours and intrigue, where wit was the most powerful currency, sentimental comedies instead espoused a discourse of what I have termed 'good breeding', an emphasis on property and exchange relations that are guided not just by aristocratic inheritance but by the cultivation of manners, politeness, sincerity and sociability, that is, by the development of a new gentility which we have come to associate with the middling classes.[57] In play after play, including Richard Steele's *The Conscious Lovers* (1722), Edward Moore's *The Foundling* (1748), George Colman the Elder's *The English Merchant* (1767) and Richard Cumberland's *The West Indian* (1771), playwrights who developed this 'species' of what Oliver Goldsmith referred to as 'Bastard Tragedy' sought to model and represent an alternative way to value character and to ensure futurity – one that would be based upon merit and upon the observance of certain kinds of conventional moral values.[58] Private woes in sentimental comedies are thus ultimately turned not only to private joy but also to public good for the nation under the guidance of a steady and sure patriarchal presence. Along with the pathetic tragedies, they proffered the kinds of cultivated sentiments and expressed the kinds of emotional sensibilities that a brute like Captain Mirvan found so odious and that refined young ladies like Evelina and her companion Miss Mirvan found so agreeable.

As I hope this excursion through some of the more sustained productions of the eighteenth-century London playhouses indicates, the repertoire in London, and by exemplary extension across England and the Continent, was a recursive operation, drawing upon older generic practices and bringing them into conjunction with new ones to suit the tastes of the times. Genres provided the cultural logics or epistemological frames that knowledgeable audiences looked to in making meaning out of representations, and playwrights could thus choose strategically either to fulfil or to frustrate those expectations. Textual meanings

FIGURE 8.4: Sarah Siddons as Isabella with her son Henry Siddons, 1785. Harry R. Beard Collection © Victoria and Albert Museum, London.

were brought to life, however, only through embodied performance, and actors and actresses played a significant role both in shaping and, at times, revising the meaning of plays and in ensuring their popularity and longevity on the stage. Out of this process emerged a repertory replete with dramatic lineages and performance genealogies of which eighteenth-century audiences would have been well-informed and which still inform our understanding today.

CHAPTER NINE

Technologies of Performance

Architecture, Scenery, Light

PANNILL CAMP

What counts as technology in the context of theatre history, and what can be said about its relationship to performance during the eighteenth century? To begin to investigate these questions, we might expand upon the idea of technology with assistance from Bernard Stiegler, who argues that 'technical objects' or 'inorganic organized beings' are integral to any understanding of human existence.[1] For Stiegler, the way human beings have manipulated nonliving materials has progressively engulfed and transformed human thought, communication and biology, producing such profound interdependencies that it is absurd to conceive of humanity apart from the tools and other sustaining external devices with which we interact.

This notion has advantages for the task of this chapter. For one, the origin of Stiegler's idea of 'technical objects' is the Greek word for art making: *techne*. This serves to remind us that theatre has always involved the deliberate arrangement of materials like earth, stone, paint and textiles, just as it has always employed the human body's expressive capabilities. For another, it helps clarify the relationship between technology and the performing body as one of interdependency without dissolving the distinction between the technological and the organic entirely. By conceiving of technology in this way we might recognize certain practices intimately connected to the body as technological – say David Garrick's wire-actuated 'fright wig' for the role of Hamlet, which the actor used to make his hair stand on end when the Danish prince saw his father's ghost, or the surgery used to change the hormones, and thus the vocal range, of the famed Italian *castrati* singers – but still maintain a bright line between these uses of tools and performance 'techniques', such as the musical way actors spoke the twelve-syllable lines of Alexandrine verse common to French tragedies, or the disciplined positioning of the limbs that defined baroque-era balletic style. Finally, Stiegler's conception of 'technics' is useful because it draws attention to a unique characteristic of the eighteenth century: a flourishing interest in what we now think of as scientific knowledge. For Stiegler, *technics* is as old as humanity itself, but *technology* arises when the organization of nonliving matter 'has functionally integrated scientific knowledge into it'.[2] What we know as technology, in other words, subordinates scientific knowledge to aims not intrinsically bound to philosophical inquiry; in the modern era these aims were often commercial, industrial, medical and military in nature. Scientifically informed technical inventions also flourished, however, in theatre and other spectacular art forms like architecture and fountain design.

The Enlightenment saw the beginnings of modern ways of seeking out and using scientific knowledge. The most promising models of the natural world at the time were mechanical, derived from the way that René Descartes and Isaac Newton understood the dynamics of the physical world. Advances in physics helped to refine and improve machines, and popular curiosity in how machines worked grew. Soon after mid-century, the philosopher and playwright Denis Diderot and the mathematician and scientist Jean le Rond d'Alembert began to publish a compendium of existing human knowledge that included intricate engraved plates illustrating all manner of technical achievements and industries for the reading public. The same *Encyclopaedia* in 1774 published plates displaying the structural plans of grand public opera houses and the complicated pulley-driven backstage machines that moved elaborate perspective scenery. Automatons, the early modern version of today's robots, reached new levels of sophistication and even made their way onto the stage. In 1750 the famed designer of automata Jacques Vaucanson designed a spring-driven serpent that hissed and struck realistically for use in the climactic moment of Marmontel's tragedy, *Cleopatra*, when the doomed queen takes her own life by pressing a poisonous asp to her breast.[3]

These inventions were not merely elaborate stage gimmicks; they participated in the rapid expansion of machine invention and manufacture which became a central part of the way Western cultures understood themselves and their place in the world. Jean d'Alembert, co-editor of the *Encyclopaedia*, rhapsodized about 'the discovery and application of a new method of philosophizing' which 'has swept away with a sort of violence everything before that stood in its way'.[4] The impressive new control over physical nature that scientifically informed machines allowed, particularly in the realms of transportation and weaponry, became, during the eighteenth century, one of the dominant factors that convinced European explorers and colonists that they were superior to other groups.[5] Elaborate, mechanically enhanced spectacles proliferated on the public stages in European capitals. As Alice Jarrard has pointed out, in the seventeenth century, military and theatrical machines were sometimes produced for similar purposes: to demonstrate powerfully to the mass audiences the wealth, sophistication and talent controlled by a king, duke or other powerful patron. Francesco d'Este, the seventeenth-century duke of the contested region of Modena, for example, produced ducal festivals for which generals and military engineers orchestrated spectacular shows of force including equestrian exercises, chivalric tournaments, and enormous mobile machines resembling mountains, castles, ships and even whales, which would transform and disgorge teams of knights and horses.[6] For such productions, engineers and architects, including Gaspare Vigarani, who would go on to design a theatre for Louis XIV in Paris, designed vast temporary arenas, and exploited the fine arts in the hopes of producing overpowering displays of magnificence.

What Jarrard calls this 'strategic relationship between politics and culture' helps explain why the late seventeenth and early eighteenth centuries witnessed the expansion of the sensory elements of theatrical performance. Besides operas such as Jean-Baptiste Lully and Philippe Quinault's *Armide*, which gave unusual emphasis to visual elements and enjoyed frequent revivals in eighteenth-century France, non-musical plays, especially tragedies, were mounted to appeal to the eyes.[7] Productions at Drury Lane transformed Shakespeare into a playwright of visual glory, rendering staged coronations into pompous affairs and favouring *The Tempest* among the Bard's comedies, perhaps because of its unique potential for spectacular effects.[8] Visual displays like these, empowered by increasingly voluminous stages, were made possible by scenic technology that originally served the implicitly political aims of seventeenth-century potentates. But as technologically sophisticated spectacular theatre was increasingly offered to mass audiences outside of court settings in the eighteenth century, stage wizardry participated in a broader cultural phenomenon generated by a myriad of Western technological achievements: it helped prop up the perception that European religion and secular knowledge placed its bearers atop a hierarchy of humankind. This sort of belief, of course, had far-reaching political and economic implications.

Certainly the eighteenth century saw the emergence of alternatives to old forms of government, the expanded circulation of consumer goods, and other changes that transformed the daily lives of people in many regions of the globe. Another change, less conspicuous at the time but ultimately just as important, concerned the way that philosophers understood the value of knowledge about the natural world. The notion that natural philosophy – the precursor to today's sciences – was valuable principally because it could be put to practical use suddenly revolutionized the way philosophy in general was done. Rather than attempting to construct grand systems of thought that amounted to a coherent picture of the whole world, thinkers aspired to create experiments that would help them observe and exactly describe a small part of nature, such as the rate of acceleration of gravity, or the way waves move through air or water. These sorts of discoveries, in turn, could be used to improve a whole range of human endeavours, medical, industrial and commercial. Intellectuals in eighteenth-century Europe believed that theatre was among the human enterprises that could be improved by making use of the latest in scientific research.

In its broad strokes, therefore, the story of theatre technology during the eighteenth century is one of ascendant rationalism and the instrumentalization of scientific knowledge. This appears in the transformation of three aesthetic facets of theatre space: architecture, scenery and light. Eighteenth-century practitioners inherited sophisticated baroque-era ways of mounting visually powerful stage pictures, but by the end of the century, architects, scenic artists and theatre-makers had concluded that optics and acoustics, practical sciences rooted in expanding fields of physical knowledge, held the key to the advancement of theatre practice. The spread of the Italian system of picture-frame proscenium arches, chariot-and-pole driven changeable painted wing flats, and retractable stage curtains into big public houses in Paris and London, as well as into more provincial courts like those of Drottningholm and St. Petersburg, shows that the early eighteenth century saw the spread of both seventeenth-century court scenic technologies and architectural models. Later came radical changes in all three components of theatre space, in theory if not always in practice.

The eighteenth century saw an unprecedented degree of communication between theatre and multiple areas of Enlightenment philosophy, and the quick application of advances in theoretical and practical optics (directional lighting), applied geometry (scenic painting), air purification (aerated wick lamps) and hydraulics (fire prevention systems). But these facts should not lead us to believe that the era was one of steady, positive accumulation of knowledge. The increasing professional specialization of artists like scene painters, backstage engineers and architects opened gulfs between areas of what had previously been the unified domain of scenic visionaries (such as Inigo Jones or Gaspare Vigarani). Moreover, the precarious state of royal finances in France in the decades just before the Revolution led the funding of new playhouses and scenic machines to financial arrangements that displayed their own form of heightened complexity. These sorts of material complications to the realization of theatrical vision prompted delays and construction crises in French cities. Technological experimentation was driven by a mixture of popular enthusiasm for reform and royal craving for dazzling novelty, but the realization of new architectural, scenic and luminous theatre spaces followed divergent and twisting paths. Nonetheless, technologically driven changes in theatre architecture, scenery and lighting that emerged in the mid-to-late eighteenth century pivoted these components of theatre production in the direction of what would later be considered modern, scientifically informed practices.

ARCHITECTURE

The eighteenth century is generally understood as a time in which the cultural capitals of Western Europe adopted the Italian baroque opera house model of playhouse design.[9] While this characterization is valid enough from a broad view of theatre history, there are some important facts that complicate this picture. First, patterns in political and social history help explain why the Italian opera house model became standard continent-wide. As the seventeenth century progressed, achievements in arts and architecture allowed kings, dukes and other leaders in what remained a largely feudal European political landscape to project their wealth and power to their subjects and to each other. Through a frequently shifting network of alliances, the theatrical achievements shown at one palace were swiftly imitated at another. So it was, for instance, that Gaspare Vigarani and his son Carlo were contracted to build an immense theatre for machine-driven spectacles in Paris soon after the elder designer had produced a number of impressive temporary shows for the Duke d'Este in Modena. Partly as a result of the expertise of artists like Vigarani, Italy and France enjoyed a kind of cultural hegemony at the outset of the eighteenth century, compelling others to see their court theatres as models of artistic achievement.

While this particular dynamic was couched in the ways that spectacle aided and produced political power, it influenced the way that public playhouses were constructed during the eighteenth century. This is true in part because of the legacy of royal support for and control of public theatres like the Comédie-Française in France and partly because, just like peripheral European courts, public audiences wanted to see versions of what so impressed the Hapsburg, Medici and Bourbon families and their ministers in more rarefied settings. The first use of perspective scenery in France had been in 1548, when King Henry II and Catherine de Medici saw a production of *La Calandria* produced by Cardinal Hippolyte d'Este in Lyon.[10] By the middle of the eighteenth century, public playhouses in London, Paris and other major and minor cities boasted stages decorated with perspective scenery. Even though over the course of the century the financing and programming of major theatre spaces became increasingly determined by the preferences of public, rather than court, audiences, the design of large urban playhouses continued to accommodate voluminous staging systems and elaborate, multi-tiered audience arrangements that essentially followed the practices of entertainments designed for the elite strata of European society. Despite this fact, architects who sought to reform theatre architecture during the eighteenth century eventually turned to the ancient theoretical programme of treating the playhouse as a sort of public building with numerous functions that could be reformed with the use of new technology.

The engineering solutions at the heart of theatre design were not overhauled during this era, but important technical challenges such as the distribution of sightlines, acoustics, fire prevention and the movement of spectators were tackled foremost with theatre's status as a public institution in mind. As the central concerns of theatre architecture gravitated towards such issues, new buildings also manifested the changing nature of political power. For example, seventeenth-century engravings show Louis XIII and Cardinal Richelieu enjoying a show in the Palais Cardinal in the centre of the room, surrounded on all sides by spectators of subordinate rank, much in the same way that James I of England and Anne of Denmark sat in 'the state' for court spectacles designed by Inigo Jones. By contrast, new French playhouses in the late eighteenth century designated positions for royal spectators in the first row of loges. In visionary new playhouse designs, monarchs were placed alongside their subjects, so that the reform of theatre spectatorship involved a new, somewhat levelling political optics that foreshadowed Revolutionary political developments to come.

Also, even though they maintained the faith in ancient secular knowledge typical of neoclassical movements in the early modern era, Italian, French and English theatre architecture reformers in the later decades of the eighteenth century also gravitated towards new sources of knowledge. We should not be misled by the term 'baroque' into thinking that playhouse design during this period was fundamentally rooted in the practices of previous centuries. As in many fields of knowledge, theories of theatre including dramatic theory, acting theory and theatre architecture theory understood that natural philosophy – what we think of today as the natural sciences – was in the process of a major transformation. Thus even though true revolutions in the sciences of engineering and acoustics would not arrive until the nineteenth century, theatre architects in the era of the Enlightenment already strived to create public playhouses informed by the latest in scientific knowledge.

The template for a public playhouse that European designers imitated and adapted developed first in Italy and was distinctly adapted in France and England. Its deepest roots, as we will see in the next section, can be traced to the rich tradition of scenic design in Italy originated by Sebastian Serlio in the sixteenth century. By the eighteenth century, Italian artists were designing theatres that allowed large numbers of spectators to see the grandest possible stage effects in permanent, indoor auditoriums. In the roughest terms, the resulting buildings joined a large rectangular box stage with space above and below for scene changing equipment to an oval or horseshoe-shaped auditorium surrounded by vertically stacked rings of boxes. The most impressive new Italian buildings of this type – the Teatro di San Carlo in Naples (1737), the Teatro

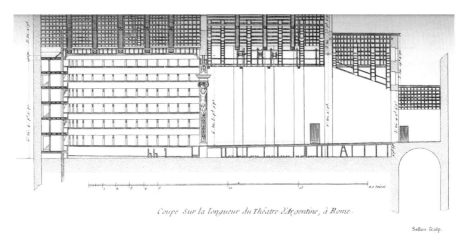

Coupe Sur la longueur du Théâtre d'Argentine, à Rome.

Sellier. sculp.

FIGURE 9.1: Longitudinal section of the Argentine Theatre in Rome, from *Parallèle des plans des plus belles salles*, Gabriel Dumont, 1774. Photo by author.

Regio in Turin (1740), the Teatro Argentina in Rome (1732) – demonstrated that housing capacity could be augmented by stacking up side and back loges five or six levels high. In order to preserve both visual and auditory access to the stage, auditoriums could not be too deep, which meant that the houses needed to be rather wide in order to maximize audience numbers and revenue.

The chief technical challenge theatre architects confronted, therefore, was the 'vaulting problem', or how to shelter a sufficiently wide auditorium space without obstructing sightlines or risking roof collapse. As George C. Izenour points out, eighteenth-century solutions followed centuries of tradition in European building construction. Bearing walls made of stone or brick masonry supported trusses made from timber beams.[11] These trusses spanned the width of the building (the dimension parallel with the front edge of the stage), and held up a slanted roof that would shed water and snow. Because timber beams longer than forty feet (twelve metres) are difficult to obtain, eighteenth-century builders devised ways to join them together, using pegs, mortise and tenon, and elaborate scarf joints reinforced with metal banding. Architectural studies and engravings of the grand modern Italian opera houses published in France dwelled on the details of truss constructions as demands for comparable theatre spaces rose across the continent.

Inspired in part by the Italian success in creating voluminous public playhouses, French architects and designers undertook to modernize the theatre design of what had become Europe's most powerful nation. In spite of what was perceived to be unexcelled attainments in dramatic literature, French plays were for the most part staged in modified buildings of various sorts. Beginning at mid-century, French architects and intellectuals began to push for new public

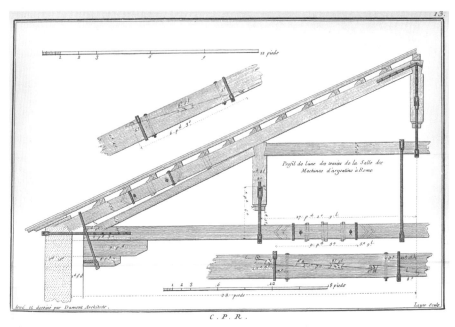

FIGURE 9.2: Profile of one of the bays of the Argentine Theatre in Rome, from *Parallèle des plans des plus belles salles*, Gabriel Dumont, 1774. Photo by author.

buildings that would match Italian advances but also go beyond them by refurbishing the fundamental principles of theatre architecture in light of recent leaps in the understanding of the physical world. The subsequent decades saw French architects confront design problems that would allow them to conquer the acoustical problems endemic to the nation's narrow modified tennis-court buildings and to bring audiences closer to the actors.

The first milestone in French modernization of theatre architecture was Germain Soufflot's new theatre in Lyon, which opened in 1754. This building was unique in France in that it was designed top to bottom for theatrical purposes and stood apart from neighbouring structures, granting theatre a prominent place in the urban milieu and aiding the ingress and egress of spectators. Soufflot adopted the oval-plus-rectangle form of his Italian contemporaries, but added distinctive, classically inspired approaches to the central technical problem of the playhouse: the arrangement of spectators around the stage with respect to the demands of seeing and hearing. In the fashion of Greek and Roman buildings, the rings of loges in his auditorium retreated slightly as they ascended, rather than rising vertically like a stack of birdcages. This alleviated the sense of obscurity, claustrophobia and detachment from the stage action that some felt afflicted the denizens of Italian loges.

Behind and between the loges on the first level, shutters could be opened to reveal tiny cabins meant to be used when the theatre was filled to capacity. Soufflot preserved the standing pit on the ground level beyond the orchestra and parquet, though later French architects eventually replaced this pit with benched seating in the hopes of producing a more absorbing and contemplative theatre-going experience.

Soufflot's playhouse at Lyon also introduced some predecessors to modern building systems by addressing the problems of climate control and fire prevention. The theatre contained niches for wood stoves on the ground level, both in the front vestibule and on either side of the parterre. To combat the spread of fire, a persistently lethal problem in public theatres throughout the century, Soufflot enclosed the stage area, where fires tended to start, in stone walls and a masonry vault. The upper part of the stage also bore a surrounding stone balcony equipped with leather pipes connected to two large reservoirs of water to be used in case of fire.[12] The Lyon theatre, much like the monumental theatres built in Paris, Bordeaux and elsewhere in the decades that followed, was also replete with accessory spaces for artists and the public: warming rooms and dressing rooms for actors, apartments for the director, coffee rooms and commodes for spectators.

While the principal site of new approaches to theatre architecture shifted in the eighteenth century from Italy to France, elsewhere in Europe court and public theatres adopted their own versions of voluminous indoor theatres featuring Italian-style scenery. Architects employed by far-flung royalty fused the delicately ornate French rococo style and the capacious volume of Italian opera houses (enabled by elaborate ways of joining wooden beams into trusses that supported wide roofs) with distinct stylistic and technical features of their own. In 1766, for instance, Carl Fredrik Adelkrantz completed work on an extravagant court playhouse for Louisa Ulrika of Prussia, and her son, King Gustav III of Sweden, which remains preserved and operational in Drottningholm today. Adelkrantz dedicated more space to his heavily mechanized stage than he did to the auditorium. The theatre boasted complicated machines above and below the stage for moving wing-flat chariots, sky borders, footlights, multiple trap doors and a thunder machine. While the Drottningholm featured an usually elaborate suite of scenic technologies even for a court playhouse, other continental court theatres introduced their own innovations. The Residenztheater of François de Cuvilliés, which opened in Munich in 1755, featured a system of stone-counterweighted levers under the auditorium floor that converted the space from a slight rake for parquet seating, to a surface flush with the stage for ballroom use.[13]

In London, meanwhile, public playhouses had supported perspective scenery since immediately after the Restoration of the Stuart monarchy. Sir William Davenant's tennis-court theatre in Lincoln's Inn Fields may have been so equipped in 1661, and when Thomas Killigrew's Theatre Royal at Drury Lane

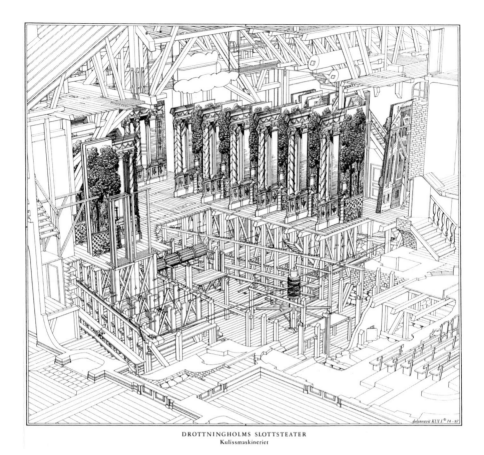

DROTTNINGHOLMS SLOTTSTEATER
Kulissmaskineriet

FIGURE 9.3: Drawing of the stage machinery of the Theatre of Drottningholm. By permission of Gustav Kull.

burned in 1672, the replacement building designed by Sir Christopher Wren dedicated extensive upstage space to perspective vista. So pervasive is Wren's attempt to incorporate the spatial device of perspective scenery that the walls of the auditorium widen out and grow as they retreat, as though in keeping with the arrangement of the perspective flats upstage – or indeed in homage to the foreshortened, three-dimensional static stage vista that Vincenzo Scamozzi had built for his Teatro Sabionetta. Renovations to the Drury Lane theatre and to the Theatre Royal at Covent Garden late in the eighteenth century granted even more space to the painted picture scene, sacrificing one of the pairs of doors that had traditionally flanked the proscenium stage. Even in England, the popular and commercial theatre had come to pursue the space-intensive scenic effects that only Italian-style scenery could deliver.

SCENERY

To discuss theatre architecture and scenery as separate technical entities in this era is somewhat misleading. This is because, especially in the seventeenth and early eighteenth centuries, the same individuals practised these arts. Members of the Bibiena family of scenic artists, for example, were frequently hired to create theatre buildings and scenic machinery and designs at the same time. The proliferation of large public and court playhouses in Italian style described above, in fact, can be read as one effect of the popularity of a style of scenic spectacle that featured painted images of unbelievably sumptuous architecture extending as far as they eye could see.[14] The dazzling, symmetrical perspectives popularized by Italian designers like Giacomo Torelli and the father–son team of Carlo and Gaspare Vigarani were refined by the Bibiena family and exported all over Europe. These artisans frequently worked as architect-scenographers, designing and constructing both the state-of-the-art machinery for changeable, large-scale perspective stage pictures, and permanent playhouses designed to hold them. Indeed, one of the defining trends of eighteenth-century stage technology in Europe is the gradual professional separation of its architectural and scenic engineering parts. In the sixteenth century, Sebastiano Serlio had thought of theatre design as an adjunct to the larger field of perspective. By the time of the Enlightenment, however, academically trained architects in France gradually took over greater responsibility for big public building projects, and ambitious new playhouse projects came under the control of people who were more familiar with theatre as spectators than as artists or backstage riggers. By the 1780s, three specialists were needed for a new theatre building: the architect, the stage engineer responsible for the machinery and a *perspecteur/* painter who would design and execute the actual images mounted on the canvas and wooden flats.

The gradual separation of theatre architecture from scenic design during the eighteenth century is important to keep in mind because it was one result of a broader trend towards greater degrees of professional separation that was definitive of the age of industrialization. But another theme will be our central concern in this section: the transformation of the scenic space of the stage as it was designed by scenic artists and viewed by growing numbers of theatregoers. We might think of the application of 'single point' or linear perspective to the stage as a distinct scenic technology. This method of projecting coherent spatial depth on a flat surface used a system of regularly ordered lines organized around a point of view ascribed to a viewer and an arbitrary vanishing point, and revolutionized painting and scene design during the Renaissance. Because it made effective use of flat, compact scenic surfaces, it complemented but was fundamentally distinct from the technology that allowed for synchronized changes in settings between or even within acts, awe-inspiring flights, or special effects like shipwrecks and storms. The combination of machine-powered changeable scenery and unified, painted perspective vistas not only defined an epoch in scenic design between the mid-seventeenth and mid-nineteenth centuries, it had a powerful effect on the design of both court and public theatre buildings that persisted deep into the modern era.

The Italian baroque 'system' of stage equipment was implemented continent-wide in a variety of configurations, but there was a discernible template that included a set of common features and mechanisms. The essential components, in George C. Izenour's terms, were 'a raked stage, a shallow substage, and an overhead grid that together provided placement, support, and guidance for the horizontal and vertical scenery-manipulating apparatus'.[15] These elements allowed as many as six sets of flat painted pieces to be installed for a given design, and thus for a variety of looks that could be easily shown during the course of a performance. Under the stage, wheeled vehicles called 'chariots' guided by tracks supported vertical posts that protruded onto the stage through slots in the stage floor. Painted and otherwise decorated scenic flats, usually constructed of wood-framed battens covered in canvas, were mounted to these posts, and walked in and out of position by stage hands in a coordinated movement. Overhead, a grid comprising parts of the roof trusses and horizontal beams supported a system of hand-driven ropes, pulleys, drums and capstan winches allowed a few backstage personnel to operate changes in the overhead scenery pieces. These frequently depicted heavens, clouds, trees or lofty pieces of architecture needed to hide the upper recesses of the stage area and complete the stage picture. Most complete scene changes took place behind a closed stage curtain, but designers often opted for transformations such as a storm, a revelation of an interior chamber, or a culminating *deus ex machina* in which actors and special decorations were flown in from above.

Over the course of the eighteenth century, artists and builders in Europe not only adopted this basic suite of stage equipment; they began to experiment with improvements to it that involved expansions of the space below the stage or above it. In France, both the creation of an enormous new opera house at Versailles and the need for a new grand opera house in Paris after the burning of the Palais-Royal opera in 1763 led to new projects that expanded scenic capacity both in terms of space and mechanics. By excavating a deep space below the stage, the French system shown in Diderot and d'Alembert's *Encyclopaedia* permitted pairs of side wing flats to be dropped through the floor entirely. This new system also included new rigging devices that controlled the vertical movement of wing flats from capstan winches above the stage, thus locating the control for all major components of the scenery in a zone above the stage. In Vienna, theatre designers explored scenic machinery from the other direction. By vaulting the space over the stage and creating the forerunners of modern fly towers, German-Austrian engineers enhanced the effects possible with horizontally moving wings by adding in the ability to fly in and out large

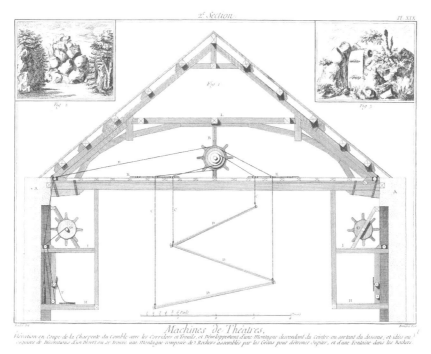

FIGURE 9.4: Cutaway section of the ceiling with corridors and pulleys, and development of a mountain descending from the hanger or rising from below, *Machines de théâtres*, 2e section, pl. xix. *Encyclopédie*, vol. 27. Engraving by Robert Bénard for Diderot and d'Alembert, 1772. Courtesy of the Department of Special Collections, Washington University Libraries.

batten sets with the aid of elaborate counterweights and guided arbours. Scene changes with these flying surfaces proved to be quicker and easier to operate successfully than the Italian or French systems.[16]

The diversity and ingenuity on display in plans of eighteenth-century stage machinery was paradoxically both driven and constrained by one common feature: the drawn and painted image of illusory depth on flat surfaces. This, too, had been an originally Italian invention. Architects including the Roman Vitruvius had written about the use of perspective compositions in scenery, and Renaissance architects including Serlio and Scamozzi helped make projections of false depth on flat surfaces part of 'modern' scenography in the fifteenth and sixteenth centuries. The innovations that captivated audiences of the seventeenth and eighteenth centuries, however, were essentially two additions that enhanced the spatial illusions of linear perspective. First, mechanized stage sets exploited the light and compact nature of painted scenic elements, combining the variety, surprise and dynamism of multiple set changes and transformations with the optical illusions inherent to linear perspective. Second, *perspecteurs* beginning with Guido Ubaldo and Scipione Chiaramonti learned to control the entire stage picture by setting distance points that governed the compositions painted across multiple stage flats.[17] Mimicking this and other methods of eliding the gaps between discontinuous wings and overhead elements, sought-after seventeenth-century scenographers mastered the creation of grand, unified vistas capable of showing their court patrons an image of space upon which a potent sense of order had been imposed, and in which monarchs and princes were apt to see a reflection of their own dominions.

Within the scope of the eighteenth century, the Bibiena family of stage decorators and theatre architects occupies a singularly important place. Originating in Florence, this family of artists, headed initially by Ferdinando Galli-Bibiena and his brother Francesco, operated professionally in Vienna and were employed foremost by the Hapsburg court, their relatives and friends continent-wide. Two of Ferdinando's sons, Giuseppe (ca. 1696–1757) and Antonio (1700–74), became the most prolific designers and architects of the century, contributing heavily to the spread of Italian baroque style abroad. Giuseppe travelled broadly, working in courts associated with the Holy Roman Empire in Austria, Poland, Bohemia and Germany, while Antonio concentrated his efforts mainly in Vienna and Italy. Actively used remnants of their creations still exist, such as Giuseppe's Markgräfliches Opernhaus at Bayreuth (1748), and Antonio's Teatro Scientifico at Mantua (1775). Giuseppe's son Carlo Galli-Bibiena designed theatre sets in Bayreuth, Berlin and London.[18]

The architectural legacy of the Bibiena's theatrical efforts is still identified with baroque style, in contrast to the more delicate French rococo creations of Cuvilliés, for example.[19] In scenic design, however, the Bibienas are thought to have modernized the uses of perspective, providing alternatives to the symmetrical, central-vanishing-point monotony that resulted from imitations of seventeenth-century impresarios like Giacomo Torelli, Gaspare and Carlo Vigarani, and Vigarani's successor as court scene designer in France, Jean Bérain I. All of these artists exploited the capacity of perspective scenery to make it seem as though the central upstage visual area projected far beyond where the back wall of the stage really was, providing the illusion of faraway horizons and rhythmic arrangements of columns, arches or trees that continued farther than the eye could see. Painted designs like these reinforced a formal feature of linear perspective, which is most visually cohesive when the whole picture is painstakingly organized around a single point of view of spectatorial view. Since the early days of perspective design, the convention had been to locate this point of view directly in front of the centre of the picture, along a line perpendicular to the canvas. Some eighteenth-century playhouses, including the Teatro Scientifico of Mantua and the Munich Residenztheater, bolstered this scenic practice by locating a royal viewing box in the centre and back of the house. In this way the represented and concrete spaces of the theatre were linked along a central axis, and each implicitly manifested a political idea: the concentration of power and judgement in the body of a single individual.

Around 1703, Ferdinando Galli-Bibiena began to create new sorts of stage pictures using a technique called *scena per angolo* oblique perspective. By fixing vanishing points for the painted composition away from the centre of the stage, and by multiplying the number of vanishing points while maintaining a unified sense of spatial composition across the whole vista, Bibiena generated more complex and imaginative stage pictures.[20] Around the same time, the Jesuit painter Andrea Pozzo published a work demonstrating advances in perspective scenery, including refinements that made it possible to depict curved architectural forms across detached flats.[21] These two advances enabled eighteenth century scenic designers to stimulate the imagination in new ways. Audiences could be placed in the midst of enormous palaces whose galleries flowed to the left and right and whose vaulted heights towered out of reach of the eye. The new compositional variety, architectural imagination, illusion and sense of magnitude dazzled audiences and promoted a new surge in perspective scenic production.

Jean-Nicolas Servandoni, a French scenic impresario who served as chief decorator to the Opéra in Paris between 1728 and mid-century, made the most of the recent refinements in perspective scenery. In sets for the opera and various other venues, Servandoni created the illusion of massive complex architecture that dwarfed the audience.[22] In the late 1730s and again in the 1750s, he produced a number of mute spectacles in his 'Salle d'optique' in Vigarani's old Salle des Machines in the Tuileries Palace. Servandoni used various means to overawe audiences: oblique lines, unusual arrangements of painted flats, dramatic, fantastical architecture inspired by the Bibienas and the painter Giovanni Panini, the real depth of his cavernous stage, and sophisticated use of lamp light to generated the effect of chiaroscuro.[23] Servandoni was uncompromising and extravagant. He bankrupted himself and very nearly the Academy of Music in the cause of his ever more dazzling productions.

The *scena per angolo* style of perspective scenery gave spectators an expansive sense of visual space, which undoubtedly contributed to its embrace by some designers. But it also stands as one of several eighteenth-century aesthetic developments that challenged centre-point perspective and the monarchical political logic that it had bolstered since becoming a mark of aesthetic taste in court milieus. The symmetrical arrangement of orthogonal lines and pictorial compositions provided the mirror image of a visual scheme organized around a central point of view associated with a single dominant place of political power and judgement. Oblique lines and multiple vanishing points therefore implicitly depicted a more complicated political order. *Per angolo* compositions still favoured a single central point of view where it was most difficult to detect the spaces that separated rows of painted flats, but abundant, irregular placement, and the oblique positions of flats themselves (as opposed to oblique pictorial lines) helped distribute the pleasures of perspective illusion to a larger nucleus of well-placed spectators.[24]

But the underlying schema of perspective scenery, even of compositions with oblique lines and multiple vanishing points, relied upon the selection of favoured locations for spectatorship. The widespread adoption of perspective painted settings in public playhouses, which depended on the revenues large audiences delivered, thus caused a problem by centralizing favourable positions for viewing the stage. The most lucrative places in baroque-style playhouses, moreover, included the first level of loges situated close to the level of the stage itself, and these wrapped around from one side of the stage picture to the other. With a mind towards democratizing theatre's visual pleasures, reform-minded architects in the decades of the high Enlightenment undertook to radically restructure spectatorial sightlines. Taking a cue from Palladio and Scamozzi's Teatro Olimpico, the stage of which featured independent perspectival scenic alleys along seven diverging axes, architects including the Italian Cosimo Morelli and the French C.-N. Cochin, Charles de Wailly and C.-N. Ledoux designed theatres where the spectatorial field of view was more or less partitioned in three, with the two side stages providing independent perspective vistas to the audiences that faced them on the right and left sides of the house respectively.[25] Rather than allowing the entire stage to be arranged in the service of a single point of view enjoyed by a few privileged spectators, these designers aspired to create multiple points around which perspective scenery could be designed. Their overt aspirations were to improve the lot of those on the margins of the auditorium, but by decentring the areas where theatre was believed to be best enjoyed and showing favour to a wider swath of the theatre-going public, reform-minded architects tried to more equally distribute theatrical pleasure. Though none would admit it, their plans translated into architectural form some of the more incendiary political writings of the era. In 1754, just as the movement to reform theatre architecture in France had begun, Rousseau had written that it was 'contrary to the law of nature, however it may be defined, . . . for a handful of people to gorge themselves on superfluities while the starving multitude lacks necessities'.[26]

For the most part, tripartite stages remained hypothetical, but in France, a nationwide wave of public theatre building spurred a great deal of investigation into theatre design and fostered enthusiasm for mould-breaking ideas.[27] Ledoux succeeded in having a three-part stage built, but the new configuration immediately caused problems for the theatrical machinists and painters hired to decorate it. One referred to Ledoux's 'crazy notion of a triple stage' in a letter.[28] This episode revealed the extent to which theatre and stage design, once a skilled artistic practice planned and executed by a select band of artisans, was morphing into something that operated more along the lines of modern

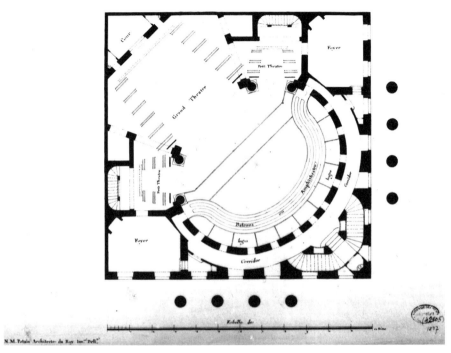

FIGURE 9.5: Theatre hall, plan of the first loges, N.M. Potain, 1763. Courtesy of l'École nationale supérieure des beaux-arts.

post-industrial modes of production. Theory and design for permanent theatre buildings came under the sway of architects with academic training who were highly versed in abstract scientific knowledge gleaned from philosophy and experimental science. But these individuals sometimes had very little first-hand understanding of how to operate scenery, or the other quirky practicalities of stagecraft.

As the narrative above suggests, the centre of theoretical and practical innovation in theatre and scenic design, as with the arts of dramatic literature, and costume design, seemed to have shifted from Italy to France during the middle of the eighteenth century. But of course artistic dynamism thrived also in Vienna, London, Milan and in untold smaller cities during this period, and savants wrote thoughtful and erudite treatises defending theories of theatre space outside France as well. But whether one reads French theorist Pierre Patte, Patte's Italian translator Paolo Landriani, or English architect George Saunders, one finds in the last decades of the eighteenth century a new method of approaching the design of theatre buildings.[29] Theatre space is now understood through a systematic evaluation of the physical conditions of spectatorship, and informed by recent discoveries in experimental science. Perhaps as much as any other single development, this transformation in the conceptual transformation of theatre space, from a place of illusory appearances to a field with physical properties, helps explain the manifold changes in theatre technology that began to emerge at the end of the century.

LIGHT

One of the principal technical features of theatre, lighting, began to transform at the end of the Enlightenment era in ways that presaged the particularly technologically dynamic era of the nineteenth century. This is not to say that other categories of stage technology remained inert. Audiences participated in a vogue for ethnographic and historical specificity in costume and stage dressing in France, prompting, for example, the unprecedented efforts to imitate Chinese dress in the 1755 production of Voltaire's *Orphan of China*, and Jacques David Louis's painstaking reconstruction of an ancient Roman chair for a 1790 production of Voltaire's tragedy *Brutus*.[30] In advance of the nineteenth-century maturity of architectural acoustics, theorists and architects across the continent experimented with a wide array of auditorium shapes (fan, bell, horseshoe, bellows, ellipse, oval, circle) that were thought to be the best for delivering sound to the audience. George Saunders carried out acoustical experiments to try to determine what form best allowed the human voice to carry.[31]

But it was lighting that truly began to transform into what would become its modern form before the turn of the nineteenth century. Previous to late Enlightenment-era experiments with directed lighting, indoor theatrical illumination both on stage and in the auditorium was supplied by candles that burned either wax or beef tallow, or simple oil lamps. These could be placed in a variety of ways. To produce general lighting, chandeliers could be suspended in the auditorium from the ceiling or the over the proscenium portion of the stage itself, and sconces could be placed on the walls near loges and around the proscenium arch. Aesthetic preferences and spectatorial practices varied across regions, with the French, for example, preferring the auditorium to remain lit during performances while Italian opera houses relied on light emanating from within semi-closed audience boxes.

Illumination of the stage came from general lighting, and from some combination of footlights in a row along the front edge of the stage and lights mounted on vertical surfaces including the proscenium sides and behind individual scenic wings. Already at the end of the seventeenth century in Venice, combinations of multi-wick oil lamps, wax candles, movable footlights and some directional capability through the manipulation of rotatable wooden rods to which lights were fixed, gave this system of stage lighting some level of sophistication, and its variations subsisted through the end of the eighteenth century.[32] Here too, practices changed over time and varied from nation to nation. After touring widely on the continent, David Garrick returned to England in 1765 and changed lighting practices at Drury Lane. Though retractable footlights had been in use before this moment in London, Garrick improved their intensity through the use of reflective backings, and reinforced scenic side lighting, which allowed him to eliminate the chandeliers that had previously hung over the apron stage at Drury Lane. Garrick's reforms to lighting at Drury Lane followed his clearing of spectators off of the stage, and a subsequent enlargement of the auditorium in order to retain the revenue they contributed. But they also imitated the French practice he had seen while on tour, where side lighting and special light directing instruments known as *réverbères* (reflectors) had been in use in the 1750s.[33]

The variety of applications that theatre-makers found for small, burning light sources should not be underestimated. Since the Renaissance, candle and lamp flames had been used to illuminate whole stages, but also to cast coloured light through tinted glass or liquors, to cause gilding, precious stones and other surfaces to shimmer and, to some degree, to support imitated light of the sort that scene painters rendered with colour, shading and direction on scenic surfaces. But eighteenth-century methods of illuminating theatres bore many difficulties. The relatively weak luminosity of oxidizing fuels like animal fats (beeswax and beef tallow) burned using simple suspended wicks severely hampered the design of stage lighting. Rather than the dynamic sense of place and mood that electric lighting now provides, early-modern theatre-makers hoped merely to generate enough light onstage to make the scenery and actors clearly visible from even remote parts of the auditorium.[34] Light could not be used to suggest the change of hour, direct audience attention or create variations in mood as it is today.

What is more, the capacious playhouses built during the eighteenth century required ever-larger quantities and dispersal of light, which led to great numbers of candle and lamp flames on stage and in the auditorium. One Venetian opera house in the late seventeenth century used an estimated 300 separate lights just to illuminate its five pairs of scenic wings, not counting footlights or instruments in the auditorium.[35] A 1757 account of the candles used in the Comédie-Française, which at that point used the same converted tennis-court space it had occupied since 1689, suggests that 116 candles and thirty-six *réverbère* instruments were placed to illuminate the stage wings, in addition to thirty-two oil lamps used as footlights.[36] Light was not only expensive in such quantities, it fouled the air, leading to complaints about the odour and atmosphere in frequently used public theatres, and magnified the risk of fire, a frequent and sometimes deadly occurrence in the eighteenth century. In 1781, for example, a backstage scenic effect in a production of Gluck's opera *Orphée et Eurydice* ignited a cloth hanging above the stage of the Paris Opéra. The building was utterly destroyed, and at least ten people were killed, including two dancers and the thirteen-year-old servant of the dancer Alexis Huart. Reportedly on this night, the relatively new building's backstage firefighting water tanks were found to be dry.[37]

New light instruments sufficiently powerful to shape the stage or change its appearance within an act would not emerge until the second half of the nineteenth century with the advent of electric carbon-arc lights. But already in the middle of the eighteenth century ideas about theatre space were changing in a way that both harkened the eventual end of perspective scenic vistas and pointed the way to modern lighting techniques. In architectural treatises written by French reformers in the third quarter of the century, playhouses began to be thought of as spaces of optics and acoustics. Some authors began to write about the 'perspective' and 'optics' as interchangeable concepts of spectatorial viewing, and in 1782, Pierre Patte declared that optical and acoustical principles should be the starting point of enlightened theatre architecture.[38] Linear perspective, which had been the central conception of space according to which baroque-era designer-builders understood what happened inside a playhouse, conceded to a new way of thinking about space. Architects now saw theatre space as a dynamic place of physical interactions and sensations, thought in terms of optics and acoustics, and availed themselves directly of the writings of experimental physicists. In other words, for the first time we see what Bernard Stiegler would consider to be the essence of modern theatre technology: the direct functional integration of the latest science with artistic techniques.

Integration with the experimental sciences appeared in the form of architectural treatises that referred to physics and employed current ways of thinking about sound and light. But it also emerged in the activities of scientists who put their instruments to use analysing the air quality, acoustics and optical problems of theatres directly. In the 1770s, a French physicist named Sigaud de Lafond included the Hôtel de Bourgogne theatre in his experiments on air quality; a reformer who advocated for the abolition of flat painted scenery in 1809 cited Lafond's results.[39] Analyses of architectural acoustics and sightlines near the turn of the century redirected the enterprise of theatre and scenic design towards the science of engineering, which is to say along the lines of complex problem solving and away from purely aesthetic concerns. Carl Ferdinand Langhans, a Prussian architect, wrote an essay on theatre and architectural acoustics in 1810 that incorporated the knowledge that sound was a form of energy that propagated and concentrated depending on the shape of the room and placement of the sound source. Langhans clarified the problems of sound propagation in theatres and refuted much of what Pierre Patte had supposed about the elliptical form of a theatre.[40]

The problems of lighting a theatre also became the locus of integration between theatrical and scientific practice. Just after Lafond reported on his tests of air quality Antoine Lavoisier, one of France's greatest scientific minds and the founder of modern chemistry, turned his attention to the design of theatre lighting instruments. During the 1770s and 1780s research expanded into new methods of lighting, including early explorations into flammable coal gas and electric sparks – precursors to the gaslights and arc lights of the next century. Having earlier studied the optimal form of reflective lamp housings for the purpose of lighting city streets, Lavoisier tried in 1781 to develop instruments that would cast light from the auditorium onto the stage in the manner of modern ellipsoidal lights. For this project Lavoisier secured the use of a voluminous hall in the Louvre, darkened the windows, and positioned his instruments to replicate the real conditions of lighting the Comédie-Française. Though it did not yield a breakthrough in directional lighting, Lavoisier's *simulacre de salle de spectacle*, or simulated playhouse, staged a precursor to work in contemporary lighting laboratories, combining geometric analysis, rigorous experimentation and aesthetic aims.[41]

A greater lasting impact on the practical technology of stage lighting, however, was made simultaneously when the Swiss inventor Aimé Argand developed a new type of brightly burning oil lamp. Carl Langhans, in 1810, explained the difference this creation made for the task of illuminating indoor theatres. Previously, the best available technology was the candle; but to light the capacious public theatres, they were required in such quantities that they

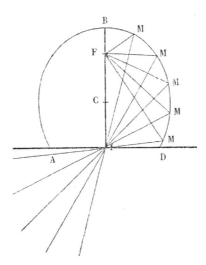

FIGURE 9.6: Geometric analysis of a reflecting lamp designed for a theatre, from *Mémoire sur la manière d'éclairer les salles de spectacle*, Antoine Lavoisier 1781. Reprinted from *Oeuvres de Lavoisier*, vol. III, 1865.

generated obnoxious amounts of smoke. Besides this problem, the smoke 'grew steadily worse and almost suffocated the flame . . . the number of candles which had to be put one above the other, behind the wings, became so numerous that the upper candles were extinguished by the heat of the lower ones'.[42] The footlights, Langhans continues, filled with wax or tallow wicks, which would cough up great amounts of smoke. Such reasons explained why proscenium openings could not be made larger – they would only expose the audience more to greater amounts of smoke. Many different types of lamps had been tried to no avail.

Argand's lamp mitigated these problems by containing both the flame (in a cylindrical glass chimney) and the oil it burned (in a separate reservoir). The glass chimney contained and was thought to reduce smoke, while both it and the enclosed fuel reservoir helped prevent fire related to oil spillage. A circular wick with a hollow inside helped the lamp burn brighter too by allowing a current of air to pass to the flame from below. This reduced the number of instruments needed and helped light upstage recesses.[43] The premiere of Beaumarchais's *Marriage of Figaro*, on 27 April 1784, is remembered in part because the play made public and explicit long-standing resentments against the aristocracy. Louis XVI is reported to have said that they only way this play would not be politically dangerous would be if the Bastille was torn down first. The debut of the play, however, also marked the first use of Argand lamps in the Comédie-Française, a notoriously conservative institution which had struggled with the question of how to light its new home, a monumental neoclassical building, finished in 1782, for which its architects had once drawn plans that included a convertible three-part stage. Late-century innovations such as these did not sweep away old ways of producing theatre in the way that the French Revolution suddenly abolished the monarchy and feudal politics. But already at that time, the expansion of experimental science, instrumental or problem-oriented thinking, and open channels between the institutional creation of theatre and cutting-edge scientific thought previewed the era of precipitous technical change that was about to arrive.

CHAPTER TEN

Knowledge Transmission

Theatrical Intelligence and the Intelligence of Theatre

DANIEL O'QUINN

To the question 'What is Enlightenment?' Kant famously answered 'man's emergence from self-incurred immaturity' and thus indicated that the very notion turns on a critical attitude towards received truths in all areas of human experience.[1] Significantly both the intellectual avatars of Enlightenment and the grassroots practitioners of enlightened social change were highly self-aware agents of transformation. After centuries of religious and sectarian wars, many eighteenth-century thinkers urgently brought this sceptical attitude to bear on organized religion and revealed a patchwork of medieval superstition. Whether that superstitious residue could be overcome, or whether it was actually constitutive of Enlightenment rationality remains a recalcitrant issue. And it was a vital issue on the eighteenth-century stage. If we look solely at the British example it is possible to describe an arc that moves from the debates surrounding Catholicism in the Restoration through satirical representations of dissenters at mid-century to enactments of toleration in the 1790s – a line that roughly links Otway's allegorization of the Exclusion Crisis in *Venice Preserv'd* to Samuel Foote's *The Minor* to Richard Cumberland's *The Jew*, but that also incorporates representations of Islam and pagan rites as allegories for superstition, enthusiasm and fanaticism.

Likewise, Peter Gay's contention that Enlightenment involved a progressive shift from monarchical absolutism to democratic governance remains a durable narrative and an unsettling problem, for if this were the case then why have freedom, equality and justice proven to be so fragile? Numerous scholars have demonstrated the importance of this grand narrative to theatre history. Indeed, one could argue that British theatre history can be effectively organized by attending to transformations in the relationship between power and knowledge.[2] Because governance was so fraught, eighteenth-century theatre continually thinks about the nature of sovereignty and control. This fixation on governance was most obvious in the Restoration when the theatre was itself part of a larger world of courtly performance and thus deeply imbricated in the changing status of kingship and new notions of the polity. In serious drama, sex became a site for thinking about the application of sovereign authority. In comedy, sex tended to operate as an allegory for the state. What is so remarkable, and beyond my remit here, is the degree to which Restoration dramatists and audiences were willing to explore the disintegration of monarchical sovereignty. The horror plays of the 1690s are perhaps the most vivid case in point, but plays such as Aphra Behn's *The Widdow Ranter* boldly examine what happens when traditional forms of authority are superseded. Important plays such as Joseph Addison's *Cato* and John Gay's *The Beggar's Opera* not only intervened in crucial contemporary political debates, but also become flashpoints for considering the changing definitions of sovereignty, liberty and virtue as they were restaged later in the century. In all three cases, we see audiences radically realigning past political arguments by selectively applying aspects of these plays to present events and situations.

The advent of sentimental theatre by mid-century can be seen as a response to both pessimistic and nostalgic accounts of the shift from absolutism to liberal governmentality. Attuned to the increasing prominence of middling audiences, sentimental tragedies such as George Lillo's *The London Merchant* explicitly explored the tissue of social obligations that maintained social order. Sentimental comedy tends to fill the vacuum opened by the breakdown in religious and political authority by scrutinizing the manners and morals of characters who were remarkably similar to the paying members of the audience. In this light, the shaming of morally dubious characters, the reformation of rakes, the abjection of independent women, the celebration of marriage, and the careful examination of property and finance are all constitutive elements of the increasing tendency towards liberal governmentality. In this regard, the theatre exhibits many of the tendencies first articulated by Michel Foucault in *Discipline and Punish*. Referring to the British example, he finds the Restoration is very much involved in an exploration of what it means to live in and to get beyond a punitive society, whereas the work of Farquhar, Centlivre and their followers Cowley, Sheridan and Inchbald are deeply engaged with the disciplinary potential of middling sociability.[3] That women playwrights should be so important to this development indicates the degree to which their bodies and lives were the ground on which much of this realignment of power and knowledge took place.

As these brief sketches of the harbingers of religious and political Enlightenment on the British stage suggest, there was a remarkable willingness to use the space of performance as a place to think about, indeed experiment with, social relations. The work of Jürgen Habermas and Robert Darnton has, in different ways, contended that Enlightenment and the emergence of the print public sphere were coextensive historical phenomena.[4] The heuristic value of their arguments is undeniable – the self-awareness of European society cannot be separated from the vast explosion in literacy and print – but these arguments need to be extended to the realms of sociability and performance in ways that will preoccupy the latter sections of this chapter. Furthermore it is important that we consider the mode of thought enabled by the proliferation of print and public venues for sociability and performance in this era. In contrast to received orthodoxy and authority, we see attempts to scrutinize and comprehend the world from empirical observation. As many theorists of the Enlightenment have suggested, the advent of the scientific method is a crucial presupposition of most enlightened thought. Propositions are made and tested against observable evidence. In an era of religious and political scepticism this could easily take on moral implications and thus become a blueprint for comedy. Indeed, Richard Brinsley Sheridan's *School for Scandal* is essentially a moral experiment: Sir Oliver Surface hides his identity and stages a series of tests to assess the worthiness of his nephews. That the younger nephew is found to be the most appropriate heir should not go unnoticed. In contrast to the laws and conventions of the *Ancien Régime* – i.e. against the prerogative of established authority – a social experiment has found a more worthy basis on which to base cultural and social continuity.

Regardless of one's position on Enlightenment itself, the very notion explicitly or implicitly involves a consideration of the status of knowledge; thus to be writing a chapter on knowledge transmission for a volume on the Enlightenment is doubly vexed. Do you explore theatre as an Enlightenment phenomenon and thus assume in advance what Enlightenment might be as I have been doing in the preceding paragraphs? Or do you track transformations in the knowledge practices inherent to and surrounding theatrical culture in order to develop a theory of theatrical Enlightenment? Either approach will necessarily veer off into unsatisfying generalizations or make some examples bear an inordinate amount of evidentiary weight. In the face of these vexations, I am going to focus on two interrelated questions that pertain directly to the epistemic transformations associated with this period: how does the theatre operate as a conduit for the burgeoning knowledge practices of the Enlightenment? And how did these same knowledge practices come to comprehend the theatrical enterprise? The distinction is roughly between utilizing the theatre as a subject of knowledge and situating theatre as an object of knowledge itself. The first two sections of this chapter outline these two antithetical approaches to the problem of knowledge transmission, and the final section attempts to perform a dialectical resolution by looking at the relationship between epistemic change and repetition. As we will see, exploring theatre as a mode of knowledge transmission in this period will force us to traverse a vast cultural field and ultimately demand that we consider theatre's role in social reproduction.

THE INTELLIGENCE OF THEATRE

It is difficult to overstate the importance of William Davenant to the knowledge practices exemplified by eighteenth-century theatre in Britain.[5] As a member of the Newcastle circle that included Thomas Hobbes and Margaret Cavendish, Davenant was well aware of the incipient transformation in political and religious thought instantiated by the scientific revolution. Two aspects of his deeply influential opera *The Siege of Rhodes* (1656/9) are important for our purposes. Devised while Charles II was still in exile, the production drew its plot from Richard Knolles' *The Generall Historie of the Turkes* (1603) and based its set designs on engravings that were themselves based on empirical observation of the situation of Rhodes.[6] This desire to capture the particularity of the foreign world signalled a new attitude towards theatrical representation: both at the level of plot and design, Davenant's opera made claims to historical and physical accuracy heretofore unattempted on the European stage. Furthermore, *The Siege of Rhodes* embraced an epistemological expansiveness whose effects were in some sense pedagogical. However imperfectly, it forcefully showed the audience what Rhodes looked like, what the Ottomans wore, how, according to the most up-to-date historical texts, Suleyman the Magnificent behaved. What this meant is that the opera was remediating new knowledge that was beginning to circulate in journey writing and in the comparative histories of empire. Since these forms of writing based their claims on ostensible empirical observation, the audience for Davenant's opera was involved in an act of repeat observation that had the potential both to consolidate knowledge about the world and to shake the foundations of received truths based on classical learning and religious doxa.

The Siege of Rhodes is rarely discussed today but it was a harbinger of much of the theatrical innovation for the next 150 years. As Bridget Orr argues, 'two notable features of [Davenant's] practice which became standard in the production of serious plays, were the deployment of backdrops representing location in perspective . . . and the situating of actors in the scene rather than on a jutting apron stage'.[7] As the century unfolds, one can discern a commitment to scenographic spectacle that is remarkable both for its expense and for its claims to verisimilitude. This is most evident in the vast array of plays that purport to represent the non-European world. The desire to systematically comprehend peoples and cultures, like the related imperative in natural history, fed the market for illustrated books, travel writing, atlases and costume albums. This last provided readers with a differential visual matrix within which to locate religion, nationality and ethnicity. As the eighteenth century unfolds these costume albums are not only 'corrected' but also begin to provide the basic

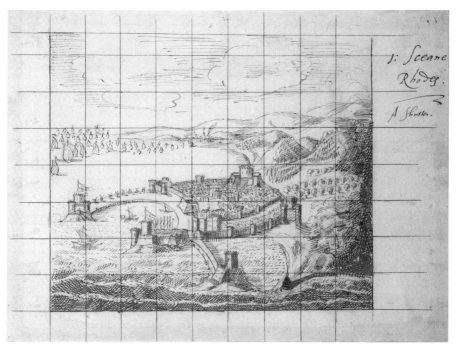

FIGURE 10.1: *View of Rhodes*, John Webb, 1656. © Devonshire Collection, Chatsworth. By permission of Chatsworth Settlement Trustees.

visual cues for performance genres. For example Jean-Baptiste Vanmour's illustrations of the Ottoman sultan and his myriad subjects that were first published in Charles De Ferriol's *Recueil de cent estampes représentant différentes nations du Levant* (1714) were quickly pirated and adapted for the stage. This process of adaptation was formalized with the publication of Thomas Jeffreys' *A Collection of the Dresses of different Nations, Antient and Modern* (4 vols, 1757–72) – a text specifically designed to guide choices for theatrical and masquerade costume. Perhaps the most extreme instance of this kind of empirical scenographic practice is O'Keefe's pantomime *Omai, or a Trip around the World*. Based on details culled from Captain Cook's third voyage to the Pacific and on the exploits of a young Raiatean visitor to London named Mai, the pantomime combines the physical humour of harlequinade with remarkably detailed representations of the peoples and spaces of Tahiti, Kamchatka, Nootka Sound and other locales. All of the advertisements and reviews for the production celebrate the involvement of John Webber, one of the principal artists among Cook's crew. Webber's drawings, taken *in situ*, became the basis for Philip-Jacques De Loutherbourg's costume and set designs and thus the *Morning Post* could argue that *Omai* 'was a source of amusement and instruction'.[8]

FIGURE 10.2: *A Dance in Otaheite*, John Keyse Sherwin after John Webber, engraving, 1784. By permission of the Trustees of the British Museum.

De Loutherbourg's career is the ultimate manifestation of the 'scientific' attitude set into motion by Davenant in the early phases of the Restoration. An absolutely vital member of Garrick's company at Drury Lane, De Loutherbourg specialized in simulating the real. His most virtuoso designs were perhaps reserved for his museum project, the Eidophusikon, in which he simulated atmospheric conditions for a paying audience. These same effects of painting, lighting and sound fundamentally altered the experience of play-going in the Georgian period, but what is so startling, from the perspective of knowledge transmission, was the concomitant claims to truth in representation. There is perhaps no better example of this than his work on *The Wonders of Derbyshire* (1779). Here was a play based on the efflorescence of local natural history in the print culture of the 1760s. As Anderson and Allen have argued, De Loutherbourg designed sets based on highly popular chorographical and geological texts.[9] Plot was fully subservient to observation and the play's perceived merit lay in the accuracy of De Loutherbourg's remediation of his geographical sources. This was even true of his work on demonstrably satirical plays: the concluding spectacle he designed for Sheridan's *The Critic* was a parody of another scenographic spectacle that was never realized, yet De Loutherbourg's staged naval battle was praised for its verisimilitude.[10]

FIGURE 10.3: *Costume Design: Dancer of Otaheite*, Philippe-Jacques De
Loutherbourg, watercolour, 1785. By permission of the National Library of Australia.

Managers understood that 'edification' could drive receipts and that audiences expected a high degree of epistemological engagement. This became even more crucial when the ethnographic imperative turned its lens on London itself. I have argued elsewhere that Georgian theatre was an auto-ethnographic enterprise through which London audiences came to know and understand themselves as a people. Many of the same aspects that animate Enlightenment proto-ethnography can be discerned in the scenography of Georgian plays. Take for instance Hannah Cowley's immensely popular comedy *The Belle's Stratagem* (1780). A thorough meditation on the politics of female sociability and the gendering of public space, Cowley's feminist analysis of marriage and gender performance is itself a virtuoso critique of the theatrical tropes used to regulate gender norms. As Gillian Russell has shown, Cowley's play is very much about the dynamics of fashionable sociability and her play counters many of interdictions placed on women's lives, especially as they are represented in Sheridan's comedies of the 1770s. Cowley's play is extremely specific about where actions happen and the play's climactic masquerade demands that the scene painters replicate the Pantheon – an innovative site of fashionable sociability. Audience members would know this space either from personal experience or from newspaper reports, and Cowley's intervention relies on the precise set of scandalous connotations associated with this entertainment venue.[11] That these connotations, like the building itself, have faded from public memory is one of the reasons why *The Belle's Stratagem* disappeared from the repertoire.

Even as the desire for 'accuracy' intensifies as the century unfolds it is important not to confuse claims for verisimilitude with realism. *Omai* is a useful reminder that harlequinade, meretricious racism, overt nationalism and protoscientific observation could be blended together to form a commercially viable pastiche. Significantly, one can find similar blends in what would appear to be more thoroughly scientific representations: as Palmira Brummett has shown, European maps of the Ottoman Empire become topographically more accurate as the century unfolded but nevertheless retained allegorical insets and racist images of the 'Turk'. Much of the complexity here has to do with the uncertain status of ethnography itself during this period. Enlightenment theories of human diversity are often a heterogeneous blend of contemporary observation, classical learning, theocratic doxa and outright invention. In many ways, the Enlightenment itself could be seen as a struggle to bring reasonable observation to bear on received accounts of character. This has significant implications for theories of acting. Joseph Roach has shown that changes in acting style mimic changes in the understanding of the human body and human subjectivity across the Enlightenment.[12] We know from audience accounts that the acting style of Thomas Betterton, marked by his equanimity and measured diction, defined the reasonable subject for much of the Restoration. Stability of posture and gesture, when combined with controlled diction exemplified the possessive individualism theorized by Locke. When David

Garrick overthrew these performance protocols at mid-century, he did so in the name of greater psychological accuracy. He was fashioning a subject more suited to the volatile world of mercantile capitalism and incipient imperialism – a world where the subject was more at risk. Audiences reacted to Garrick's innovations with extraordinary levels of identification and it became the actor's task to enact the spirit of the age. To put it somewhat bluntly, Garrick, and later Sarah Siddons, were essaying subjectivity itself; a performance of Hamlet or of Lady Macbeth thus became more than the exemplification of certain passions. It offered implicitly a theory of human motivation that was portable to circumstances beyond those dictated by the script.

These enactments of personality and motivation were inherently political. The control or loss of control of emotions on stage allowed audiences to experiment with new social formations, new modes of subjectivity and new forms of affective relations. Knowledge here became a speculative endeavour but it was one based on a set of performative hypotheses and it operated according to increasingly empirical notions of probability. It is this notion of probability that lends much of the theatre in this era its satirical and disruptive edge. Although highly 'unrealistic' scripts abound, the will to correlate events or characters on stage with historical events and people was ubiquitous. We still do not have a fully theorized understanding of this kind of topical reception, but we know from memoirs and from the press that audiences frequently drew historical resemblances from the slightest of gestures or utterances. The most profound implication of this kind of nimble will to correlate is that every aspect of performance in this era constituted and challenged the very notion of the public. The theatre in this light would necessarily be a physical zone where power and knowledge coalesced, not in an abstract Habermasian sphere of reasonable discussion, but rather in a far more volatile matrix where history was understood viscerally among a crowd of other observers. It is no surprise that such a laboratory would erupt into violence and would be the subject of such long-standing governmental censorship.

Returning momentarily to Davenant, it is worth remembering that *The Siege of Rhodes* was derived from a historical text. History had always provided material for serious drama, but during the eighteenth century its function and significance underwent significant changes. In the Restoration, Rome remained of vital importance for exploring the complex relationship between republicanism, absolutism and empire. It is hardly surprising that *All for Love* (1677), *Lucius Junius Brutus* (1680) and *Cato* (1712) played to such acclaim and remained canonical scripts for this era. But as the period unfolded, classical history was supplemented with Ottoman and Asian histories. As Bridget Orr has powerfully argued, plays set in Turkey, Persia, China and other Eastern locales not only proliferated in the late seventeenth and early eighteenth centuries, these settings became alternative zones for the analysis of sovereignty and governance.[13] Later in the century, the surge in antiquarianism in Britain brought a host of medieval and Germanic subjects to the stage. Often the site of nationalist discourse, these gothic plays would emerge as a significant genre in their own right during the politically volatile years of British Romanticism.

But more important than any expansion in the historical milieu represented on stage was a widespread tendency to search for systematic patterns within human and natural history. Just as the philosophers of the Scottish Enlightenment were developing stadial theories of human development or the French philosophes were building systems based on climatological difference, so too did playwrights locate characters within larger human systems. For example, Cumberland's *The West Indian* (1771) clearly differentiates its eponymous hero Belcour from the surrounding English and Irish characters by invoking the warm climate of his homeland. As he normalizes himself to English life, the play explicitly indicates that he will slowly lose the impetuous qualities that characterize his West Indian descent. From the 1760s onward stadial and climatological theories of human difference increasingly define the agency and potential of characters on the British stage. As Michael Ragussis argues, many plays in the period offer multi-ethnic spectacles that not only build human hierarchies, but also implicitly argue that such hierarchies are substantively akin to those exhibited in the world.[14]

This careful segmentation of the social is arguably one of the most profound instances of Enlightenment governmentality. By setting the limits on what a character can be, the theatre, like the novel, was regulating the social from within its very domain – only now character was thoroughly ingrained in the timbre of the player's voice and the very gestural economy that defined his or her performance. In a very real, tangible sense, the theatre not only exemplified how men and women should and should not behave, but also established the norms of sociability itself. This is especially acute when one turns to the way that the theatre both represented and activated the eighteenth-century sex/gender system because there was often little difference between what was happening on the stage and in the house. Perhaps because of the prevalence of women playwrights it is in this power/knowledge nexus that we can discern the most intense levels of active dissent. Whereas stadial and climatological theories of human difference seem to inhere on the Georgian stage, playwrights such as Centlivre, Cowley and Inchbald continually reveal the regulatory mechanisms of emergent liberal society and in doing so demand a level of scrutiny from their audiences. Certain female players had a similar effect – Charlotte Charke, Kitty Clive, Frances Abington, Sarah Siddons and Dora Jordan come immediately to mind – in that they could use their celebrity to test the boundaries of normativity. I would argue that the will to test, the desire to consider the social as an open problematic, constitutes a form of intelligence fully in keeping with most definitions of the Enlightenment.

THEATRICAL INTELLIGENCE

As we have seen, the emergent commercial theatre of the eighteenth century can be understood as an epistemic practice that parallels transformations in the knowledge practices of the Enlightenment. This is perhaps most readily seen by the late century impulses to systematize the theatrical canon. This desire had its impetus from the simultaneous efforts of David Garrick and Samuel Johnson to restore and consolidate the Shakespearean canon from seventeenth- and early eighteenth-century adaptations. In spite of the fact that Garrick was constantly adapting Shakespeare's plays he, more than any other player or manager, was responsible for valorizing the Shakespearean corpus, but his efforts were not as solitary as he would have liked to suggest. Fiona Ritchie has argued that the women players in his company and a significant group of female critics were also committed to establishing the centrality of Shakespeare to British theatre history.[15] Johnson's edition of Shakespeare's works and his surrounding criticism firmly established Shakespeare's place in the cultural patrimony and provided much of the critical lexicon through which value would be assessed. The lectures of Coleridge and Hazlitt pushed this critical project even further by looking carefully at the dramatic text and at the decisions inherent to late eighteenth-century performances of the Shakespearean repertoire. The importance of these endeavours has been long known, but we should not let them occlude the key systematizing activities of Elizabeth Inchbald. Her anthology of British theatre not only compiled the canon, but also offered prefatory notes for every play in the tradition.[16] Her supplemental anthologies sought to do the same thing for contemporary theatrical production and for afterpieces. All of these anthology projects made 'theatre' the object of knowledge and introduced crucial methods of organization. Chronology organizes the entire multivolume anthology, but genre and author are invoked in specific volumes. This is in stark contrast to the actual living and breathing deployment of the repertoire in the theatres themselves. Many of the plays collected by Inchbald were rarely performed by the end of the eighteenth century; if anything, genre and profitability were the chief concerns of managers. What this meant was that plays, for better or worse, could be considered as dramatic literature separate from their enactment as theatre.

Johnson's edition of Shakespeare and Inchbald's *British Theatre* stand as palpable evidence of the increasing importance of print culture for preserving and normalizing the transient world of performance. Just as one cannot comprehend the epistemic shifts of Enlightenment culture without accounting for the remarkable transformations in mediation – the emergence of the print public sphere, the stunning proliferation of newspapers and the periodical press, and the democratization of reading – one cannot address theatrical knowledge without considering how audiences gained their knowledge of the theatre. Anthologies were only the latest development in a long history of interaction between print and performance. The key issue for the eighteenth century was the symbiotic relationship between the newspapers and the theatres. In part because of the example set by Addison and Steele in *The Tatler* and *The Spectator*, reporting on the theatre was the most significant form of cultural information in the daily press.[17] Theatrical advertising was a vital source of revenue for the papers. But more importantly the theatre provided a steady stream of social and theatrical intelligence and this heady mix of scandal and culture was crucial for the papers' commercial success.

By the mid-century all of the London papers were printing reviews under the heading 'Theatrical Intelligence'. Even when, in the late 1760s, newspapers finally gained the right to print parliamentary debate, 'Theatrical Intelligence' held its own and in many ways continued to drive the desire for scandal and cultural information.[18] The information imparted in puffs and reviews directly influenced the success or failure of productions and thus theatrical managers were deeply involved in manipulating the press. Garrick was renowned for his skill at influencing 'Theatrical Intelligence' at a time when paragraphs could be bought and sold, but he was hardly alone. Successful management in the commercial theatre required intimate hands-on interaction with the dailies.[19] One of the most important ways of keeping a play in the press, and arguing for its viability, was first enacted in the playhouse. All mainpieces were framed by a Prologue and Epilogue that argued explicitly for audience favour. The texts of these addresses to the audiences were frequently printed in the daily papers a day or two after the initial review.[20] Similarly the lyrics to popular songs from comic operas or musical afterpieces were printed both to keep the production in the public eye and to elicit audience participation at ensuing performances.

This tight relationship between the daily press and the nightly theatre had considerable impact on reception because material from the press, in the form of political news, was frequently inserted or referenced in the plays advertised for that evening. This meant that topical knowledge suffused the eighteenth-century playhouse in a way that reinforced the economic interdependence of the newspapers and the theatres. It is not an exaggeration to suggest that the ideal audience in this theatrical world was thoroughly enmeshed in the consumption of both media. From accounts of how quickly topical knowledge was activated in the playhouse and from the extensive evidence of topical reference in the plays themselves, we can surmise that this was the norm.

Audiences were also remarkably knowledgeable about the plays themselves. There was an extensive market in printed scripts, so audiences became familiar with plays either through reading or through a remarkable level of repeat attendance. We know from diaries – Pepys is especially notable here – letters, collections of ephemera and from receipts that people would see the same plays repeatedly throughout their runs and throughout their lifetime. For highly successful plays like *The Beggar's Opera* or Sheridan's *The Duenna*, many audience members would see the play on successive nights in part because it was a social cause célèbre. Play-going was inseparable from the broader contours of sociability, so audiences were both knowledgeable and distracted. Regardless of the level of distraction, audience's deeply ingrained knowledge of scripts and performance protocols meant that the slightest variations in presentation style were noted and scrupulously judged. Frequently celebrity was grounded on a player's capacity to change long-standing performance protocols. The fame of Macklin, Garrick and Siddons was based on performative interventions in acting style but their lives became culturally significant beyond their specific contributions to the theatre. They became emblems for sociable norms and forms of subjectivity.

Celebrity was in many ways the bread and butter of 'Theatrical Intelligence'. Famous players crafted their personae in the playhouses through their performances and through the careful management of their character. The daily press's role in the inculcation of celebrity was crucial, but its strategies were quickly supplemented by other materials. Shearer West has shown the importance of painting and the expanding market for engravings to the inculcation of fame and thus the generation of custom for specific performances.[21] But often celebrity was secured by scandal. Innuendo about players in the newspapers often erupted into more elaborate narratives, poems and printed rebuttals in a variety of media. Some players and booksellers recognized early on that there was a market for scandalous memoirs and the publication of these materials impinged on the theatrical economy and on audience relation with particular actors and actresses. The memoirs of Colley Cibber, Charlotte Charke and Mary Robinson to name but a few sold myriad copies and thus had a profound impact on how the theatrical world was known by non-professionals. Of further importance was the publication of retrospective memoirs of play-going and performing by figures such as John Genest, James Boaden and William Charles Macready. Either through personal or professional relationships, all of these men were sources of insider knowledge that would eventually become vital sources of information about the repertory itself.

KNOW THY SELF, AGAIN AND AGAIN AND AGAIN

Thus far I have outlined two ways of thinking about knowledge transmission in the eighteenth-century theatre. On the one hand we have theatre as a practice actively constructing and promulgating knowledge of the world and on the other hand we see theatre itself becoming the object of typically Enlightenment forms of knowledge acquisition and circulation. If we look at these as two moments in a dialectic, then what we find at the heart of both is a complex relationship to repetition. When theatre is operating as a subject of knowledge it is constantly remediating information derived from the tangible archive of print culture or from the amorphous repertoire of social practice. When theatre is the object of knowledge these same practices remediate performance so that it gets incorporated into the horizon of social meaning and cultural significance. If we can point to one fundamental difference between the commercial theatre of the Enlightenment and its precursors, it is the intensification of this epistemic feedback loop. As we will see shortly, theatre practitioners and audiences were so aware of this phenomenon that it became the topic of dramatic representation and one could argue that by mid-century the theatre emerges as an autonomous cultural and social system suddenly aware of itself as a social generator. To put this in Hegelian terms, the theatre comes into a form of self-consciousness. But everything about its self-perceived systematicity turns on the repeated experience of seeing the same plays performed over and over again on consecutive nights, across consecutive seasons, often with the same players reprising their performances in signature roles. This is a theatre where everything happens again and again and again. This intense repetition is the experience from which a dialectical synthesis of the contrasting knowledge practices of the theatre can be resolved: it is what allows us to postulate a resolution between theatre's subjective and objective claims to knowledge.

In the eighteenth century, the repertory was a mode of knowledge in its own right that lived and breathed in the memory and affective responses of its audience. Because the repertory itself was so repetitive, audiences were constantly re-experiencing and reconsidering the same plays, the same performance protocols and their own relation to prior performances. New plays and performances frequently modelled themselves on or specifically invoked precursor scripts, gestures and utterances. Sets and music were reused and effectively reterritorialized to suit present needs. Audiences knew this world in ways that are hard for us to appreciate because the very restriction of the number of playhouses and the simultaneous explosion of extra-theatrical commentary on the theatre made theatrical culture a saturated zone of cultural and social exchange. Perhaps the most vivid way of imagining this is to envision Covent Garden or Drury Lane as a hothouse of topicality that channelled the nutrients cast up from print culture and from the practice of everyday life into dynamic cultural organisms that were themselves the object of discussion and elaboration beyond the playhouse walls. What this means is that the eighteenth-century theatre was integrally tied to its historical moment and this helps to explain why so few of its plays can be effectively remounted in our present day. Because the topical substrate has been largely lost, eighteenth-century scripts either exist in a kind of rootless condition or must be supplemented either with nostalgic fantasies of the past – usually signalled by elaborate period costume – or completely relocated to some version of the present that seems to resonate with the play's original situation.

Perhaps the most remarkable aspect of eighteenth-century theatre history is the degree to which knowledge of the repertoire is assumed, enacted and scrutinized both on the stage and in the audience. Because that repertoire was so thoroughly part of the lifeworld of eighteenth-century London, I would suggest that it is in this period that we see the theatre coming into dialectical self-consciousness. In perhaps the culminating moment of Enlightenment Hegel famously argued that self-consciousness requires the subject to see itself as it is seen by an other. Kant's injunction in 'What is Enlightenment?' to 'Dare to know' requires for Hegel a level of externality.[22] For our purposes here that externality can be found in the daily press. For at every nightly performance both the players and the audience could see themselves reflected back in the morning dailies and that external representation had a profound impact on performance and reception protocols the next night. The complexity of this dialectical relation should not be underestimated because the press captured performance in imperfect ways and players and audiences related to the representation of themselves in a variegated fashion. But the fact that the dynamic was incessantly repeated to meet the commercial needs of both the theatrical institution and the periodical press meant that a kind of aggregate cultural self-consciousness not only emerged, but also actively constructed the society around it.

There is no better sign of the coming into consciousness of the repertoire than the sheer number and importance of plays about the theatre. There are far too many plays that comment upon or allude to other plays (often being performed simultaneously in the other patent house) to discuss here – one would be hard-pressed to find a play that did not call up some other performance. Vanbrugh's *The Relapse* assumes knowledge of Cibber's *Love's Last Shift*; Cowley's *The Belle's Stratagem* assumes knowledge not only of Farquhar's *The Beaux's Stratagem*, but also of characters and situations from Sheridan's *The Duenna* and *The School for Scandal*; Fielding's and Foote's comedies are constantly reworking their own prior work, which in turn was always engaged with notable plays in the repertoire. But I want to conclude this chapter by focusing on a series of canonical plays and performances that literally scrutinized the practice of theatre in their own moment. Arguably the most important – in terms of audience approbation – is also one of the earliest: George Villiers, the Duke of Buckingham's *The Rehearsal* of 1671. Often understood as a burlesque of heroic drama, *The Rehearsal* retained its appeal well into the early nineteenth century – it was performed as late as 1817 – and as we will see it played a key role in the consolidation of David Garrick's acting career and in the culmination of Sheridan's critique of the British cultural patrimony during the American war.

The Rehearsal is a satire on the bombast of heroic drama that was patronized by Charles II during the early phases of his reign. Over the course of five acts the audience watches the playwright Bayes stage a rehearsal of his new play. Two surrogate viewers named Smith and Johnson scrutinize Bayes' play as it unfolds; Bayes for his part defends his play from their observations in increasingly ridiculous terms. Buckingham's satire on 'new Wit' is not simply theoretical: Bayes' play incorporates recognizable elements from Davenant's *The Siege of*

Rhodes, Dryden's *The Conquest of Granada*, and a host of other plays by lesser followers of these two poet laureates, hence the name 'Bayes'.[23] According to contemporary reports, Buckingham coached John Lacy to mimic Dryden's mannerisms, and audiences for the early productions of the plays would yell out the names of the plays and playwrights being parodied as the play progressed. But Buckingham's satire is not limited to the theatre. As George McFadden and Margarita Stocker have persuasively argued, Bayes is also a figure for Buckingham's political rival Arlington, Charles II's Secretary of State.[24] Stocker's detailed accounting of the play's topical allegory shows that Buckingham was using the parallel between poetry and the polity to suggest that the Ministry's domestic policy was as nonsensical as Bayes' play. By operating a double allegory, Buckingham was able to mount an opposition play under cover of an attack on playwriting. As Stocker states, 'that tactic . . . assumes . . . the alert pluralism of the seventeenth-century reader, upon which such writers as Dryden depended for the recognition of historiographic parallels with the present, and for the deduction of political principles'.[25] In a crucial observation Stocker adds that this form of recognition – itself a form of knowledge production – did not require full and consistent articulation of the allegory; it could operate through momentary flashes of correlation.[26]

One need not lay out the complex matrix of political allusions and resonances to recognize that *The Rehearsal* itself is enacting a form of dialectical self-scrutiny, for the aesthetic and the political critiques are not merely coincidental, they are coextensive. Heroic drama as practised by Dryden and theorized by Davenant in *Preface to Gondibert* 'reflect a Stuart conception of kingship and a fundamentally conservative ideology' because it was designed expressly for Charles II.[27] Likewise Arlington serves the King no less than Dryden does. What is so fascinating about this play is how it seems to have pulled the historical/political function of the theatre into the realm of public scrutiny. When the audience – made up of the various factions of Charles II's court – are induced to name and ridicule the plot contrivances of Dryden's plays, and by extension the political contrivances of the ministry, are they not involved in speaking truth to power? In other words, can we not infer that the thrill of such a play lies precisely in its activation of the nexus between power and knowledge. For its initial, all too knowing audience, its hilarity must have been remarkably proximate to the politically dangerous world of the 1670s.

The Rehearsal was printed almost immediately after its first performance and went through multiple editions, but it was not until 1704 that a *Key to The Rehearsal* was printed and subsequently added to all subsequent editions. What this means is that the play's knowledge effects remained operative well after its initial production. After a passage of thirty years many of its aesthetic targets had been consigned to oblivion and many of its immediate political imperatives ceased to signify. With the *Key* now circulating in the print public sphere, the play itself could stand as fully formed critique of an outmoded dramatic genre. But that same consolidation of the play's meaning could also liberate Bayes' idiocy and the vacuity of his play for further allegorical deployment. Unmoored from its political/aesthetic target, the play's entertainment value shifted away from the repetition of specific plays to the form of repetition nascent in Lacy's mimicry of Dryden. Significant actors such as Estcourt, Colley Cibber and Theophilus Cibber indulged their capacity for impersonation to ridicule theatrical personalities.[28] With knowledge of the heroic drama in decline players were now shifting the locus of entertainment by assuming audience knowledge of things as transitory as a player's voice or gesture.

This trend culminated in David Garrick's extraordinary reinvention of the role of Bayes and of the play itself. Garrick first performed Bayes on 3 February 1742 at Goodman's Fields and he forcefully shifted the play away from a satire on an obsolete genre and the pretensions of playwrights to a virtuoso attack on the acting of contemporary players. In an uncanny act of historical repetition, audiences once again starting shouting out names, this time not of plays, but of players. In Garrick's hands, Bayes became a controversial showpiece for his mimicry, and the thrill of the play lay in its personal irreverence. But because Garrick's mimicry was ubiquitous – he imitated all and sundry with the famous exception of Quin – it also became a highly self-conscious instantiation of the theatre system. Fully subordinating the play to the celebrity of the player, Garrick not only cast himself forth as the embodiment of theatrical artifice, but also pulled the entire panoply of actors he was putting on with him. In a highly tangible way, Garrick was making those he imitated known to themselves by externalizing their most characteristic qualities. In the aggregate this had the effect of making the theatre system aware of itself as a system.

We know from an early acting copy of *The Rehearsal* that was part of Garrick's personal library that initially he did not add a great deal to the play.[29] But he did cut almost all of speeches and business satirizing Dryden and Davenant's plays. Shorn of this material it is clear that he progressively added improvised scenes mimicking other players. It is on the strength of these improvisations that his early fame was based. But he did not let the play lie. In later years he started to add increasingly spectacular scenes and cast many of the players he was mimicking so that they were present on stage before the audience. The most famous of these was the 'new-rais'd Troops' that supplemented Bayes' battle scene in Act V of Buckingham's original. Punning on the word 'Troops' the entire troupe of actors was called upon to imitate their most famous roles and they were now deployed to exemplify theatre's willingness to defend 'culture' in the face of Jacobite insurrection. In these scenes, he resuscitated the topicality of Buckingham's script, only now he was simultaneously parodying the repertoire and using it to evoke contemporary extra-theatrical events. The dialectical imperative increasingly moves towards subsuming Buckingham's revelation of the proximity

FIGURE 10.4: *Muster of Bays's Troops*, anonymous, engraving,1745. By permission of the Library of Congress.

of knowledge, power and art into a larger recognition of theatre's ideological function in a post-courtly age. Bayes, as played by Garrick, is no longer speaking truth to power – i.e. to his King and his political rivals – because the theatre he plays in is now a thoroughly commercial enterprise whose efficacy relies not on the plays of courtier poets, but rather on the virtuosity of middling players. Thus the role and the play become self-conscious acts of commodification and explicitly align themselves with the imperatives of the state. That Garrick's mimicry made his compatriots uneasy is hardly surprising for it revealed that theatrical and social value are a function of an illusory form of autonomy.

The moral quandary posed by Garrick's intervention is one of the most important aspects of his theatrical persona, for it brought the question of legitimation to the fore. In this world where identities can be exchanged so easily, where the individual is so quickly fungible, how does one make moral judgements? The question applied as much to the world of commerce, where credit was a form of acting, as it did to the stage and to the social world it purported to represent. Enlightenment philosophers would explore this dilemma in various ways, but Garrick, controversially, sought legitimation in precisely the place obliterated in his adaptation of *The Rehearsal* – namely in the forms and genres of an earlier theatrical era. Garrick's role in consolidating Shakespeare's canonicity has already been mentioned, but he also actively aligned himself with Shakespeare and with Shakespeare's characters. On 7 December 1772 Garrick played Bayes for the last time, but by that time he was more fully aligned with Coriolanus, Richard III, Lear and above all Hamlet. Having established the autonomy of the commercial theatrical system, Garrick and others falling within his sphere of influence attempted to legitimate the theatre as a site of national identity by remediating Shakespeare for a new age. This process has been extensively discussed by Michael Dobson, Christian Deelman, Fiona Ritchie, Kristina Straub[30] and others; but it was Garrick's death that prompted perhaps the most profound meditation on the dangers of predicating knowledge transmission in the theatre on the transient body of the actor. And once again audiences had to contend with *The Rehearsal*.

Richard Brinsley Sheridan was the chief mourner at Garrick's pageant-like funeral and the performance of his *Monody on the Death of David Garrick* starkly raised the problem of how theatrical knowledge persists beyond the death of the actor. With the passing of the actor's body, Sheridan argued that the repertoire persisted in the memory of the audience. But he also recognized and baldly stated that audience memory is also subject to decay; unless some other actor comes along to fill the vacuum left by a figure like Garrick there is the very real possibility that theatrical culture will revert to a state of entropy. Roughly eight months after these related acts of mourning, Sheridan brought *The Critic* to the stage as an afterpiece to Drury Lane's new production of *Hamlet*. *The Critic* is a radical adaptation of Buckingham's *The Rehearsal* and a complex diagnosis of the Britain's cultural predicament in the final years of the American war.[31] Replicating Buckingham's meta-theatrical gesture, Sheridan also stages a very bad play for the audience's consideration, but he makes two crucial alterations to Buckingham's conceit. First, the surrogate viewers of the play and the playwright himself all work as critics or writers for the daily press. Smith, Johnson and Bayes become Sneer, Dangle and Puff and the entire first act amounts to a scathing critique of the public's inability to discern the difference between matters of poesy and matters of politics. Act I is thus an explicit reckoning with the interpenetration of the papers and the theatre in this period. At a moment of national crisis, Dangle prefers to read the 'Theatrical Intelligence' and Puff makes a living not only actively inventing facts and opinions about the war, but also writing propaganda for the stage. The play rehearsed in the second and third acts, entitled 'The Spanish Armada', is one such production and here we see Sheridan's second intervention. He returns to the spirit of *The Rehearsal* and creates a nonsensical pastiche of patriotic plays such as Richard Cumberland's *The Battle of Hastings* and King's *The Prophecy, or Elizabeth at Tilbury*. Even at a moment when it was evident that America would not be reconquered, these plays continued to suggest that history would repeat itself and Britain would emerge victorious. With repeated references to Buckingham's precursor, Sheridan's attack on the degradation of the stage carried the larger political implication that audiences had lost the capacity to make sound political judgements. Because historical knowledge was being distorted to suit the demands of ministry propaganda, *The Critic* was suggesting that historical consciousness itself was under threat.

The radicalness of this latter argument was brought home by his subtle deployment of the intertwined legacies of Shakespeare and Garrick. That *The Critic* was staged as an afterpiece to *Hamlet* was not a coincidence. Speeches from Shakespeare's masterpiece as well as props and costumes from that evening's production of the play make their way into Puff's 'The Spanish Armada' in much the same way as fragments of the patriotic propaganda Sheridan was explicitly satirizing. The levelling gesture is startling and deeply disturbing because it suggests that King's spectacle and Shakespeare's tragedy are of equal value. Significantly, the period following Garrick's death was not a good time for productions of *Hamlet*. His absence was acutely felt and seemed to signal a disconnection from the very cultural patrimony that Garrick had argued was the legitimating force behind British theatrical history. For a brief period theatre's place in the propagation of national fantasy was interrupted. This interruption coincided with the identity crisis prompted by American decolonization. By deploying *Hamlet* in *The Critic* in much the same way that Buckingham satirized Dryden's *Conquest of Granada* Sheridan pushed the question of obsolescence in a new direction. Sheridan is not saying that *Hamlet* is no longer playable, but rather that there will be a historical gap before it can signify properly again. Or to put this differently, Sheridan uses Buckingham's tactics to argue that knowledge of *Hamlet* was so essential that audiences and players would have to imagine a way to keep it alive in the repertoire. This is why the play ends with an injunction to repeat: a more 'perfect' performance may be rehearsed 'tomorrow'.[32] This demand on the future of players and audiences alike amounts to a radical reactivation of the politics of Buckingham's original play, for it counters state-sponsored obfuscation and bombast with a sober analysis of the current state of affairs both on stage and off. This had extraordinary implications for understanding Britain's precarious situation in the spring of 1780, a moment where knowledge that the time was out of joint was beginning to permeate the culture at large.

Sheridan's afterpiece pushed the dialectical self-consciousness of the theatrical system to the recognition that its very survival relied not only on aggregate acts of remembrance – i.e. on repetition – but also on creative acts of forgetting – i.e. on invention. If we think of the various iterations of *The Rehearsal* I have discussed here as increasingly sophisticated dialectical resolutions to the problem of theatrical knowledge transmission, then what we see is a shift from script to performance to culture. Each step in this cascade of sublations assumes increasingly intimate modes of engagement as we move from words on the page to the texture of the voice and motion of the hand to the deeply interior experience of remembering what is no longer there. By the time we get to this latter situation, knowledge begins to confront its very limits and theatre begins to aspire to the condition of life. We can summarize this movement of theatre beyond itself by returning to Kant's 'What is Enlightenment?' by way of Foucault's recasting of the same question.[33] In quite tangible ways, Buckingham's *The Rehearsal* and Garrick's adaptation of it 'dare to know' in Kant's terms: as attempts to free oneself from self-incurred tutelage they strike out powerfully for the autonomy of the theatrical/political subject and the theatrical enterprise more generally. In keeping with Foucault's radicalization of Kant's question, *The Critic* dares to know in order to do otherwise – its project is oriented towards future reform because it emerges from a moment where autonomy, with all its concomitant dangers, emerged as a historical possibility. If America could reterritorialize liberty and thus momentarily embody the dream of Enlightenment, then why could not culture and society itself be reinvented? That is the question posed by Sheridan as he moved from the theatre to the world of politics, thus enacting the very transition that Buckingham struggled for and failed to achieve.

NOTES

Introduction: Theatre and the Enlightenment Matrix

1. Carlson 1966: 1.
2. Darlow 2012: 18; see Leon 2013.
3. Hunt 1984: 12–13.
4. Hunt 1984: 15.
5. Friedland 2002: 3.
6. Burke 2008: 9.
7. Balme and Davis 2015: 403.
8. Chartier 1991: 17.
9. Munck 2008: 142.
10. Foucault 1984: 43.
11. Foucault 1984: 42.
12. Edelstein 2010: 13.
13. Edelstein 2010: 19.
14. Edelstein 2010: 32. Edelstein draws this argument for the primacy of the social in conceptions of the Enlightenment from, most especially, Keith Baker, Daniel Gordon and Yair Mintzker.
15. Edelstein 2010: 32.
16. Rousseau 1960: 17.
17. Rousseau 1960: 18.
18. Rousseau 1960: 17.
19. Rousseau 1960: 20–1.
20. Brewer 2004: 171–4.
21. Diderot 1980: 143.
22. Diderot 1980: 92.
23. Diderot 1980: 29.
24. Quoted in Fried 1980: 95.

25. Fried 1980: 10.
26. Fried 1980: 104–5.
27. Roach 1985: 122.
28. Roach 1985: 118.
29. Johnson 1996: 65.
30. Camp 2014: 131.
31. Voltaire 1749: 20–1.
32. Voltaire 1749: 21.
33. Mittman 1981: 8.
34. Voltaire 1749: 22.
35. Ravel 1999: 211.

Chapter One: Institutional Frameworks: The State, the Market and the People in the Age of Enlightenment

1. Little and Kahrl 1963: 755.
2. Thomas 1989: 4; Clay 2013: 6.
3. Meech 2006: 65.
4. Howarth 1997: 398–400.
5. Marker and Marker 1975: 69–73.
6. Clay (2013) demonstrates how rarely the central government paid attention to regional theatres.
7. Thomas 1989: 44.
8. Collier 1698: 15.
9. Hédelin 1657.
10. Raysor 1927: 1–9.
11. On the London theatre of the 1730s and the Stage Licensing Act, see Liesenfeld 1984; Hume 1988.
12. See Kinservik 2007.
13. See Dobson 1992.
14. Rymer 1693: 4.
15. Taylor 2014: 79.
16. Thomas 1989: 50.
17. Collier 1698: 1.
18. Thompson 1993.
19. See Baer 1992.
20. Habermas 1991.
21. Fielding, J. 1758: 8.
22. See Fielding, H. 1752.
23. Quoted in Marker and Marker 1975: 67.
24. Quoted in Sharpe 2002: 123.
25. Quoted in Sharpe 2002: 117.
26. Howarth 1997: 684.

Chapter Two: Social Functions: Audiences and Authority

1. Wilson 2003: 63, 70. See also Wilson 2002: 62–93.
2. O'Quinn 2005.
3. Shaffer 2007.
4. Now available as Mackintosh 2008.
5. Scotland and Wales are poorly represented. The drawings are available from a Houghton Library site. See Winston 1805.
6. Johnson and Burling 2001.
7. Johnson 2003: 29–42.
8. Lawrence 1813. Lawrence quotes these figures from *The Morning Chronicle* 29 February 1812.
9. *The True Briton* 1797.
10. Folger Ms. W.a. 12, *Nightly receipts of Edward Warren in Order of Amount*.
11. GB Historical GIS 2014.
12. Bryan 1993: 237–8.
13. Hill 1767: 11–12, original emphasis.
14. Folger W.b. 104 (3) 1756.
15. Hare 1958: 41–2.
16. Newitt 1995: 157–9; Folger W.a. 32 1721.
17. Worrall 2013a: 157–82.
18. Notes for a Biography 1768.
19. Hill 1767: 14.
20. Colman 1829: 2.
21. Tilly 1995.
22. Baer 1992.
23. McPherson 2002.
24. Thompson 1998: documents 35–40, 67. Hewlett was reported by the comedian, Charles Mathews, as acting in Liverpool around January 1825.
25. Lindfors (2006) now updates all previous accounts of Aldridge's first British appearances.
26. Anon., *Calamity at Richmond* 1812: 19, 39–40. The play was an unidentified adaptation of M.G. Lewis's novel, *The Monk* (1796).
27. Playbill 1805.
28. Hoole 1946: 38.
29. Anon., *Polyanthos* 1805: 68, 70.
30. Playbill 1815.
31. Playbill 1754.
32. Pollock 1933: 335; Arnould 1797: 10.
33. Le Gardeur 1963: 12–13.
34. The 'Shake' refers to her grace notes or trills, much sought after skills for a singer; Folger W.a. 104 (13) 1775.
35. Oliver 1972: 80.
36. Probably from 'buss', 'a type of large cargo ship designed for heavy loads' (*OED*).
37. Dann 1988: 152–3.
38. Folger Ms. M.A. 125 n.d.
39. Gay 1969; Garrick 1759; Farquhar 1702; Anna Larpent Diaries 1774.

40. Adams 1783.
41. Liu 1953; Ou 2008.
42. Marsh, J. 1785.
43. Adams 1785.
44. Adams 1786.
45. Wilson 2009.
46. *The Times* 1788.
47. Waterfield, French and Craske 2003: 128–9, cat. 67; Anon., 'High Life below Stairs' 1774.
48. Walpole 1785.
49. Wilson 2008.
50. Worrall 2013b.

Chapter Three: Sexuality and Gender: Changing Identities

1. Anderson 2002: 25.
2. *The London Chronicle for the year 1757*: 223.
3. Topham 1805: 207.
4. Cumberland 1791: 20.
5. Haslewood 1792; vol. I: 9.
6. Philips 1712: 59.
7. Oldys 1741: 28.
8. Oldys 1741: 32.
9. See Pullen 1995: 22–54.
10. Blackstone 1765: 430.
11. Emsley, Hitchcock and Shoemaker 2014; Milling 2008b; 'Articles of Agreement' 1709.
12. Milhous and Hume 1990: 226; Meldrum 2014: 193.
13. Highfill, Burnim and Langhans 1973–93, vol. 1: 13; vol. 3: 64.
14. Kearsley 1787: 97.
15. See Earle 1989: 64; Milling 2008a.
16. Picard 2003: 55; Chapman 1992: 22; Cave 2004; Milhous and Hume 1990: 228.
17. Highfill et al. 1973–93, vol. 3: 278; Cave 2004.
18. Fothergill 1965: 105.
19. See Brooks 2015: 20; Hay and Rogers 1997: 21.
20. Milhous and Hume 1990: 231; Highfill et al. 1973–93, vol. 3: 275; Garrick's salary is detailed in his contract with James Lacy dated 9 April 1747, see Little and Kahrl 1963, vol. 3: 1347.
21. Wilkinson 1795, vol. 2: 141.
22. See Milhous and Hume 1993: 29.
23. Pasquin 1789: 268.
24. See 'an establishment for ye company' 1703.
25. Milhous and Hume 1993: 42.
26. Milhous and Hume 1993: 47.
27. Perkin 2002: 18.
28. For wages at Covent Garden this season, see Milhous and Hume 1990: 211.

Chapter Four: The Environment of Theatre: Power, Resistance and Commerce

1. Wiles 2003: 7.
2. Tuan 1977: 149.
3. *Cours d'Architecture*, 1771–7. Quoted in Sajous D'Oria 2007: 209. All translations from the French are mine unless otherwise noted.
4. Voltaire 1749. Quoted in Sajous D'Oria 2007: 16.
5. Lefebvre 1991: 221.
6. Olsen 1986: 9.
7. Carlson 1989: 50.
8. Tidworth 1973: 73.
9. Mullin 1970: 59.
10. Mullin 1970: 60.
11. Clay 2013: 43.
12. Martine de Rougemont places theatre as third among city halls and churches, 1988: 164.
13. Tidworth 1973: 112.
14. Clay 2013: 52.
15. Sajous D'Oria 2007: 204. Quoted from his memoires.
16. Sajous D'Oria 2007: 204–8.
17. Clay 2013: 66.
18. Clay 2013: 43.
19. Rudé 1972: 54.
20. Newman 2007: 2.
21. DeJean 2014: 12.
22. Newman 2007: 3.
23. Vries 1984: 10–13.
24. Sajous D'Oria 2007: 209.
25. Radicchio and Sajous D'Oria 1990: 12–14.
26. Rougemont 1988: 155; Rabreau 2008: 31.
27. Rabreau 2008: 31. Today the Place d'Odéon, the terrain was that of the Hôtel de Condé.
28. Carlson 1989: 79.
29. Voltaire 1749. Quoted in Carlson 1989: 74–5.
30. Mumford 1961: 390.
31. Rabreau 2008: 42.
32. Trott 2005: 6. The website *Théâtres de société: Rayonnement du répertoire français entre 1700 et 1799* at the University of Toronto catalogues 350 such places. See http://homes.chass.utoronto.ca/ trott/societe/societe.htm. David Trott of the University of Toronto, deceased in 2005, was instrumental in developing this data source that he hoped would provide, in tandem with others, a comprehensive look at a complex and vast phenomenon in its key traits: size, heterogeneity, spatiality, production and reception (see Trott 2005. Also http://www.cesar.org.uk).
33. Trott 2005: 10.
34. Lilti 2002: 283.
35. Carlson 1989: 50.

36. Trott 2000: 167.
37. Carlson 1989: 50.
38. On Italy's private theatres see Macé 2005: 171–2; Carlson 1989: 52–4.
39. Jullien 1875: 7.
40. Rougemont 1988: 297.
41. Lever 2001: 273.
42. Rougemont 1988: 301. See also Lagrave 1992: 328–30.
43. Rougemont 1988: 303.
44. Carlson 1989: 50.
45. Rougemont 1988: 309.
46. Rougemont 1988: 309–10.
47. Lagrave 1992: 330.
48. Rougemont 1988: 306.
49. Kümin 2008: 202.
50. Schaich 2008: 127.
51. Trott, 2005: 10.
52. Crogiez Labarthe 2005. The ruins of the theatre remain, although they are not open to the public.
53. Trott 2000: 177–8. Quoting Germain Bapst, *Essai sur l'histoire du théâtre* (1893).
54. Trott 2000: 178.
55. Lagrave 1992: 328–30.
56. Lilti 2002: 286.
57. Rougemont 1988: 314.
58. Lagrave 1992: 330.
59. Trott 2005: 20.
60. Lilti 2002: 293.
61. Ravel 2005: 219.
62. Ravel 2005: 219.
63. Trott 2000: 137.
64. See Rosenfeld 1960.
65. A theatre at the Saint-Laurent fair was reported to have crystal chandeliers lighting its double row of box seating with finely decorated balustrades. While there are few theatres described, what information exists tells of spaces that grew in development and stage technology. See Martin 2002: 17–24.
66. Lever 2001: 215–54.
67. Martin 2002: 17.
68. Isherwood 1986: 216.
69. Isherwood 1986: 33.
70. Gascar 1980: 6.
71. Root-Bernstein 1984: 25–6.
72. Isherwood 1986: 163.
73. Mercier 1990: 118.
74. Root-Bernstein 1984: 235–6.
75. Radicchio and Sajous D'Oria 1990: 12. See also Isherwood 1986: 217–27.
76. Isherwood 1986: 217.
77. Lefebvre 1991: 56.

Chapter Five: Circulation: Emergent Modalities of Intercultural Performance

1. The definition of circulation used here is a derivative of Bruce McConachie's observation that '[t]heatrical performances do cultural work of historical significance through their repeated circularity over time'. See McConachie 1998, particularly his discussion of the method of 'cultural systems analysis': vol. I, 111–81 and specifically 111.

2. Beyond the purview of this chapter is the history of the King's Theatre in the Haymarket – a satellite of the Court and patronized by rich and influential entities – which was the exclusive venue for performances of foreign opera in eighteenth-century London. For a history of the recruitment of European (mostly Italian but also German and other) composers and singers for the Haymarket, see Price, Milhous and Hume 1992 on the season of 1763–4.

3. This information is culled from the best source of biographical information on Zoffany: Treadwell 2009: 3–9 and specifically 6.

4. Treadwell 2009: 11–19 and specifically 12.

5. The rhetoric of theatrical portraiture and the meaning of a theatrical scene in this period require special consideration, as Kalman Burnim and Andrew Wilton remind us:

   > [A] theatrical scene generally falls into one of two categories: either it is an artificial reconstruction of a specific dramatic performance, or it is a collection of individual theatrical portraits, combined, according to the skill of the artist to create a stronger, more artistically impressive whole. Although the term 'theatrical portrait' may be understood to include portraits of actors and actresses out of costume, more accurately it applies to portraits of actors in character, in which the artist is trying to convey the essence of the performance by reproducing a significant moment in the play. The theatrical scene is often the most effective type of theatrical portrait because it concentrates the essence of the performance of several players into one moment

   See Wilton 1997, specifically, xxvi.

6. I use the term 'live' in the sense in which Auslander 1999 has used it in his seminal work.

7. Mrs William Pritchard (Hannah née Vaughan, 1709–68), 'six years older than Garrick, had begun her career singing in Fielding and Hippisley's Booth during Bartholomew Fair in 1733, from which she graduated to the Haymarket Theatre, singing as Nell in the popular Devil to Pay'. Her last performance as Lady Macbeth on 25 April 1768 was also her last performance on stage: 'For her final performance . . . Garrick played Macbeth to her Lady Macbeth, and wrote a "Simple, modest, short & pathetick" epilogue for her farewells speech'. See Stone 1979: 72–5. See also Baskett 2003: 160–1.

8. Zoffany had been trained by Benjamin Wilson (1721–88), who is now best known for his oil on canvas depicting David Garrick and Anne Bellamy in *Romeo and Juliet* (1753). There were other theatrical portrait and scene painters in London, but none as influential as Zoffany. More important for the purpose of this discussion is the widely held assumption that 'Zoffany's introduction to Garrick . . . is said to have taken place in Wilson's studio'. Penelope Treadwell rightly points out that in terms

of theatrical portraiture Garrick saw in Zoffany 'a worthy successor' to Hogarth. See Treadwell 2009: 59 and 61.

9. Wilkinson 1790, vol. 1: 1–2.
10. Theatres could only operate under royal patent; they were then deemed legitimate. After the Restoration of monarchy in 1660, for instance, Charles II granted royal patents to the King's Company (led by Tomas Killigrew) and the Duke's Company (led by William Davenant). A 'duopoly' was thus created and both Killigrew and Davenant became the patentees of the Drury Lane and Dorset Garden theatres.
11. Little and Kahrl 1963: li.
12. Little and Kahrl 1963: 'Introduction', specifically li–liv.
13. Davies 1780, vol. II: 83.
14. *Garrigues* is the 'French term for the semibarren areas of scrub, oak, broom, cistus, and fragrant herbs east of Bordeaux stretching into Provence'. See Stone and Kahrl 1979: 293–312, specifically 293.
15. Clair Josèphe Hippolyte Leris (1723–1803). According to Thomas Davies, Garrick's encounters with Madame Clairon, as she was called, were always productive. At one meeting, for instance,

> [t]he conversation turned for some time on the belles lettres, in which the merits of several eminent writers were discussed with equal judgment and candour. Many critical observations were made on the action and eloquence of the French and English theatres, and, at the request of this very brilliant circle, La Clairon and Garrick consented to exhibit various specimens of their theatrical talents, which produced much entertainment.

See Davies 1780, vol. II: 81.
16. Physicist, philosopher and music theorist, d'Alembert was the co-editor with Denis Diderot of the *Encyclopédie* (1751–77).
17. See Stone and Kahrl 1979: 'Friendships with Women', specifically 412–19.
18. Garrick's extensive connections with the French performance industry is described at length in 'Heir to the Classical Traditions' in Stone and Kahrl 1979: 293–8. According to these biographers, Jean Monnet was also 'the versatile and tireless bookseller who kept Garrick in touch with the French publications and secondhand book market'. See Stone and Kahrl 1979: 171.
19. Stone and Kahrl 1979: 294.
20. Stone and Kahrl 1979: 718, n43. For the uses of lycopodium torches on the eighteenth-century stage, see Rice 2015: 23–40.
21. Stone and Kahrl 1979: 299.
22. The Temple was built in 1757 when Garrick commissioned Jean Francois Roubiliac for the statue of Shakespeare, which now sits at the entrance of the British Library at St Pancras.
23. Treadwell 2009: 71.
24. Treadwell 2009: 72.
25. This is a reference to the work of Diana Taylor in Balme and Davis 2015: 413.
26. Defoe 1728: 17–18.
27. The cast list for *Astyanax* appears under the 6 May 1727 record in Avery 1960–8, pt. 2, vol. II: 924. In this production Senesino played Pyrrhus.

28. Highfill, Burnim and Langhans 1973–93, vol. 5, under entry on 'Signora Faustina': 189.
29. The aristocracy – having greater access to continental cultures as both travellers and as consumers of travel narratives – were the main subscribers of opera as well as the patrons of Handel (who was kapellmeister to George I) and Heidegger.
30. Highfill, Burnim and Langhans 1973–93, vol. 5: 188–90, specifically 188–9.
31. John Gay, in a letter to Jonathan Swift (3 February 1723), said the following of Senesino: 'People have now forgot Homer, and Virgil, and Caesar, or at least, they have lost their ranks; for, in London and Westminster, in all polite conversations, Senesino is daily voted to be the greatest man that ever lived'. Highfill, Burnim and Langhans 1973–93, vol. 13: 249–55, passage quoted in 253.
32. Highfill, Burnim and Langhans 1973–93, vol. 4: 112–18, specifically 112.
33. Highfill, Burnim and Langhans 1973–93, vol. 5: 189.
34. Quoted in Highfill, Burnim and Langhans 1973–93, vol. 4: 112.
35. Anon., *Devil to Pay at St. James's* (1727). The title page continues as follows: 'Also of a hot skirmish between Signor Boschi and Signor Palmecini. Moreover, how Senesino has taken snuff, is going to leave the opera, and sing psalms at Henley's oratory. Also About the Flying Man, and how the doctor of St. Martin's has very unkindly taken down the scaffold, and disappointed a world of good company'. See specifically 3.
36. Anon., *Devil to Pay at St. James's* (1727): 4–5.
37. Anon., *The Contre Temps; Or, Rival Queans* (1727) is in a more innovative form: It is a dramatic script which also claims to be an eyewitness account: 'As it was lately acted with great applause, at H__d__r's private th__re near the H__y M___t'. The scene is set near the 'temple of discord' at the Haymarket and, in addition to the rival queens, the characters include Heidegger, Handel and Senesino, who is the high priest. The scene opens to the Temple of Discord, which is described as: 'An altar with crowns, globes, sceptres and other ensigns of royalty' (5).
38. Davies 1780, vol. II: 177.
39. Davies 1780, vol. II: 178–9.
40. Davies 1780, vol. II: 180, 182.
41. See McConachie 1998, specifically vol. I: 113–26.
42. For a detailed account of the many circuitries in early American drama, see, for instance, 'British Author, American Text: *The Poor Soldier* in the New Republic' and 'American Author, British Source: Writing Revolution in Murray's *Traveller Returned*' in Richards 2005: 60–104.
43. McConachie 1998, vol. I: 121–2.
44. McConachie 1998, vol. I: 125.
45. McConachie 1998, vol. I: 221. For the impact of various legislation on theatre at the turn of the century, see McConachie passim.
46. One of the frequently cited sources of the 'home and social life' of the British in India in the late eighteenth century remains Busteed's *Echoes from Old Calcutta* (1908), 'being chiefly reminiscences of the days of Warren Hastings, Francis, and Impey'. Writing in the late nineteenth century, Busteed was removed from his subject by hundred years or more. In any in-depth study of British culture in eighteenth-century India, Busteed's references to source materials – newspaper articles, diaries

and letters of colonial administrators – need to be verified and cross-checked against other extant records of British culture and theatrical practices in eighteenth-century India.

47. Busteed 1908: 121.
48. Busteed 1908: 143.
49. This is a reference to Folger manuscript W.a. 237 which I have described and discussed at length in Choudhury 2000: 87–108.
50. Choudhury 2000.
51. Choudhury 2000, specifically 98.
52. Aurangzeb was Mughal Emperor Shah Jahan's son and ruled India from 1658 to 1707.
53. Davies 1784, vol. III: 94.
54. Davies 1784, vol. III: 93.

Chapter Six: Interpretations: From Theatrephobia to a Theatrical 'Science of Man'

1. Cabanis 1980 [1796]: 254. All translations are mine unless otherwise indicated.
2. Cabanis 1980 [1796]: 264.
3. I use the same definition of science as Christa Knellwolf, who points out that, during the Enlightenment, 'the term "science" did not yet have its twenty-first-century sense, but was still more or less equivalent with the Latin *scientia*, so that "science of man" can essentially be paraphrased as *knowledge* of man'. Knellwolf 2004: 194.
4. Vidal 2006: 13.
5. Two paramount examples of this type of theorization are Diderot's *Observations on the Natural Son* (*Entretiens sur le Fils naturel*, 1757; discussed at length in this chapter) and Beaumarchais' preface to his *drame, Eugenia*, entitled *Essay on Serious Drama* (*Essai sur le drame sérieux*, 1767).
6. In her book on the relationship between science and sensibility, Jessica Riskin argues that philosophers gradually interlaced internal, affective processes with moral and social issues during the 1750s and 1760s in France. For example, Diderot believed that sensibility 'attuned the animal to the world outside and governed its inner processes' and that 'sensibility can also be used with regard to morals'. Riskin 2002: 2.
7. Editors of this series in documents communicated to contributors.
8. Diderot 2005a.
9. The ending is 'happy' in that it prescribes specific bourgeois norms of happiness at the time, such as romantic harmony, pro-social behaviour, and financial success. For an astute problematizing of Enlightenment notions of happiness in Diderot's works, see Pucci 1997; Bryson 1991.
10. For more information on the relationship between Diderot and classical drama, see Haquette 2000.
11. Diderot 2005a: 79.
12. Frantz 1998: 5. For Diderot's description of the *tableau* see Diderot 1996: 1136–8.
13. It is important to note, however, that Diderot was not the first dramatist in France who tried to close the distance between spectator and character. During the 1730s,

writers of France's *comédies larmoyantes* (tearful comedies), such as Nivelle de la Chaussée, offered positive images of bourgeois characters, compared to their traditional ridicule in classical comedy (i.e. Molière). For more information on the connection between La Chaussée and Diderot, see Leichman 2016; Dagen 2012: 9–22.

14. Diderot wrote *drames* and co-edited the famous *Encyclopédie*. Other authors of *drames*, such as Michel-Jean Sedaine and Jean-François Marmontel, either contributed to the *Encyclopédie* or maintained close ties with *encyclopédistes*.

15. Roach 1981: 51. See also Roach 1993.

16. Diderot 2005b: 344.

17. For more information on the unity of Diderot's dramatic theory from the *Dialogues* to the *Paradox*, see Frantz 1993: 685–701.

18. Roach 1981: 53. For more information on the connections between Diderot's *Paradox* and physiological treatises of the time, see Roach 1993.

19. Roach 1981: 64.

20. Not all classical theorists sought to establish a rational set of rules for art. In his work on *Ancients* vs. *Moderns* polemic, Larry Norman brings to light a group of *Ancients* who consistently spurned rule-making by emphasizing the power of the ineffable in works of art and literature. For more information see Norman 2011: 185–212.

21. Lyons 1999: xi.

22. Harris 2014: 4.

23. Harris 2007: 152.

24. Several scholars have questioned the distinction between the seventeenth-century 'Spectator' and eighteenth-century *spectators*. For a keen analysis on the role of a judging public during the seventeenth century, see DeJean 1997: 35–50. Whereas DeJean demonstrates the advent of modern notions of the spectator, my argument pertains to the inclusion of those concerns in new theoretical texts and dramatic genres during the eighteenth century. For more information on this theoretical distinction, see Connors 2012: 3–28.

25. Jean Dagen grounds several Diderotian concepts in serious theatre of the 1730s. See Dagen 2012: 16–23.

26. For more information on the visual sources of Diderot's dramatic theories, see Creech 1986: 46–61.

27. For more information on theatre and personal transformation, see Fischer-Lichte 1997.

28. For general introduction to Nicole and his writings, see Thirouin 1998: 8–34. For a detailed reading of both Nicole's *Treatise* and Bossuet's *Maxims*, see Barish 1981: 190–214. See, for example, Phillips 1980; Dubu 1997; and Thirouin 1997 for more information about anti-theatrical criticism in seventeenth-century France.

29. See Merlin-Kajman 2004.

30. For more information on religious writing against the theatre in both Italy and France during the late sixteenth and early seventeenth centuries, see Fumaroli 1970.

31. For more information on the relationship between Descartes and Nicole, see Thirouin 1997: 173–180.

32. Nicole's argument that theatrical affect leads to moral harm was rampant during the seventeenth century. For example, Bernard Lamy, author of the *Nouvelles réflexions*

sur l'art poétique, a virulent anti-theatrical text, attached the physiology of voice to negative moral consequences. Erec R. Koch (2008: 12) argues that

> Lamy's account of the power of voice to produce an affective response represents a radical departure from rhetorics earlier in the seventeenth century. In those works, such as Nicolas Caussin's *Eloquentiae Sacrae et Humanae Parallela, Libri 16* (1619), the affective efficacy of voice in discourse is not based on an analysis of sound and material force that act on the body, but on voice as a mode of expression that represents the affect as something phenomenally to be appropriated and grasped by the soul. Little more than fifty years later, Lamy asserts that passion is stirred by a material force that acts on the body, that provokes sensibility, and that produces an affective response

33. Koch 2008: 12.
34. Nicole 1998: 37.
35. Barish 1981: 195.
36. Rousseau detailed his arguments against theatre in a 1758 letter to Diderot's friend and fellow *encyclopédiste*, Jean le Rond d'Alembert. About the possibility of catharsis, Rousseau writes: 'Je sais que la poétique du théâtre prétend faire tout le contraire, et purger les passions en les excitant: mais j'ai peine à bien concevoir cette règle'. Rousseau 1967: 71–2.
37. Nicole 1998: 41.
38. Nicole peppers his text with food and poison metaphors. For example, he compares theatre-going to eating tasty but spoiled meat. See Nicole 1998: 85.
39. Nicole 1998: 43.
40. Nicole 1998: 47.
41. Nicole 1998: 59.
42. Phillips 1980: 98.
43. Phillips 1980: 98.
44. Nicole argues that spectatorship is dangerous precisely because we use our visual apparatus at the theatre. See Nicole 1998: 59.
45. Racine 1873: 354.
46. Racine 1873: 354.
47. Bossuet writes that the hearts of spectators are moved by the skin, facial expressions and tears of the actors just as much as any fictional elements of the drama. See Bossuet 1862: 34–6.
48. Le Gallois de Grimarest 1707: 330.
49. Leichman 2016: 56.
50. Dubos 1967: 27.
51. See Nicole 1998: 43.
52. Nicole 1998: 30–1.
53. Harris 2014: 139.
54. For more information on the theatrical arm of this important dramatic and emotional regime change see Marchand 2009.
55. See Feilla 2013 for an important assessment of emotion and theatre during the tumultuous Revolutionary years. Diderot's influence on Lessing is most evident in the *Hamburg Dramaturgy* (1769) in which the German playwright cites Diderot's' *The Natural Son* as

well as his *On Dramatic Poetry* (1758). Goethe translated a number of Diderot's prose
works, including parts of the famous *Jacques the Fatalist* (trans. 1785).
56. Reddy 2001: ix.
57. Rousseau 1967: 65.

Chapter Seven: Communities of Production: Eighteenth-Century Acting Companies

1. Alpers 1988.
2. Wiley 1960: 92.
3. Van Lennep et al. 1960–8, part I, vol. 1: xxxvii–ix.
4. Stern 2000: 145, 246–7.
5. Wiley 1960: 111. Non-sharing, mid-level actors were salaried.
6. Habermas 1989.
7. Foucault 1972, *passim*.
8. Wiley 1960: 107.
9. Gurr 1985: 28–33.
10. McKendrick 1989: 49.
11. The grant giving the theatre manager William Davenant permanent rights to his own
    plays, along with several pre-Civil War titles, also stipulated that actors could not
    transfer from one company to another. See Milhous and Hume 1991: 15.
12. Brockett 1999: 281.
13. Hume 1975: 250–1.
14. Garlick 2004: 175.
15. Highfill 1980: 156.
16. DiPiero 2014: 141.
17. Crochunis 2014: 572.
18. Crochunis 2014: 572.
19. Davis 2000: 115.
20. Howarth 1997: 426.
21. See, for instance, the 'Regulation' issued in the early 1720 for the *Comédie-Italienne*
    or the 'act of association' drawn up by the *Comédie-Française* in 1758. Howarth
    1997: 429.
22. McDermott 1998: 183.
23. McDermott 1998: 191.
24. McDermott 1998: 192.
25. Downes 1987: 66–7.
26. Worrall 2013a: 42–3.
27. Highfill 1980: 179.
28. Worrall 2013a: 43.
29. Howarth 1997: 430.
30. McPherson 2002: 237.
31. DiPiero 2014: 142–3.
32. As quoted in DiPiero 2014: 143.
33. As quoted in DiPiero 2014: 143.
34. Stern 2000: 277.

35. As described in Stern 2000: 278.
36. As quoted in Stern 2000: 281.
37. Both incidents recounted in Stern 2000: 278.
38. Brown 2006: 121.
39. See Smith 2002; Brewer and Porter 1993.
40. Johnson 2014: 658.
41. Harrington 2010: 78–9.
42. As quoted in Johnson 2014: 665.
43. As quoted in Johnson 2014: 659.
44. Johnson 2014: 661.
45. Roach 2007: 8, original emphasis.
46. Spratt 2013: 61.
47. Roach 2007: 149.
48. Thomson 2007: 14.
49. Wanko 2003.
50. See Foucault 2006, 1973, 1977.
51. Banham 1995: 949.
52. Foucault 1980: 106–7.
53. Fischer-Lichte 2002: 149.
54. Senelick 1991: 23–4.
55. Senelick 1991: 73.
56. Senelick 1991: 192–3.
57. Brockett 1999: 282, 248.
58. Sharpe 2002: 124–5.
59. As quoted in Fischer-Lichte 2002: 152.
60. See, for instance, how often various contributors reference this speech in Karim-Cooper and Stern 2013.
61. Leichman 2015: 423.
62. Leichman 2015: 423.
63. Leichman 2015: 420.
64. Downes 1987: 51.
65. Leichman 2015: 429.

Chapter Eight: Repertoire and Genres: Cultural Logics and the Trick of Theatrical Longevity

1. On David Garrick's theatrical history and repertoire, see 'David Garrick' in Highfill, Burnim and Langhans 1973–93.
2. Burney 1997: 63.
3. Burney 1997: 70–1.
4. In her discussion of the nineteenth-century repertoire, Tracy C. Davis has characterized this anticipation as a knowledge of the day-to-day of theatrical performance, remarked upon only when an actor or actress defers from those expectations. In this respect and drawing on Jacky Bratton's work on the idea of 'intertheatricality', she argues that

'performance texts are relational, and their interpretability is coextant between theatre artists and audiences'. See Davis 2009; Bratton 2003: especially 17–66.

5. Inchbald 1990.

6. Burney 1997: 124, 126.

7. Inchbald 1990.

8. On the unequal distribution of stock plays from the pre-Civil War era and the competition that ensued, see Hume 1976: 20–1.

9. Van Lennep et al. 1960–8, pt. I: cxxii.

10. These generic trends are documented in standard histories of Restoration drama; for three classic examples, see Nicoll 1952; Hume 1976; Hughes 1996.

11. Van Lennep et al. 1960–8, pt. I: cxxvii.

12. Van Lennep et al. 1960–8, pt. III: cli.

13. Van Lennep et al. 1960–8, pt. I: cxxvi.

14. Van Lennep et al. 1960–8, pt. III: cxlvi–cxlvii.

15. Van Lennep et al. 1960–8, pt. II: cxvii.

16. Van Lennep et al. 1960–8, pt. IV: clxx.

17. See Freeman 2015.

18. For an account of Macklin's Shylock and the celebrity it engendered, see Anderson 2011.

19. Van Lennep et al. 1960–8, pt. IV: xxx. For a recent account of this event, see Ritchie 2015.

20. Richard Brome's *A Jovial Crew* was performed at the Cockpit Theatre by the King and Queen's Young Company, also known as Beeston's Boys, on 2 September 1642. Its first printed edition appeared in 1652. For a complete stage history of *A Jovial Crew* and other resources associated with the works of Richard Brome, see Richard Brome Online.

21. For an account of possible sources, see Stern 2014: 30–4.

22. Brome 2014: I.1.11.

23. Stern 2014: 13.

24. Gay 1969: I.1.10.

25. Brome 2014: II.1.191–2.

26. Brome 2014: II.1.199–202.

27. Butler 1984: 274.

28. Brome 2014: V.1.35.

29. Brome 2014: V.1.328–36.

30. Brome 2014: V.1.337–8.

31. Brome 2014: V.1.438–440.

32. Brome 2014: V.1.352.

33. This conclusion echoes that of Butler (1984) who argues that 'the play is about escapism rather than escapist' (271).

34. Gay 1969: Introduction, 16–30.

35. Gay 1969: II.3.1–3.

36. Gay 1969: II.3.19–20.

37. Gay 1969: III.15.18.

38. Gay 1969: I.15.15–17.

39. Gay 1969: III.16.10–14.
40. Gay 1969: III.16.15.
41. Miller 1983.
42. Gay 1969: III.17.9.
43. During the 1735/6 season at Drury Lane, for instance, Theophilus Cibber mounted a campaign for his wife Susannah Cibber to take the part of Polly and relegate Kitty Clive to the part of Lucy. Clive triumphed after a prolonged public battle and gained especial leverage in citing a 'receiv'd Maxim in the Theatre, *that no Actor or Actress shall be depriv'd of a Part in which they have been well receiv'd, until they are render'd incapable of performing it either by Age or Sickness*' ('Kitty Clive' in Highfill, Burnim and Langhans 1973–93). For a more extensive discussion of this rivalry and Kitty Clive's particular success at developing and maintaining her theatrical property, see Nussbaum 2010: 58–9, 151–88.
44. For a useful discussion of these performance practices and the popularity of *The Beggar's Opera* in the eighteenth-century repertory, see Brewer 1997: 428–49. The transvestite practice originated with two actresses famous for their performances in male parts, Peg Woffington in 1732 and Charlotte Charke in 1736.
45. Stern 2014: 57.
46. Marsden 2006: 61.
47. For an extensive discussion of she-tragedy, see Marsden 2006: 60–99.
48. Freeman 2002: 125.
49. Behn 1996: 42.
50. Southerne 1694: II.2, p. 25.
51. Southerne 1694: I.3, p. 19.
52. Southerne 1694: V.1, p. 79.
53. Staves 1979: 175.
54. Garrick 1757.
55. Southerne, 1694: Epistle Dedicatory.
56. For a reading of this event and of Siddons's strategic emphasis on motherhood as a central feature of her public persona, see Brooks 2015: 134–41.
57. See Freeman 2002: 193–234.
58. See Goldsmith 1966: 212.

Chapter Nine: Technologies of Performance: Architecture, Scenery, Light

1. Stiegler 1998: 17.
2. Stiegler 2010: 202.
3. Doyon and Liaigre 1966: 224–5.
4. Quoted in Cassirer 1951: 46–7.
5. Adas 1989: 73.
6. Jarrard 2003: 27.
7. Thomas 2002: 102–3.
8. Carlson 1998: 25.
9. Izenour 1997: 47–63.
10. Kernodle 1970: 202; Lawrenson: 1986: 137–9.
11. Izenour 1997: 2–3.

12. Leacroft and Leacroft 1984: 86–9; Dumont 1968.
13. Izenour 1997: 51.
14. Izenour 1997: 47.
15. Izenour 1998: 13.
16. Izenour 1998: 18.
17. Schöne 1961.
18. Baur-Heinhold 1967: 129–31.
19. Izenour 1997: 47.
20. Brockett, Mitchell and Hardberger, 2010: 132–5.
21. Pozzo 1700.
22. On the archival remnants of Servandoni's designs, see Bjurstrom 1961 and Gorce 2009.
23. Pelletier 2006: 26–30.
24. Bergman 1977: 109–16.
25. Lawrenson 1980.
26. Rousseau 1987: 81.
27. On the scope of theatre construction in France during this period, see Clay 2013: 15–17.
28. Camp 2014: 211–12.
29. See Patte 1782; Landriani 1815; and Saunders 1790.
30. Rougemont 2001: 138. See also Herbert 1973.
31. Izenour 1997: 59–63.
32. Bergman 1977: 89–98.
33. Bergman 1977: 171.
34. See Izenour 1998: 34–5.
35. Bergman 1977: 97.
36. Bergman 1977: 171.
37. Camp 2013: 56.
38. See Chaumont 1769: 113, and Patte 1782: 3–23.
39. Lafond 1779: 187–95; Grobert 1809: 8.
40. Langhans 1810.
41. Lavoisier 1862–93, vol. III: 100.
42. Quoted in Izenour 1997: 67.
43. Izenour 1998: 36; Bergman 1977: 196–201.

Chapter Ten: Knowledge Transmission: Theatrical Intelligence and the Intelligence of Theatre

1. Kant 1991: 54.
2. See Backsheider 1993; Staves 1979; and Canfield 2000.
3. See Foucault's (1995) distinction between sovereign punishment and the disciplinary strategies of liberal states.
4. See Habermas 1991; Darnton 1987; and Warner 2002.
5. My argument revolves around theatrical practice in London and thus the plurality of theatrical cultures in Europe, no less than the variety of Enlightenments, lies beyond the horizon of analysis. That said, it is my hope that the overall methodological

intervention will be of interest to scholars working in roughly contemporaneous but distinct archives.

6. See Orr's discussion of Webb's designs for *The Siege of Rhodes* in *Empire* 2001: 49–55.
7. Orr 2001: 49.
8. *Morning Post* 26 December 1785. See Joppien 1975 and O'Quinn 2005: 74–124.
9. See Allen 1962 and Misty G. Anderson's forthcoming *God on Stage*. My observations here are indebted to Anderson's work on wonder.
10. O'Quinn 2011: 231.
11. See Russell 2010: 216–18.
12. Roach 1985.
13. Orr 2001: 61–134.
14. See Ragussis 2010: 43–86.
15. Ritchie 2014.
16. Inchbald's introductions have been compiled as *Remarks for the British Theatre* 1990.
17. See Sherman 2015.
18. See Werkmeister 1967: 4–26, and O'Quinn 2011: 6–29 for discussions of these transformations in the daily press and the nightly offerings at the theatre.
19. See Sherman 2011.
20. See Russell 2010: 126–35.
21. West 1993.
22. Kant 1991: 54. Hegel's most iconic account is the master–slave dialectic in the *Phenomenology of Spirit*. As he states in paragraph 179: 'On approaching the other it has lost its own self, since it finds itself as another being; secondly, it has thereby sublated that other, for this primitive consciousness does not regard the other as essentially real but sees its own self in the other' (1977: 111).
23. Crane's edition of *The Rehearsal* finds allusions to at least thirty-seven different plays, many of which are parodied extensively. See Villiers 1976: 78–80.
24. See McFadden 1974 and Stocker 1988.
25. Stocker 1988: 14.
26. Stocker 1988: 14–15.
27. Stocker 1988: 16.
28. Summers 1914: xiv–xv.
29. For a full discussion of Garrick's alterations see Pedicord and Bergman 1982: 301–14.
30. Deelman 1964; Dobson 1992; Ritchie 2014; Straub 1991.
31. See O'Quinn 2011: 186–239 for a more comprehensive reading of both the *Monody* and *The Critic*.
32. Sheridan 1989: *The Critic*, III.2.291.
33. Foucault's 'What is Enlightenment?' (1984) radicalizes the notion of freedom in Kant's text and argues that the ultimate objective of enlightenment is to make a disjunctive break with the past.

BIBLIOGRAPHY

Adams, A. to Elizabeth Smith Shaw. 4 March 1786. *Founders Online*. Accessed 29 December 2015. http://founders.archives.gov/documents/Adams/04-07-02-0021.

Adams, A. to William Stephens Smith. 17 September 1785. *Founders Online*. Accessed 29 December 2015. http://founders.archives.gov/documents/Adams/04-06-02-0116.

Adams, J.Q. 31 October 1783. Diary 9, Massachusetts Historical Society, online edition. Accessed 2 February 2010. http://www.masshist.org/jqadiaries/diaries.cfm.

Adas, M. 1989. *Machines as the Measure of Men: Science, Technology, and Ideologies of Western Dominance*. Ithaca, NY: Cornell University Press.

Allen, R. 1960. 'The Stage Spectacles of Philip James de Loutherbourg'. PhD diss., Yale University.

Allen, R. 1962. 'De Loutherbourg and Captain Cook'. *Theatre Research/Recherches théâtrales* 4 (3): 195–213.

Alpers, S. 1988. *Rembrandt's Enterprise: The Studio and the Market*. Chicago: University of Chicago Press.

Anderson, E.H. 2011. 'Celebrity Shylock'. *PMLA* 126 (4): 935–49.

Anderson, M. 2002. *Female Playwrights and Eighteenth-Century Comedy*. Basingstoke: Palgrave Macmillan.

Anna Larpent Diaries. 1774. HM 31201, vol. 17. The Huntington Library, San Marino, CA.

Anonymous. 1727. *The Contre Temps; or Rival Queens, a Small Farce*. London: A. Moore.

Anonymous. 1727. *The Devil to Pay at St. James's: Or, A Full and true Account of a most horrid and bloody battle between Madam Faustina and Madam Cuzzoni*. London: A. Moore. In *The London Stage, 1660–1800: A Calendar of Plays, Entertainments, and Afterpieces*, vol. 2 (1960–8), edited by E.L. Avery. Carbondale: Southern Illinois University Press.

Anonymous. 1774. 'High Life below Stairs'. 23 February. Call no. 774.2.23.1.1 and 774.2.23.1.2, Lewis Walpole Library, Farmington, CT.

Anonymous. 1805. *Polyanthos*. December. Boston, MA.

Anonymous. 1812. *Calamity at Richmond, Being a Narrative Of the affecting circumstances attending the Awful Conflagration of the Theatre, in the city of*

Richmond, On the Night of Thursday, the 26th of December, 1811. Philadelphia: J.F. Watson.

Arnould, M. 1797. *The American Heroine, A Pantomime, In Three Acts . . . Originally performed at the Theatre of L'Ambigu-Comique*. Philadelphia.

'Articles of Agreement on 24 May 1709 between Owen Swiney and Mary Porter of St Paul's Covent Garden, Spinster'. 1709. In The National Archives at Kew, LC 7/3 f.117.

Auslander, P. 1999. *Liveness: Performance in a Mediatized Culture*. London: Routledge, reprinted 2008.

Avery, E.L., ed. 1960–8. *The London Stage, 1660–1800: A Calendar of Plays, Entertainments, and Afterpieces*, vol. 2. Carbondale: Southern Illinois University Press.

Backsheider, P. 1993. *Spectacular Politics: Theatrical Power and Mass Culture in Early Modern England*. Baltimore: The Johns Hopkins University Press.

Baer, M. 1992. *Theatre and Disorder in Late Georgian London*. Oxford: Oxford University Press.

Balme, C., and T.C. Davis. 2015. 'A Cultural History of Theatre: A Prospectus'. *Theatre Survey* 56 (3): 402–21.

Banham, M., ed. 1995. *The Cambridge Guide to Theatre*. Cambridge: Cambridge University Press.

Barish, J. 1981. *The Anti-Theatrical Prejudice*. Berkeley: University of California.

Baskett, K.A. 2003. *Brief Lives: Sitters and Artists in the Garrick Club Collection*. London: The Garrick Club.

Baur-Heinhold, M. 1967. *The Baroque Theatre: A Cultural History of the 17th and 18th Centuries*. New York: McGraw-Hill.

Beaumarchais, P.-A.C. de. 1767. *Eugénie, drame en cinq actes en prose [. . .] avec un essai sur le drame sérieux*. Paris: Merlin.

Behn, A. 1996. *The History of the Nun; Or, The Fair Vow-Breaker* (1689). In *Popular Fiction by Women 1660–1730*, edited by P. Backscheider and J.J. Richetti, 1–42. Oxford: Clarendon Press.

Benedict, P. 1990. 'Was the Eighteenth Century an Era of Urbanization in France?' *The Journal of Interdisciplinary History* 21 (2): 179–215.

Bergman, G.M. 1977. *Lighting in the Theatre*. Stockholm: Almqvist & Wiksell International.

Bjurstrom, P. 1961. 'Servandoni et la salle des machines'. *Revue de la société d'histoire du théâtre* 43 (3): 222–4.

Blackstone, W. 1765. *Commentaries on the Laws of England in Four Books*, vol. 1. Oxford: Clarendon.

Bossuet, J.-B. 1862. *Maximes et réflexions sur la comédie*. In *Œuvres complètes de Bossuet*, vol. XVII. Paris: Louis Vivès.

Brant, C., and S.E. Whyman, eds. 2007. *Walking the Streets of Eighteenth-Century London: John Gay's* Trivia *(1716)*. Oxford: Oxford University Press.

Bratton, J. 2003. *New Readings in Theatre History*. Cambridge: Cambridge University Press.

Brewer, D. 2004. 'Lights in Space'. *Eighteenth-Century Studies* 37 (2): 171–86.

Brewer, J. 1995. 'This, That and the Other: Public, Social and Private in the Seventeenth and Eighteenth Centuries'. In *Shifting the Boundaries: Transformation of the Languages of Public and Private in the Eighteenth Century*, edited by L. Sharpe and D. Castiglione, 1–21. Exeter: University of Exeter Press.

Brewer, J. 1997. *The Pleasures of the Imagination: English Culture in the Eighteenth Century*. Chicago: The University of Chicago Press.

Brewer, J., and R. Porter, eds. 1993. *Consumption and the World of Goods*. London: Routledge.

Brockett, O. 1999. *History of the Theatre*. Boston: Allyn and Bacon.

Brockett, O., M. Mitchell, and L. Hardberger. 2010. *Making the Scene: A History of Stage Design and Technology in Europe and the United States*. San Antonio, TX: Tobin Theatre Arts Fund.

Brome, R. 2014. *A Jovial Crew, Or, The Merry Beggars* (1652), edited and introduced by T. Stern. London: Bloomsbury.

Brooks, H.E.M. 2015. *Actresses, Gender and the Eighteenth-Century Stage: Playing Women*. Basingstoke: Palgrave Macmillan.

Brown, G.S. 2006. *Literary Sociability and Literary Property in France, 1775–1793: Beaumarchais, the Société des Auteurs Dramatiques and the Comédie Française*. Aldershot: Ashgate.

Brummett, P. 2015. *Mapping the Ottomans: Sovereignty, Territory, and Identity in the Early Modern Mediterranean*. Cambridge: Cambridge University Press.

Bryan, G.B. 1993. *American Theatrical Regulation, 1607–1900: Conspectus and Texts*. Metuchen, NJ: The Scarecrow Press.

Bryson, S.S. 1991. *The Chastised Stage: Bourgeois Drama and the Exercise of Power*. Saratoga, CA: Anma libri.

Burke, Peter. 2008. *What is Cultural History?* Cambridge: Polity.

Burney, F. 1997. *Evelina* (1778), edited by K. Straub. Boston: Bedford Books.

'buss, n.1'. 2015. *OED Online*, Oxford: Oxford University Press. Accessed 29 December 2015. http://www.oed.com.www2.lib.ku.edu/view/Entry/25256?rskey#=qIaVqK&result=1.

Busteed, H.E. 1908. *Echoes from Old Calcutta*. London: W. Thacker and Company.

Butler, M. 1984. *Theatre and Crisis 1632–1642*. Cambridge: Cambridge University Press.

Cabanis, P.-J.G. 1980. *Rapports du physique et du moral de l'homme* (1796). In S. Moravia, 'The Enlightenment and the Sciences of Man'. *History of Science* 18: 245–68.

Camp, P. 2013. 'Belle Horreur: Hubert Robert's Scenic Space the Paris Opera Fire of 1781'. *Performance Research* 18 (1): 56–63.

Camp, P. 2014. *The First Frame: Theatre Space in Enlightenment France*. Cambridge: Cambridge University Press.

Canfield, J.D. 2000. *Heroes and States: On the Ideology of Restoration Tragedy*. Lexington: University of Kentucky Press.

Carlson, M. 1966. *The Theatre of the French Revolution*. Ithaca, NY: Cornell University Press.

Carlson, M. 1978. *Goethe and the Weimar Court Theatre*. Ithaca, NY: Cornell University Press.

Carlson, M. 1989. *Place of Performance: The Semiotics of Theatre Architecture*. Ithaca, NY: Cornell University Press.

Carlson, M. 1998. *Voltaire and the Theatre of the Eighteenth Century*. Westport, CT: Greenwood Publishing Group.

Cassirer, E. 1951. *The Philosophy of the Enlightenment*. Princeton, NJ: Princeton University Press.

Cave, R.A. 2004. 'Woffington, Margaret [Peg] (1720?–1760)'. *Oxford Dictionary of National Biography*. Oxford: Oxford University Press. Accessed 4 April 2016. http://www.oxforddnb.com/view/article/29820.

Certeau, M. de. 1984. *The Practice of Everyday Life*, translated by S. Rendall. Berkeley: University of California Press.

Chapman, S. 1992. *Merchant Enterprise in Britain: From the Industrial Revolution to World War I*. Cambridge: Cambridge University Press.

Chartier, R. 1991. *The Cultural Origins of the French Revolution*, translated by L.G. Cochrane. Durham, NC: Duke University Press.

Chaumont, C. de. 1769. *Exposition des principes qu'on doit suivre dans l'ordonnance des théâtres modernes*. Paris: C.A. Jombert.

Choudhury, M. 2000. *Interculturalism and Resistance in the London Theater: Identity, Performance, Empire, 1660–1800*. Lewisburg, PA: Bucknell University Press.

Choudhury, M. 2007. 'Universality, Early Modernity, and the Contingencies of Representing Race'. In *Players, Playwrights, Playhouses: Investigating Performance, 1660–1800*, edited by M.C. Holland and G.E. Peter Holland, 231–47. Basingstoke: Palgrave Macmillan.

Clay, L.R. 2013. *Stagestruck: The Business of Theater in Eighteenth-Century France and Its Colonies*. Ithaca, NY: Cornell University Press.

Collier, J. 1698. *A Short View of the Immorality, and Profaneness of the English-Stage*. London: Printed for S. Reble at the Turk's-Head in Fleetstreet.

Colman the Younger, G. 1829. *Observations on the Notice of a Motion to Rescind Certain Powers of His Majesty's Lord Chamberlain*. Westminster.

Connors, L.J. 2012. *Dramatic Battles in Eighteenth-Century France:* Philosophes, Anti-*philosophes and Polemical Theatre*. Oxford: Voltaire Foundation.

Coudreuse, A. 2001. *Le Refus du pathos au XVIIIe siècle*. Paris: Honoré Champion.

Creech, J. 1986. *Diderot: Thresholds of Representation*. Columbus: Ohio State University.

Crochunis, T.C. 2014. 'Women Theatre Managers'. In *The Oxford Handbook of the Georgian Theatre, 1737–1832*, edited by J. Swindells and D.F. Taylor, 568–84. Oxford: Oxford University Press.

Crogiez Labarthe, M. 2005. 'Le Théâtre du château de La Roche-Guyon'. In *Les Théâtres de société au XVIIIe siècle*, edited by M.-E. Plagnol-Diéval and D. Quéro, 119–29. Brussels: Editions de l'Université de Bruxelles.

Csengei, I. 2012. *Sympathy, Sensibility and the Literature of Feeling in the Eighteenth Century*. Basingstoke: Palgrave Macmillan.

Cumberland, R. 1791. 'Observer No. 123'. In *The Observer. Being a Collection of Moral, Literary and Familiar Essays*, vol. 4. Dublin: P. Byrne, R. Marchbank, J. Moore and W. Jones.

Curtis Price, J.M. 1992. *The Impresario's Ten Commandments: Continental Recruitment for Italian Opera in London 1763–64*. London: Royal Musical Association.

Dagen, J. 2012. 'Introduction'. In *La Chaussée, destouches et la comédie nouvelle au XVIIIe siècle*, edited by J. Dagen, C. François-Giappiconi and S. Marchand. Paris: Presse Universitaire du Paris-Sorbonne.

Dann, J.C. 1988. *The Nagle Journal: The Diary of the Life of Jacob Nagle, Sailor, From the Year 1775 to 1841*. New York: Weidenfeld & Nicolson.

Darlow, M. 2012. *Staging the French Revolution: Cultural Politics and the Paris Opéra, 1789–1794*. Oxford: Oxford University Press.

Darnton, R. 1987. *The Business of Enlightenment: Publishing History of the* Encyclopédie, *1775–1800*. Cambridge, MA: Belknap Press.

Davies, T. 1780. *Memoirs of the Life of David Garrick*, vol. II. London: Printed for the Author.

Davies, T. 1784. *Dramatic Miscellanies: Consisting of Critical Observations on Several Plays of Shakespeare*, vol. III. Dublin: S. Price et al.

Davis, T.C. 2000. 'Female Managers, Lessees and Proprietors of the British Stage (to 1914)'. *Nineteenth Century Theatre* 28 (2): 114–44.

Davis, T.C. 2009. 'Nineteenth-Century Repertoire'. *Nineteenth-Century Theatre and Film* 36 (2): 6–28.

Deelman, C. 1964. *The Great Shakespeare Jubilee*. New York: Viking.

Defoe, D. 1728. *Augusta Triumphans*. London: J. Roberts.

DeJean, J. 1997. *Ancients Against Moderns: Culture Wars and the Making of a Fin de Siècle*. Chicago: University of Chicago.

DeJean, J. 2014. *How Paris Became Paris: The Invention of the Modern City*. London: Bloomsbury.

Delehanty, A.T. 2013. *Literary Knowing in Neoclassical France: From Poetics to Aesthetics*. Lewisburg, PA: Bucknell University.

Diderot, D. 1980. *Œuvres complètes*, edited by J. Chouillet and A.-M. Chouillet, Tome X. Paris: Hermann.

Diderot, D. 1996. *Entretiens sur Le Fils naturel*. In *Œuvres* III, 1131–90. Paris: Robert Laffont.

Diderot, D. 2005a. *Entretiens sur Le Fils naturel* (1757). In *Entretiens sur Le Fils naturel, De la Poésie dramatique, Paradoxe sur le comédien*, 69–155. Paris: Flammarion.

Diderot, D. 2005b. *Paradoxe sur le comédien* (1773). In *Entretiens sur Le Fils naturel, De la Poésie dramatique, Paradoxe sur le comédien*, 269–344. Paris: Flammarion.

DiPiero, T. 2014. 'Enlightenment Literature'. In *The Cambridge Companion to the French Enlightenment*, edited by D. Brewer, 137–52. Cambridge: Cambridge University Press.

Dobson, M. 1992. *The Making of the National Poet: Shakespeare, Adaptation, and Authorship, 1660–1769*. Oxford: Clarendon Press.

Dobson, M. 2007. 'Theatre for Nothing'. In *Players, Playwrights, Playhouses: Investigating Performance, 1660–1800*, edited by M. Cordner and P. Holland, 175–88. Basingstoke: Palgrave Macmillan.

Downes, J. 1987. *Roscius Anglicanus*, edited by J. Milhous and R.D. Hume. London: The Society for Theatre Research.

Doyon, A., and L. Liaigre. 1966. *Jacques Vaucanson: Mécanicien de génie*. Paris: Presses Universitaires de France.

Dubos, J.-B. 1967. *Réflexions critiques sur la poésie et sur la peinture*. Paris: Pissot (1719). Geneva: Slatkine Reprints.

Dubu, J. 1997. *Les Eglises chrétiennes et le théâtre, 1550–1850*. Grenoble: Presses Universitaires de Grenoble.

Dumont, G. 1986. *Parallèle de plans des plus belles salles d'Italie et de France*. New York: Benjamin Blom.

Earle, P. 1989. *The Making of the English Middle Class: Business, Society, and Family Life in London, 1660–1730*. Berkeley: University of California Press.

Edelstein, D. 2010. *The Enlightenment: A Genealogy*. Chicago: University of Chicago.

Emsley, C., T. Hitchcock, and R. Shoemaker. 2014. 'London History – Currency, Coinage & the Cost of Living'. In *Old Bailey Proceedings Online*. Accessed 7 March 2014. www.oldbaileyonline.org, version 7.0.

Engel, L. 2007. *Fashioning Celebrity: Eighteenth-Century British Actresses and the Politics of Image Making*. Columbus: Ohio University Press.

'an establishment for ye company'. 1703. The National Archives at Kew, LC7/3, f.161.

Farquhar, G. 1702. *The Inconstant; or, the Way to Win Him.*

Feilla, C. 2013. *The Sentimental Theater of the French Revolution.* London: Ashgate.

Fielding, H. 1752. *A Plan of the Universal Register Office.* London.

Fielding, J. 1758. *An Account of the Origins and Effects of a Police.* London: Andrew Millar.

Fischer-Lichte, E. 1997. *The Show and the Gaze of Theatre.* Iowa City: University of Iowa Press.

Fischer-Lichte, E. 2002. *History of European Drama and Theatre*, translated by J. Riley. London: Routledge.

Folger Ms. M.A. 125, n.d., Folger Shakespeare Library, Washington, DC.

Folger Ms. W.a. 12, *Nightly Receipts of Edward Warren in Order of Amount.* 1813–14. Folger Shakespeare Library, Washington, DC.

Folger W.a. 104 (13), 28 October 1775, Folger Shakespeare Library, Washington, DC.

Folger W.a. 32, 27 April 1721, 2–3 May 1721, Folger Shakespeare Library, Washington, DC.

Folger W.b. 104 (3), 4 May 1756, Folger Shakespeare Library, Washington, DC.

Forestier, G. 2003. *Passions tragiques et règles classiques.* Paris: Presses Universitaires de France.

Fothergill, B. 1965. *Mrs Jordan: Portrait of an Actress.* London: Faber and Faber.

Foucault, M. 1972. *The Archaeology of Knowledge* and *The Discourse on Language*, translated by A.M. Sheridan Smith. New York: Pantheon Books.

Foucault, M. 1973. *The Birth of the Clinic: An Archaeology of Medical Perception*, translated by A.M. Sheridan Smith. New York: Pantheon Books.

Foucault, M. 1977. *Discipline and Punish: The Birth of the Prison*, translated by A. Sheridan. New York: Pantheon Books.

Foucault, M. 1980. *Power/Knowledge: Selected Interviews and Other Writings, 1972–1977*, edited by Colin Gordon. New York: Pantheon Books.

Foucault, M. 1984. 'What Is Enlightenment?' In *The Foucault Reader*, edited by P. Rabinow, 32–50. New York: Pantheon.

Foucault, M. 1995. *Discipline and Punish: The Birth of the Prison*, translated by A. Sheridan. New York: Vintage.

Foucault, M. 2006. *History of Madness*, introduction by J. Khalfa. London: Routledge.

Frantz, P. 1993. 'Du Spectateur au comédien: Le *Paradoxe* comme nouveau point de vue'. *Revue d'histoire littéraire de la France* 93 (5): 685–701.

Frantz, P. 1998. *L'Esthétique du tableau dans le théâtre du XVIIIe siècle.* Paris: Presses Universitaires de France.

Freeman, L.A. 2002. *Character's Theater: Genre and Identity on the Eighteenth-Century English Stage.* Philadelphia: University of Pennsylvania Press.

Freeman, L.A. 2015. 'Mourning the "Dignity of the Siddonian Form"', *Eighteenth-Century Fiction* 27 (3/4): 597–629.

Fried, M. 1980. *Absorption and Theatricality: Painting and Beholder in the Age of Diderot.* Berkeley: University of California Press.

Friedland, P. 2002. *Political Actors: Representative Bodies and Theatricality in the Age of the French Revolution.* Ithaca, NY: Cornell University Press.

Fumaroli, M. 1970. 'La Querelle de la moralité du théâtre avant Nicole et Bossuet'. *Revue d'histoire littéraire de la France* 70 (5): 1007–30.

Garlick, G. 2004. 'Theatre Outside London, 1660–1775'. In *The Cambridge History of British Theatre*, vol. 2, edited by J. Donohue, 165–82. Cambridge: Cambridge University Press.

Garrick, D. 1757. *Isabella; Or, The Fatal Marriage. A Play Alter'd from Southern*. London: ECCO.

Garrick, D. 1759. *Harlequin's Invasion*.

Garrick, D. 1982. *The Rehearsal*. In *The Plays of David Garrick, vol. 5, Garrick's Alterations of Others, 1742–1750*, edited by H.W. Pedicord and F.L. Bergmann, Carbondale: Southern Illinois University Press.

Gascar, P. 1980. *Le Boulevard du crime*. Paris: Atelier Hachette/Massin.

Gay, J. 1969. *The Beggar's Opera* (1728), edited by E.V. Roberts and E. Smith. Lincoln: University of Nebraska Press.

Gay, P. 1996. *The Enlightenment: An Interpretation*. New York: W.W. Norton & Company.

GB Historical GIS. 2014. 'Inner London through Time, Population Statistics, Total Population'. In *A Vision of Britain through Time*, University of Portsmouth. Accessed 9 May 2015. http://www.visionofbritain.org.uk/unit/10076845/cube/TOT_POP.

Gheeraert, T. 2002. 'La *Catharsis* impensable: La passion dans la théorie classique de la tragédie et sa mise en cause par les moralistes augustiniens'. *Études Epistémè* 1: 104–40.

Goldsmith, O. 1966. 'An Essay on the Theatre, or A Comparison between Laughing and Sentimental Comedy' (1773). In *Collected Works of Oliver Goldsmith*, vol. 3, edited by A. Friedman, 209–13. Oxford: Oxford University Press.

Gorce, J. de la. 2009. 'Une Scénographie de Servandoni conservée pour les spectacles de l'Opéra à Paris: Le Décor de la ville de Thèbes du triomphe de l'harmonie (1737)'. *Journal for Eighteenth-Century Studies* 32 (4): 577–90.

Grobert, J.-F.-L. 1809. *De l'Exécution dramatique, considérée dans ses rapports avec le matériel de la salle et de la scène*. Paris: Schoell.

Gurr, A. 1985. *The Shakespearean Stage, 1572–1642*, 2nd edition. Cambridge: Cambridge University Press.

Habermas, J. 1989. *The Structural Transformation of the Public Sphere: An Inquiry into a Category of Bourgeois Society*, translated by T. Burger and F. Lawrence. Cambridge: Polity Press.

Habermas, J. 1991. *The Structural Transformation of the Public Sphere: An Inquiry into a Category of Bourgeois Society* (1962), translated by T. Burger. Boston, MA: The MIT Press.

Haquette, J.-L. 2000. 'Le Public et l'intime: Réflexions sur le statut du visible, *Le Fils naturel* et *Les Entretiens*'. In *Diderot, l'invention du drame*, edited by Marc Buffat, 59–76. Paris: Klincksieck.

Hare, A. 1958. *The Georgian Theatre in Wessex*. London: Phoenix House.

Harrington, D. 2010. 'Remembering the Body: Eighteenth-Century Elocution and the Oral Tradition'. *Rhetorica* 28: 67–95.

Harris, E.P. 1981. 'From Outcast to Ideal: The Imagine of the Actress in Eighteenth-Century Germany'. *The German Quarterly* 54: 177–87.

Harris, J. 2007. 'Between Interest and Identification: Early Modern Theatre and the Invention of the Spectator'. In *Theatre, Fiction, and Poetry in the French Long Seventeenth Century / Le Théâtre, le roman, et la poésie à l'âge classique*, edited by William Brooks and Rainer Zaiser, 143–56. Oxford: Peter Lang.

Harris, J. 2014. *Inventing the Spectator: Subjectivity and the Theatrical Experience in Early Modern France*. Oxford: Oxford University.

Haslewood, J. 1792. *The Secret History of the Green Room: Containing Authentic and Entertaining Memoires of the Actors and Actresses in the Three Theatres Royal*, 2 vols. London: H.D. Symmonds.

Hay, D., and N. Rogers. 1997. *Eighteenth-Century English Society: Shuttles and Swords*. Oxford: Oxford University Press.

Hédelin, F. 1657. *La Pratique du théâtre*. Paris.

Hegel, G.W.F. 1977. *Phenomenology of Spirit*, translated by A.V. Miller. Oxford: Clarendon Press.

Herbert, R.L. 1973. *David, Voltaire, Brutus and the French Revolution: An Essay in Art and Politics*. New York: Viking Press.

Highfill, P.H. 1980. 'Performers and Performing'. In *The London Theatre World, 1660–1800*, edited by R.D. Hume. Carbondale: Southern Illinois University Press.

Highfill, P.H., K.A. Burnim, and E.A. Langhans. 1973–93. *A Biographical Dictionary Of Actors, Actresses, Musicians, Dancers, Managers & Other Stage Personnel In London, 1660–1800*, 16 vols. Carbondale: Southern Illinois University Press.

Hill, R. 1767. *A Letter from Richard Hill, Esq; To His Friend near Shrewsbury, Containing Some Remarks on a Letter Signed by a Player Which Letter Is also Prefixed . . . Sold for the Benefit of the Prisoners in Shrewsbury Goal*. Shrewsbury.

Hoole, W.S. 1946. *The Ante-Bellum Charleston Theatre*. Tuscaloosa: University of Alabama Press.

Houdar de La Motte. 1859. 'Discours à l'occasion de la tragédie d'Œdipe' (1720). In *Les Paradoxes littéraire de La Motte: Discours écrits par cet académicien sur les principaux genres de poèmes*, 2–15. Paris: Hachette.

Houdar de La Motte. 2002. *Textes critiques: Les raisons du sentiment*, edited by F. Gevrey and B. Guion. Paris: Honoré Champion.

Howard, J.E. 2007. *Theatre of a City: The Places of London Comedy, 1598–1642*. Philadelphia: University of Pennsylvania Press.

Howarth, W.D. ed. 1997. *French Theatre in the Neo-classical era, 1550–1789*. Cambridge: Cambridge University Press.

Huet, M.-H. 1982. *Rehearsing the Revolution: The Staging of Marat's Death, 1793–1797*. Berkeley: University of California Press.

Hughes, D. 1996. *English Drama 1660–1700*. Oxford: Clarendon Press.

Hume, D. 1975. *Enquiries Concerning Human Understanding and Concerning the Principles of Morals* (1777). Oxford: Clarendon Press.

Hume, R.D. 1976. *The Development of English Drama in the Late Seventeenth Century*. Oxford: Clarendon Press.

Hume, R.D. 1988. *Henry Fielding and the London Theatre 1728–1737*. Oxford: Clarendon Press.

Hunt, L. 1984. *Politics, Culture, and Class in the French Revolution*. Berkeley: University of California Press.

Inchbald, E. 1990. *Remarks for the British Theatre (1806–1809)*. Delmar, NY: Scholars' Facsimiles and Reprints.

Isherwood, R.M. 1986. *Farce and Fantasy: Popular Entertainment in Eighteenth-Century Paris*. Oxford: Oxford University Press.

Izenour, G.C. 1997. *Theater Design*, 2nd edition. New Haven, CT: Yale University Press.

Izenour, G.C. 1998. *Theater Technology*, 2nd edition. New Haven, CT: Yale University Press.

Jarrard, A. 2003. *Architecture as Performance in Seventeenth-Century Europe: Court Ritual in Modena, Rome, and Paris*. Cambridge: Cambridge University Press.

Jauss, H.R. 1982. 'Literary History as a Challenge to Literary Theory'. In *Toward an Aesthetic Theory of Reception*, translated by T. Bathi, introduced by P. de Man, 3–45. Minneapolis: University of Minnesota Press.

Jefferys, T. 1757–72. *A Collection of the Dresses of different Nations, Antient and Modern*, 4 vols. London.

Johnson, J.H. 1996. *Listening in Paris: A Cultural History*. Berkeley: University of California Press.

Johnson, O. 2003. 'The Leeward Islands Company'. *Theatre Survey* 44: 29–42.

Johnson, O. 2014. 'The Georgian Theatre in Colonial America'. In *The Oxford Handbook of the Georgian Theatre, 1737–1832*, edited by J. Swindells and D.F. Taylor. Oxford: Oxford University Press.

Johnson, O., and W.J. Burling. 2001. *The Colonial American Stage, 1665–1774: A Documentary Calendar*. Madison, NJ: Fairleigh Dickinson University Press.

Joppien, R. 1975. 'Philippe Jacque de Loutherbourg's Pantomime *Omai, or, A Trip round the World* and the Artists of Captain Cook's Voyages'. In *The British Museum Yearbook: Captain Cook and the South Pacific*, vol. III, edited by T.C. Mitchell, 81–137. London: British Museum Publications.

Jullien, A. 1875. *La Comédie à la cour: Les Théâtres de société royale pendant la siècle dernier*. Paris: Firmin-Didot.

Kant, I. 1991. 'What Is Enlightenment?' In *Political Writings*, edited by H. Reiss. Cambridge: Cambridge University Press.

Karim-Cooper, F., and T. Stern, eds. 2013. *Shakespeare's Theatres and the Effects of Performance*. London: Bloomsbury.

Kearsley, G. 1787. *Kearsley's Table of Trades*, a new edition. London.

Kernodle, G. 1970. *From Art to Theatre: Form and Convention in the Renaissance*. Chicago: University of Chicago Press.

Kinservik, M. 2007. 'Reconsidering Theatrical Regulation in the Long Eighteenth Century'. In *Players, Playwrights, Playhouses: Investigating Performance, 1660–1800*, edited by M. Cordner and P. Holland, 152–71. Basingstoke: Palgrave Macmillan.

Knellwolf, C. 2004. 'The Science of Man'. In *The Enlightenment World*, edited by M. Fitzpatrick, P. Jones, C. Knellwolf, and I. McCalman, 194–216. London: Routledge.

Knolles, R. 1603. *The Generall Historie of the Turke*. London.

Koch, E.R. 2008. *The Aesthetic Body: Passion, Sensibility, and Corporeality in Seventeenth-Century France*. Newark: University of Delaware.

Kümin, B. 2008. 'Popular Culture and Sociability'. In *A Companion to Eighteenth-Century Europe*, edited by P.H. Wilson, 192–207. Oxford: Blackwell.

Lafond, J.-A.S. de. 1779. *Essais sur différentes espèces d'air*. Paris: Gueffier.

Lagrave, H. 1992. 'Privilèges et Libertés'. In *Le Théâtre en France*, edited by J. de Jomaron, 269–330. Paris: Armand Colin.

Landriani, P. 1815. *Osservazioni sui difetti prodotti nei teatri*. Milan: Dalla Ceserea.

Langhans, C.F. 1810. *Ueber Theater; oder, Bemerkungen über Katakustik in Beziehung auf Theater*. Berlin: Gottfried Hayn.

Larlham, D. 2012. 'The Felt Truth of Mimetic Experience: Motions of the Soul and the Kinetics of Passion in Eighteenth-Century Theatre'. *The Eighteenth Century* 53 (4): 432–54.

Lavoisier, A.-L. de. 1862–93. *Oeuvres de Lavoisier*, 6 vols. Paris: Imprimerie Impériale.

Lawrence, J.H. 1813. *Dramatic Emancipation, or Strictures on the State of the Theatres, and the Consequent Degeneration of the Drama; on the Partiality and Injustice of London Managers; on Many Theatrical Regulations; and on the Continent for the Security of Literary and Dramatic Property. Particularly Deserving the Attention of the Subscribers for a Third Theatre*. [London: The Pampleteer.]

Lawrenson, T.E. 1980. 'The Ideal Theatre in the Eighteenth Century'. *Themes in Drama II: Drama and Mimesis*, 51–64. Cambridge: Cambridge University Press.

Lawrenson, T.E. 1986. *French Stage and Playhouse in the XVIIth Century: A Study in the Advent of the Italian Order*. New York: AMS Press.

Le Gallois de Grimarest, J.-L. 1707. *Traité du récitatif dans la lecture, dans l'action publique, dans la déclamation et dans le chant. Avec un traité des accents, de la quantité et de la ponctuation*. Paris: Le Fevre.

Le Gardeur, R.J., Jr. 1963. *The First New Orleans Theatre 1792–1803*. New Orleans: Leeward Books.

Leacroft, R., and H. Leacroft. 1984. *Theatre and Playhouse: An Illustrated Survey of Theatre Building from Ancient Greece to the Present Day*. New York: Methuen Publishing.

Lefebvre, H. 1991. *The Production of Space* (1971), translated by D. Nicholson-Smith. Oxford: Blackwell.

Leichman, J.M. 2015. 'What They Talked About When They Talked About Acting: Clairon via Diderot and Talma'. *Eighteenth-Century Studies* 48 (4): 417–36.

Leichman, J.M. 2016. *Acting Up: Staging the Subject in Enlightenment France*. Lewisburg, PA: Bucknell University.

Leon, M. 2013. Review of *Staging the French Revolution: Cultural Politics and the Paris Opéra, 1789–1794* by Mark Darlow. *French Studies* 67 (4): 567–8.

Lessing, G.E. 1962. *Hamburg Dramaturgy* (1769), edited by V.L. Lange. Dover: Dover Publications.

Lever, M. 2001. *Théâtre et lumières: Les spectacles de Paris au XVIIIe siècle*. Paris: Fayard.

Liesenfeld, V.J. 1984. *The Licensing Act of 1737*. Madison: University of Wisconsin Press.

Lilti, A. 2002. 'Public ou Sociabilité? Les théâtres de société au XVIIIe siècle'. In *De la publication: Entre renaissance et lumières*, edited by C. Jouhaud and A. Viala, 281–300. Paris: Fayard.

Lilti, A. 2005. *The World of the Salons: Sociability and Worldliness in Eighteenth-Century Paris*, translated by L. Cochrane. Oxford: Oxford University Press.

Lilti, A. 2014. 'Private Lives, Public Space: A New Social History of the Enlightenment'. In *The Cambridge Companion to the French Enlightenment*, edited by D. Brewer, 14–28. Cambridge: Cambridge University Press.

Lindfors, B. 2006. 'Ira Aldridge's London Debut'. *Theatre Notebook* 60: 30–44.

Little, David M., and George M. Kahrl. 1963. *The Letters of David Garrick*, vol. I. Cambridge, MA: The Belknap Press of Harvard University.

Liu, W.-C. 1953. 'The Original *Orphan of China*'. *Comparative Literature* 5: 193–212.

The London Chronicle for the Year 1757. 1757. Vol. I. London: J. Wilkie.

Lyons, J.D. 1999. *Kingdom of Disorder: The Theory of Tragedy in Classical France*. West Lafayette, IN: Purdue University.

Macé, L. 2005. 'Les Représentations d'Auteurs Français sur les Scènes Privées Italiennes'. In *Les Théâtres de société au XVIIIe siècle*, edited by M.E. Plagnol-Diéval and D. Quéro, 169–78. Brussels: Editions de l'Université de Bruxelles.

Mackintosh, I., ed. 2008. *The Theatric Tourist: A Facsimile* (1805), introduced by M. Ridsell. London: Society for Theatre Research.

Marchand, S. 2009. *Théâtre et Pathétique au XVIIIe siècle: Pour une esthétique de l'effet dramatique*. Paris: Honoré Champion.

Marie, L. 2014. 'A "perfectly honest comedian" is "a metaphysical abstraction": From The Moral Condemnation of Acting to its Aesthetic Promotion in the Eighteenth Century'. *Restoration and 18th Century Theatre Research* 29: 75–95.

Marker, F.J., and L.-L. Marker. 1975. *The Scandinavian Theatre: A Short History*. Totowa, NJ: Rowman and Littlefield.

Marsden, J. 2006. *Fatal Desire: Women, Sexuality, and the English Stage, 1660–1720*. Ithaca, NY: Cornell University Press.

Marsh, J. 1785. *History of my Private Life (autobiography)*, vol. 9, HM 54457. The Huntington Library, San Marino, CA.

Marshall, D. 1988. *The Surprising Effects of Sympathy: Marivaux, Diderot, Rousseau, and Mary Shelley*. Chicago: University of Chicago.

Martin, I. 2002. *Le Théâtre de la foire: Des Tréteaux aux boulevards*. Oxford: SVEC.

Maslan, S. 2005. *Revolutionary Acts: Theatre, Democracy, and the French Revolution*. Baltimore: Johns Hopkins University Press.

McConachie, B. 1998. 'American Theatre in Context, from the Beginnings to 1870'. In *The Cambridge History of American Theatre*, vol. I, edited by D.B. Wilmeth and C. Bigsby, 111–81. Cambridge: Cambridge University Press.

McDermott, D. 1998. 'Structure and Management in the American Theatre from the Beginning to 1870'. In *The Cambridge History of American Theatre*, vol. I, edited by D.B. Wilmeth and C. Bigsby, 182–215 Cambridge: Cambridge University Press.

McFadden, G. 1974. 'Political Satire in *The Rehearsal*'. *Yearbook of English Studies* 4: 120–8.

McKendrick, M. 1989. *Theatre in Spain 1490–1700*. Cambridge: Cambridge University Press.

McPherson, H. 2002. 'Theatrical Riots and Cultural Politics in Eighteenth-Century London'. *Eighteenth Century: Theory & Interpretation* 43 (3): 236–52.

Meech, A. 2006. 'Classical Theatre and the Formation of a Civil Society, 1720–1832'. In *A History of German Theatre*, edited by S. Williams and M. Hamburger, 65–91. Cambridge: Cambridge University Press.

Meldrum, T. 2014. *Domestic Service and Gender 1660–1750: Life and Work in the London Household*. Abingdon, UK: Routledge.

Mercier, L.S. 1990. *Tableau de Paris & Le Nouveau Paris*. Paris: Editions Robert Laffont.

Merlin-Kajman, H. 2004. *Public et littérature en France au XVIIe siècle*. Paris: Société des Belles Lettres.

Milhous, J., and R.D. Hume. 1990. 'John Rich's Covent Garden Account Books for 1735–36'. *Theatre Survey* 31 (2): 200–41.

Milhous, J., and R.D. Hume, eds. 1991. *A Register of English Theatrical Documents, 1660–1737*. Carbondale: Southern Illinois University Press.

Milhous, J., and R.D. Hume. 1993. 'Opera Salaries in Eighteenth-Century London'. *Journal of the American Musicological Society* 46 (1): 26–83.

Miller, J., director. 1983. *The Beggar's Opera*, with R. Daltrey, B. Hoskins and P. Routledge, BBC TV.

Milling, J. 2008a. 'Oldfield, Anne (1683–1730)'. In *Oxford Dictionary of National Biography* online ed. Oxford: Oxford University Press. Accessed 4 April 2016. http://www.oxforddnb.com/view/article/20677.

Milling, J. 2008b. 'Porter, Mary (*d.* 1765)'. In *Oxford Dictionary of National Biography* online ed. Oxford: Oxford University Press. Accessed 4 April 2016. http://www.oxforddnb.com/view/article/22575.

Mittman, B. 1981. 'Make Way for the Mailman! Spectators on the Stage in Paris Theatres'. *Theatre Survey* 22 (1): 1–15.

Morning Post. 26 December 1785.

Mullin, D.C. 1970. *The Development of the Playhouse*. Berkeley: University of California Press.

Mumford, L. 1961. *The City in History: Its Origins, Its Transformations, and Its Prospects*. New York: Harcourt Brace.

Munck, T. 2008. 'Enlightened Thought, Its Critics and Competitors'. In *A Companion to Eighteenth-Century Europe*, edited by P.H. Wilson, 141–57. London: Blackwell.

Newitt, M. 1995. *A History of Mozambique*. London: C. Hurst.

Newman, K. 2007. *Cultural Capitals: Early Modern London and Paris*. Princeton, NJ: Princeton University Press.

Nicole, P. 1998. *Traité de la comédie et autres pièces d'un procès du théâtre* (1667), edited by L. Thirouin. Paris: Champion.

Nicoll, A. 1952. *A History of English Drama 1660–1800*, 3 vols, 4th edition. Cambridge: Cambridge University Press.

Norman, L.F. 2011. *The Shock of the Ancient: Literature and History in Early Modern France*. Chicago: University of Chicago Press.

Notes for a Biography. 1768. HM 64533, vol. 1, *John Kendall Correspondence and Papers*. The Huntington Library, San Marino, CA.

Nussbaum, F. 2010. *The Rival Queens: Actresses, Performance, and the Eighteenth-Century British Theatre*. Philadelphia: University of Pennsylvania Press.

O'Quinn, D. 2005. *Staging Governance: Theatrical Imperialism in London, 1770–1800*. Baltimore: The Johns Hopkins University Press.

O'Quinn, D. 2011. *Entertaining Crisis in the Atlantic Imperium, 1770–1790*. Baltimore: The Johns Hopkins University Press.

Oldys, W. 1741. *Memoirs of Mrs Anne Oldfield*, London.

Oliver, A., ed. 1972. *The Journal of Samuel Curwen, Loyalist*, vol. I. Cambridge, MA: Harvard University Press for the Essex Institute Salem, Massachusetts.

Olsen, D.J. 1986. *The City as a Work of Art: London. Paris, Vienna*. New Haven, CT: Yale, University Press.

Orr, B. 2001. *Empire on the English Stage, 1660–1714*. Cambridge: Cambridge University Press.

Ou, H.-Y. 2008. 'Gender, Consumption, and Ideological Ambiguity in David Garrick's Production of *The Orphan of China* (1759)'. *Theatre Journal* 60: 383–407.

Ozouf, M. 1991. *The Festivals of the French Revolution*. Cambridge, MA: Harvard University Press.

Pasquin, A. 1789. *Poems*. London: printed for J. Strahan.

Patte, P. 1782. *Essai sur l'architecture théâtrale*. Paris: Chez Moutard.

Pedicord, H.W., and F.L. Bergmann, eds. 1982. *The Plays of David Garrick*, vol. V, *Garrick's Alterations of Others, 1742–1750*. Carbondale: Southern Illinois University Press.

Pelletier, L. 2006. *Architecture in Words: Theatre, Language and the Sensuous Space of Architecture*. London: Routledge.

Perkin, H. 2002. *The Origins of Modern English Society*, 2nd edition. London: Routledge.

Philips, A. 1712. *The Distrest Mother*. London.

Phillips, H. 1980. *The Theatre and Its Critics in Seventeenth-Century France*. Oxford: Oxford University.

Picard, L. 2003. *Dr. Johnson's London: Life in London, 1740–1770*. London: Phoenix.

Plagnol-Diéval, M.E., and D. Quéro, eds. 2005. *Les Théâtres de société au XVIIIe siècle*. Brussels: Editions de l'Université de Bruxelles.

Playbill. 4 August 1815. Theatre, Stamford.

Playbill. 20 November 1754. Newcastle Upon Tyne, England.

Playbill. 24 December 1805. Charleston Theatre, South Carolina.

Pollock, T.C. 1933. *The Philadelphia Theatre in the Eighteenth Century together with the Day Book of the Same Period*. Philadelphia: University of Pennsylvania Press.

Pozzo, Andrea. 1700. *La Perspective propre des peintres et des architectes*. Rome: J.J. Komarek.

Price, C., J. Milhous, and R.D. Hume. 1992. *The Impresario's Ten Commandments: Continental Recruitment for Italian Opera in London, 1763–64*, Royal Musical Association Monographs, vol. VI. New York: Routledge.

Pucci, S. 1997. 'The Nature of Domestic Intimacy and Sibling Incest in Diderot's *Le Fils naturel*'. *Eighteenth-Century Studies* 30 (1): 271–87.

Pullen, K. 1995. *Actresses and Whores: On Stage and in Society*. Cambridge: Cambridge University Press.

Rabreau, D. 2008. *Apollon dans la ville: Essai sur le théâtre et l'urbanisme à l'époque des lumières*. Paris: Editions du Patrimoine, Centre des Monuments Nationaux.

Racine, J. 1873. 'Seconde lettre à l'auteur des *Hérésies imaginaires et des deux visionnaires*' (1666). In *Œuvres de Jean Racine*, 352–8. Paris: Laplace.

Radicchio, G., and M. Sajous D'Oria. 1990. *Les Théâtres de Paris pendant la révolution*. Fasano, Italy: Elemond periodici.

Ragussis, M. 2010. *Theatrical Nation: Jews and Other Outlandish Englishmen in Georgian Britain*. Philadelphia: University of Pennsylvania Press.

Ravel, J. 1999. *The Contested Parterre: Public Theater and French Political Culture, 1680–1791*. Ithaca, NY: Cornell University Press.

Ravel, J. 2005. 'Le Derrière du cocher: Une soirée interrompue au XVIIIè siècle'. In *Les Théâtres de société au XVIIIe siècle*, edited by M.E. Plagnol-Diéval and D. Quéro, 217–24. Brussels: Editions de l'Université de Bruxelles.

Raysor, T.M. 1927. 'The Downfall of the Three Unities'. *Modern Language Notes* 42 (1): 1–9.

Reddy, W.M. 2001. *The Navigation of Feeling: A Framework for the History of Emotions*. Cambridge: Cambridge University Press.

Restif de La Bretonne, N.-E. 1990. *Les Nuits de Paris*. Paris: Editions Robert Laffont.

Rice, J.A. 2015. 'Operatic Pyrotechnics in the Eighteenth Century'. In *Theatrical Heritage: Challenges and Opportunities*, edited by B. Forment and C. Stalpaert. Leuven: Leuven University Press.

Richard Brome Online. 2016. Accessed 13 May 2016. http://www.hrionline.ac.uk/brome/home.jsp.

Richards, J.H. 2005. *Drama, Theatre, and Identity in the American New Republic*. Cambridge: Cambridge University Press.

Riskin, J. 2002. *Science in the Age of Sensibility: The Sentimental Empiricists of the French Enlightenment*. Chicago: University of Chicago.

Ritchie, F. 2014. *Women and Shakespeare in the Eighteenth Century*. Cambridge: Cambridge University Press.

Ritchie, L. 2015. 'Pox on Both Your Houses: The Battle of the Romeos'. *Eighteenth-Century Fiction* 27 (3/4): 373–93.

Roach, J. 1981. 'Diderot and the Actor's Machine'. *Theatre Survey* 22 (1): 51–68.

Roach, J. 1985. *The Player's Passion: Studies in the Science of Acting*. Ann Arbor: University of Michigan Press.

Roach, J. 1993. *The Player's Passion: Studies in the Science of Acting*, new edition. Ann Arbor: University of Michigan Press.

Roach, J. 2007. *It*. Ann Arbor: University of Michigan Press.

Root-Bernstein, M. 1984. *Boulevard Theatre and Revolution in Eighteenth-Century Paris*. Ann Arbor: UMI Research Press.

Rosenfeld, S. 1960. *The Theatre of the London Fairs in the 18th Century*. Cambridge: Cambridge University Press.

Rosenfeld, S. 1978. *Temples of Thespis: Some Private Theatres and Theatricals in England and Wales, 1700–1820*. London: Society for Theatre Research.

Rougemont, M. de. 1988. *La Vie théâtrale en France au XVIIIe siècle*. Geneva: Slatkine.

Rougemont, M. de. 2001. *La Vie théâtrale en France au XVIIIe siècle*. Paris: Champion.

Rousseau, J.-J. 1960. 'Letter to M. d'Alembert on the Theatre' (1758). In *Jean-Jacques Rousseau: Politics and the Arts*, translated and introduced by A. Bloom. Ithaca, NY: Cornell University Press.

Rousseau, J.-J. 1967. *Lettre à d'Alembert* (1758). Paris: Flammarion.

Rousseau, J.-J. 1987. *The Basic Political Writings*, translated by D.A. Cress. Indianapolis, IN: Hackett.

Rudé, G. 1972. *Europe in the Eighteenth Century: Aristocracy and the Bourgeois Challenge*. London: Weidenfeld and Nicolson.

Russell, G. 1995. *The Theatres of War: Performance, Politics, and Society 1793–1815*. Oxford: Clarendon Press.

Russell, G. 2010. *Women, Sociability and Theatre in Georgian London*. Cambridge: Cambridge University Press.

Rymer, T. 1693. *A Short View of Tragedy; Its Original, Excellency, and Corruption*. London: Richard Baldwin.

Sajous D'Oria, M. 2007. *Bleu et Or: La Scène et la salle en France au temps des lumières, 1748–1807*. Paris: CNRS Editions.

Saunders, G. 1790. *Treatise on Theatres*. London.

Schaich, M. 2008. 'The Public Sphere'. In *A Companion to Eighteenth-Century Europe*, edited by P.H. Wilson, 125–40. Oxford: Blackwell.

Schöne, G. 1961. 'Les Traités de perspective, sources historiques du théâtre'. *Theatre Research/Recherches théâtrales* 3 (3): 176–90.

Senelick, L., ed. 1991. *National Theatre in Northern and Eastern Europe, 1746–1900*. Cambridge: Cambridge University Press.

Shaffer, J. 2007. *Performing Patriotism National Identity in the Colonial and Revolutionary American Theater*. Philadelphia: University of Pennsylvania Press.

Sharpe, L. 2002. 'Goethe and the Weimar Theatre'. In *The Cambridge Companion to Goethe*, edited by L. Sharpe, 116–28. Cambridge: Cambridge University Press.

Sheridan, R.B. 1989. *The Critic*, edited by D. Crane. New York: Norton.

Sherman, S. 2011. 'Garrick among Media: The "*Now* Performer" Navigates the News'. *PMLA* 126 (4): 966–82.

Sherman, S. 2015. '"The General Entertainment of My Life": The *Tatler*, the *Spectator*, and the Quidnunc's Cure'. *Eighteenth-Century Fiction* 27 (3/4): 343–71.

Smith, W.D. 2002. *Consumption and the Making of Respectability, 1600–1800*. New York: Routledge.

Southerne, T. 1694. *The Fatal Marriage, Or, The Innocent Adultery*. London, EEBO.

Spratt, D. 2013. '"Genius Thus Munificently Employed!!!": Philanthropy and Celebrity in the Theaters of Garrick and Siddons'. *Eighteenth-Century Life* 37 (3): 55–84.

Staves, S. 1979. *Players' Scepters: Fictions of Authority in the Restoration*. Lincoln: University of Nebraska Press.

Stern, T. 2000. *Rehearsal from Shakespeare to Sheridan*. Oxford: Clarendon Press.

Stern, T. 2014. Introduction to *A Jovial Crew, Or, The Merry Beggars* (1652), by R. Brome. London: Bloomsbury.

Stiegler, B. 1998. *Technics and Time, 1: The Fault of Epimetheus*. Stanford, CA: Stanford University Press.

Stiegler, B. 2010. *Technics and Time, 3: Cinematic Time and the Question of Malaise*. Stanford, CA: Stanford University Press.

Stocker, M. 1988. 'Political Allusion in *The Rehearsal*'. *Philological Quarterly* 67 (1): 11–35.

Stone, G.W., Jr, and George M. Kahrl. 1979. *David Garrick: A Critical Biography*. Carbondale: Southern Illinois University Press.

Straub, K. 1991. *Sexual Suspects: Eighteenth Century Players and Sexual Ideology*. Princeton, NJ: Princeton University Press.

Summers, M., ed. 1914. Prefatory Note to *The Rehearsal* (1672) by G. Villiers. Stratford-upon-Avon: Shakespeare Head Press.

Taylor, D.F. 2014. 'Theatre Managers and the Managing of Theatre History'. In *The Oxford Handbook of the Georgian Theatre 1737–1832*, edited by J. Swindells and D.F. Taylor, 70–88. Oxford: Oxford University Press.

Thirouin, L. 1997. *L'Aveuglement salutaire: Le réquisitoire contre le théâtre dans la France classique*. Paris: Honoré Champion.

Thirouin, L. 1998. 'Introduction'. In *Traité de la comédie et autres pièces d'un procès du théâtre* (1667), edited by L. Thirouin. Paris: Champion.

Thomas, D.A., ed. 1989. *Theatre in Europe, A Documentary History: Restoration and Georgian England 1660–1788*. Cambridge: Cambridge University Press.

Thomas, D.A. 2002. *Aesthetics of Opéra in the Ancien Régime, 1647–1785*. Cambridge: Cambridge University Press.

Thompson, E.P. 1993. *Customs in Common: Studies in Traditional Popular Culture*. New York: New Press.

Thompson, G.A., Jr. 1998. *A Documentary History of the African Theatre*. Evanston, IL: Northwestern University Press.

Thomson, P. 2007. 'Acting and Actors from Garrick to Kean'. In *The Cambridge Companion to British Theatre, 1730–1830*, edited by J. Moody and D. O'Quinn, 3–20. Cambridge: Cambridge University Press.

Tidworth, S. 1973. *Theatres: An Illustrated History*. London: Pall Mall Press.

Tilly, C. 1995. *Popular Contention in Great Britain 1758–1834*. Cambridge, MA: Harvard University Press.

The Times. 11 August 1788. 'Madras Theatricals of Ton'.

Topham, E. 1805. *Public Characters of 1805*, vol. VII. London: Richard Phillips.

Treadwell, P. 2009. *Johan Zoffany: Artist and Adventurer*. London: Paul Holberton Publishing.

Trott, D. 2000. *Théâtre du XVIIIe siècle: Jeux, écritures, regards*. Montpellier: Editions Espaces 34.

Trott, D. 2005. 'Qu'est-ce que le théâtre de société?' *Revue d'histoire du théâtre* 225: 7–21.

The True Briton. 7 July 1797.

Tuan, Y.-F. 1977. *Space and Place: The Perspective of Experience*. Minneapolis: University of Minnesota Press.

Van Lennep, W., E.L. Avery, A.H. Scouten, G.W. Stone, Jr, and C.B. Hogan, eds. 1960–8. *The London Stage 1660–1800: A Calendar of Plays, Entertainments and Afterpieces*, 5 parts, 11 vols. Carbondale: Southern Illinois University Press.

Vidal, F. 2006. *Les Sciences de l'âme, XVIe–XVIIIe siècles*. Paris: Honoré Champion.

Villiers, G., Duke of Buckingham. 1914. *The Rehearsal*, edited by M. Summers. Stratford-upon-Avon: Shakespeare Head Press.

Villiers, G., Duke of Buckingham. 1976. *The Rehearsal*, edited by D.E.L. Crane. Durham: University of Durham.

Voltaire, F.M.A. de. 1749. *La Tragédie de Sémiramis*. Paris: P.-G. Le Mercier.

Vries, J. de. 1984. *European Urbanization, 1500–1800*. Cambridge, MA: Harvard University Press.

Walpole, H. 1785. *A Collection of Prologues and Epilogues and Other Pieces Relative to the Stage in the Reign of King George the Third, from the Year 1785*, newspaper cutting. Lewis Walpole Library, Farmington, CT, Call No. LWL 49 1810 58.

Wanko, Cheryl. 2003. *Roles of Authority: Thespian Biography and Celebrity in Eighteenth-Century Britain*. Lubbock: Texas Tech University Press.

Warner, M. 2002. *Publics and Counterpublics*. Brooklyn, NY: Zone Books.

Waterfield, G., A. French, and M. Craske, eds. 2003. *Below Stairs: 400 Years of Servants' Portraits*. London: National Portrait Gallery Publications.

Werkmeister, L. 1967. *A Newspaper History of England, 1792–93*. Lincoln: University of Nebraska Press.

West, S. 1993. *The Image of the Actor: Verbal and Visual Representation in the Age of Garrick and Kemble*. London: Frances Pinter.

Wiles, D. 2003. *A Short History of Western Performance Space*. Cambridge: Cambridge University Press.

Wiley, W.L. 1960. *The Early Public Theatre in France*. Cambridge, MA: Harvard University Press.

Wilkinson, T. 1790. *Memoirs of His Own Life*, vol. I. London: Wilson, Spence, and Mawman.

Wilkinson, T. 1795. *The Wandering Patentee; or, a History of the Yorkshire Theatres, From 1770 to the Present Time*, 4 vols. York: Wilson, Spence, and Mawman.

Wilson, K. 2002. 'Pacific Modernity: Theatre, Englishness, and the Arts of Discovery, 1760–1800'. In *The Age of Cultural Revolutions: Britain and France, 1750–1820*, edited by C. Jones and D. Wahrman. Berkeley: University of California Press.

Wilson, K. 2003. *The Island Race: Englishness, Empire and Gender in the Eighteenth Century*. London: Routledge.

Wilson, K. 2008. 'Rowe's *Fair Penitent* as Global History: Or, a Diversionary Voyage to New South Wales'. *Eighteenth-Century Studies* 41: 231–51.

Wilson, K. 2009. 'The Performance of Freedom: Maroons and the Colonial Order in Eighteenth-Century Jamaica and the Atlantic Sound'. *William and Mary Quarterly* 66: 45–86.

Wilton, K.A. 1997. *Pictures in the Garrick Club: A Catalogue*. London: The Garrick Club.

Winston, J. 1805. *The Theatric Tourist: Being a Genuine Collection of Correct Views, with Brief and Authentic Historical Accounts of All the Principal Provincial Theatres in the United Kingdom*. In Houghton Library, HEW 13.4.2 vol. II. London: Printed by T. Woodfall, sold by H.D. Symonds. Accessed 28 December 2015. http://nrs.harvard.edu/urn-3:FHCL.HOUGH:2309664.

Winton, C. 1993. *John Gay and the London Theatre*. Lexington: University Press of Kentucky.

Worrall, D. 2013a. *Celebrity, Performance, Reception: British Georgian Theatre as Social Assemblage*. Cambridge: Cambridge University Press.

Worrall, D. 2013b. 'Theatre in the Combat Zone: British Military Theatricals at Philadelphia, 1778'. In *Urban Identity and the Atlantic World*, edited by E. Fay and L. von Morz, 219–36. Basingstoke: Palgrave Macmillan.

INDEX

Abington, Frances, 71–2, 153
   Love for Love, 154 fig.7.4
   School for Scandal, 114 fig.5.5
Abrams, Harriet, 44
'Act for Preventing Stage Plays'
   (Massachusetts, 1750–1779), 39
acting
   companies, 39–40, 141–2, 145, 148
   lines of business, 162–3, 240 n.43
   manuals, 156–7
   schools, 141, 155
actresses
   attacks on sexuality, 68
   in Europe, 56
   gender norms, 212
   government regulation, 142
   introduction in England, 55–6
   marriage, 68–9
   motherhood, 65–8
   pregnancy and labour, 62–5
   wages, 71–4
Adams, Abigail, 49–50
Adams, John Quincy, 48
Addison, Joseph
   Cato, 21, 26, 36, 52, 204
   The Spectator, 29
Adelkrantz, Carl Fredrik, 189
affect, 5, 49, 119, 122–3, 125, 128, 134,
   136, 143, 175, 211
   see also emotion
African Theatre (New York), 42

American colonial theatre, 38–9, 43,
   110–11, 144–5, 150–1
American theatre, indigenous performance,
   44, 110
Andromache (role), *see* Philips, *The Distrest*
   Mother
Anti-theatricalism, 8, 125–30, 131–2,
   137
Arabin, Major William John, 51
architecture, theatres
   civic symbols, 83
   French, 187–9
   Italian, 186–7
   public monuments, 78–9
   seating, 37–8, 186
   seating capacity, 25–6
   vaulting, 187
Argentine Theatre (Rome), 187 fig.9.1, 188
   fig.9.2
Arne, Thomas, *Artaxerxes*, 45
Arnould-Mussot, François, *American*
   Heroine (or *Fair American*), 44
audiences
   behaviour, 35–6, 42, 48–50, 146–7
   expectations of, 160, 164, 178, 180,
   experience, 44–8, 214–15
   foreign members in, 40
   as public, 30–3
   seating on stage, 12
   taste, 32, 92
Austen, Jane, *Mansfield Park*, 50–1